*What They Don't Tell You*
*In Schools of Education*
*About School Administration*

# WHAT THEY DON'T TELL YOU
## IN SCHOOLS OF EDUCATION
## ABOUT
## SCHOOL ADMINISTRATION

### John A. Black, Ph.D.
### Fenwick W. English, Ph.D.

TECHNOMIC
PUBLISHING CO., INC.

LANCASTER · BASEL

*Published in the Western Hemisphere by*
Technomic Publishing Company, Inc.
851 New Holland Avenue
Box 3535
Lancaster, Pennsylvania 17604 U.S.A.

*Distributed in the Rest of the World by*
Technomic Publishing AG

While many organizations and persons mentioned in this book
are real, certain organizations and persons, particularly those
in examples, are fictitious, and any resemblance to actual
organizations or to actual persons, living or dead, is purely
coincidental.

Printed in the United States of America
10  9  8  7  6  5  4

Main entry under title:
  What They Don't Tell You in Schools of Education
    About School Administration
A Technomic Publishing Company book
Bibliography: p. 309
Includes index p. 319

Library of Congress Card No. 86-50183
ISBN No. 87762-461-5

# Table of Contents

*Preface*                                                                    xi

*Acknowledgement*                                                            xiii

### I  POWER AND THE CONTEXT OF SCHOOL ADMINISTRATION

**1  Power and Politics**                                                    **3**

JFK, Stalin, Churchill, and Iacocca—Who Would
Make It as a School Administrator? . . . . . . . . . . . . . . . . . .7
Ideas about Power: The Big "P" or Who Has It
and Who Doesn't . . . . . . . . . . . . . . . . . . . . . . . . . . . . .8
Power Plays, Politics, and Politicians . . . . . . . . . . . . . . . .11
The Zero Sum Game as Organizational Poker Playing . . . . .12
Building Coalitions: The Chess Game . . . . . . . . . . . . . . .15
Is School Administration for You? . . . . . . . . . . . . . . . . . .17
Caveats, Codicils, and Conundrums about
Power and Politics . . . . . . . . . . . . . . . . . . . . . . . . . . . .20

**2  Are You Ready to Play the Game?**                                       **23**

The Game, the Players, the Stakes, and the Rules . . . . . . .23
The Nature of School Administration . . . . . . . . . . . . . . . .24
Winning, Losing, Winners, and Losers . . . . . . . . . . . . . . .25
Jocks, Jive, and Jokers . . . . . . . . . . . . . . . . . . . . . . . . . .29
Caveats, Codicils, and Conundrums about
Playing the Game . . . . . . . . . . . . . . . . . . . . . . . . . . . . .32

**3  Bureaucracies, Babus, and Baksheesh**                                   **35**

Vacuums, Inertia, and Administrivia . . . . . . . . . . . . . . . .35
Competency and Potency . . . . . . . . . . . . . . . . . . . . . . . .38
Rocking in the Boat vs Rocking the Boat . . . . . . . . . . . . . .40
Beating the System vs Being Beaten by the System . . . . . .41
Blunders and Business Acumen . . . . . . . . . . . . . . . . . . . .44
Caveats, Codicils, and Conundrums about
Bureaucracies, Babus, and Baksheesh . . . . . . . . . . . . . .48

II CONNECTIONS

**4  The Community**      **53**

The "Community" Is a Mirage . . . . . . . . . . . . . . . . . . . . . . . .53
Tapping the Power Bases of the Communities . . . . . . . . . .54
Spotting the People in Power—The Informal Network . . . .55
Using the Power Bases of a Community . . . . . . . . . . . . . . .60
Caveats, Codicils, and Conundrums about
  the Community . . . . . . . . . . . . . . . . . . . . . . . . . . . . . . . . .61

**5  The PTA**      **63**

What the PTA Is Not: Teachers and Men . . . . . . . . . . . . . .63
Gossip, "Gotchas," and Gripe Sessions . . . . . . . . . . . . . . .64
Payoffs, Potholes, and Parsimony . . . . . . . . . . . . . . . . . . . .65
Virulence at the Secondary School . . . . . . . . . . . . . . . . . .67
And Virulence at the Elementary School . . . . . . . . . . . . .68
Caveats, Codicils, and Conundrums about PTA's . . . . . . . .71

**6  The Staff**      **73**

The Staff vs the Faculty . . . . . . . . . . . . . . . . . . . . . . . . . . . .73
The Faculty: Superstars, Superchargers, Turkeys,
  Stool Pigeons, and Wimps . . . . . . . . . . . . . . . . . . . . . . . .75
Morale and Networking . . . . . . . . . . . . . . . . . . . . . . . . . . . .82
Pedagogues, Poker Games, and Privies:
  Faculty Room Dynamics . . . . . . . . . . . . . . . . . . . . . . . . . .82
Caveats, Codicils, and Conundrums about the Staff . . . . . .83

**7  The Media**      **85**

The Truth Never Gets in the Way of a Good Story . . . . . . .85
Stroking the Press . . . . . . . . . . . . . . . . . . . . . . . . . . . . . . . .87
Developing a Media "Presence" That Sells . . . . . . . . . . . . .90
Turning Bad News into Good News:
  Being Your Own Press Agent . . . . . . . . . . . . . . . . . . . . . .91
Two Sources of Information about
  the Schools You Should Know . . . . . . . . . . . . . . . . . . . . .92
Caveats, Codicils, and Conundrums about the Media . . . . .93

**8  Students**      **95**

The Pawns and the Powerful . . . . . . . . . . . . . . . . . . . . . . . .95
A Student-Centered Value System . . . . . . . . . . . . . . . . . . .96
Students as a Power Group . . . . . . . . . . . . . . . . . . . . . . . . .98
Students as Problems to Students as Solutions . . . . . . . . .102
Pots, Pot, and Pets . . . . . . . . . . . . . . . . . . . . . . . . . . . . . . .103
Caveats, Codicils, and Conundrums about Students . . . . .105

### III  THE CAREER LADDER

**9  Career Planning—The Legend of the "Chairs"**      **109**

The Legend and the Fraternity ..................... 109
The Play Is the Thing—The Difference Between
Scenery and the Players ........................... 111
Getting the Position You Want: Two Strategies ........ 115
The Right People—Who Are They? .................. 116
Caveats, Codicils, and Conundrums about
Career Planning ................................ 118

**10  Resumes, Headhunters, and Interviewing**      **119**

The Resume as Doublespeak ....................... 119
On Bogus Degrees: Avoiding Dipscam ............... 123
Headhunters, Cannibals, and the OBN .............. 124
Interviewing Your Interviewers ................... 126
Leads: Dead Ends, Deadbeats, Detours,
and Dividends ................................. 127
Caveats, Codicils, and Conundrums about
Resumes, Headhunters, and Interviewing .......... 128

**11  Academics and Abecedarians**      **131**

The Ph.D. and Ed.D. or Initials Are Everything ........ 135
The Alphabet Jungle: Reading the Letterhead ........ 137
Picking the Right Place to Get Placed ............... 137
Professors as Partners ........................... 138
Life in College Classrooms ........................ 138
Caveats, Codicils, and Conundrums about
Acedemics and Abecedarians .................... 139

### IV  GETTING THE JOB DONE RIGHT

**12  The Job vs the Job Description**      **143**

What Makes Up a Job? ........................... 145
Data, People, and Things ......................... 146
Control vs Controls Over the Job ................... 146
Retrofitting the Job Description to the Job ........... 147
Caveats, Codicils, and Conundrums about
the Job vs the Job Description .................... 149

**13  Ploys to Avoid**      **151**

Givers, Takers, and Flimflam Artists ............... 151
Memo Wars and Turf Battles ...................... 157

Forcing Democracy on Dopes ...................... 160
Your Title and You, When to Take It Seriously ........ 164
Caveats, Codicils, and Conundrums about
   Ploys to Avoid .................................. 167

**14 Hiring, Shifting, and Firing**                         **169**
Where Loyalties Begin and End:
   Have Gun Will Travel ........................... 169
The Proper Attitude .............................. 170
The Subtleties of Staffing ......................... 171
Hiring Good People or Hiring People
   Who Hire Good People ......................... 172
Con Games in Letters of Reference ................. 174
Shifting Personnel: Keep Your Eyes on the Pea! ........ 176
Who Must Be Fired and Making It Stick .............. 178
Theory X and Theory Y .......................... 178
Taking Your Lumps, the Dirty Work
   Is Part of the Job ............................. 185
The Only Thing That Lasts ........................ 186
Retrospective ................................... 186
Caveats, Codicils, and Conundrums about
   Hiring, Shifting, and Firing ..................... 187

**15 The Emmetropia of Evaluation**                      **189**
Growth vs Performance ........................... 189
The Search for the One "Perfect" System ............ 190
Hard vs Soft Data ............................... 193
Flattery Will Lose You a Grievance .................. 196
Facts Only Count for So Much ..................... 197
Caveats, Codicils, and Conundrums about Evaluation ... 200

**16 Budget Skullduggery**                                   **201**
Budget Control and Hieroglyphics ................... 201
What Is a Budget? ............................... 201
All Budgets Are Padded .......................... 202
How Not to Be Caught with Your Padding Down ....... 203
The Telltale Evidence: The Sawdust on the Floor ....... 204
Controlling Costs ................................ 205
Caveats, Codicils, and Conundrums about
   Budget Skullduggery ........................... 207

**17 Textbook Tyranny, Curriculum Chicanery, and Testing Insanity**   **209**
The Educational Mugwumps ....................... 209
Putting It Together in the Schools .................. 211
Testing Insanity ................................. 214

Caveats, Codicils, and Conundrums about
Textbook Tyranny, Curriculum Chicanery,
and Testing Insanity . . . . . . . . . . . . . . . . . . . . . . . . . . . . .217

V  ADVERSARIES AND FRIENDS

**18  Secretaries and Custodians**                                    **221**

The "Shadow" Administrators:
Secretaries Behind the Throne . . . . . . . . . . . . . . . . . . . . .221
Secretaries as Mediators and Power Brokers . . . . . . . . . . .222
Secretarial Sign Language Everybody Knows . . . . . . . . . .225
The Real Basics Are Always Custodial . . . . . . . . . . . . . . . .226
Caveats, Codicils, and Conundrums about
Secretaries and Custodians . . . . . . . . . . . . . . . . . . . . . . .228

**19  Unions**                                                       **231**

The Avon Lady Is Calling:
Cosmetic vs Custodial Roles . . . . . . . . . . . . . . . . . . . . . . .231
Union Tactics and Victims . . . . . . . . . . . . . . . . . . . . . . . . .233
Living, Loving, and Laughing with Unions . . . . . . . . . . . .234
Grievances and Arbitration . . . . . . . . . . . . . . . . . . . . . . . .235
The Godfather: Understanding Union Leaders . . . . . . . . .237
Caveats, Codicils, and Conundrums about Unions . . . . . .239

**20  The Lunatic Fringe**                                           **241**

Prudes, Censors, Wackos, and Birchers . . . . . . . . . . . . . . .241
The Last Crusade: The Religious Fanatics . . . . . . . . . . . . .244
The Assassins—When the Bullets Are Real . . . . . . . . . . . .247
The Power of Humor . . . . . . . . . . . . . . . . . . . . . . . . . . . . . .248
Caveats, Codicils, and Conundrums about
the Lunatic Fringe . . . . . . . . . . . . . . . . . . . . . . . . . . . . . .249

**21  Arch Rivals and Competitors**                                  **251**

Et tu Brutus? Knowing Who Wants Your Job . . . . . . . . . .251
Plots, Plotters, and Psychopaths . . . . . . . . . . . . . . . . . . . .252
Case Study: Stanley Friend's First Failure . . . . . . . . . . . .254
Motivation for Advancement . . . . . . . . . . . . . . . . . . . . . . .259
Assistants . . . . . . . . . . . . . . . . . . . . . . . . . . . . . . . . . . . . . . .261
Caveats, Codicils, and Conundrums about
Arch Rivals and Competitors . . . . . . . . . . . . . . . . . . . . . .263

VI  SURVIVING

**22  Knowing Who Is the Boss**                                      **267**

You Don't Work for Everyone:
How to Tell Who Is the Boss . . . . . . . . . . . . . . . . . . . . . . .267

Case Study: Todd Laker Knocks 'em Dead
  but Is Knocked Out . . . . . . . . . . . . . . . . . . . . . . . . . . . . . 268
All the President's Men: Are They Men? . . . . . . . . . . . . . . 273
Does Your Boss Want Your Competence
  or Your Strokes? . . . . . . . . . . . . . . . . . . . . . . . . . . . . . . 274
Who Is Your Boss's Boss and Who Cares? . . . . . . . . . . . . . 275
Caveats, Codicils, and Conundrums about
  Knowing Who Is the Boss . . . . . . . . . . . . . . . . . . . . . . . . 277

**23 Staying in Power and Staying Power**　　　　　　**279**

Real Lessons from the Real World . . . . . . . . . . . . . . . . . . 287
How to Survive Losing to *The Turk:* Getting Fired . . . . . . 289
Caveats, Codicils, and Conundrums about
  Staying in Power and Staying Power . . . . . . . . . . . . . . . 291

**24 Idealism vs Ideology**　　　　　　**293**

Machiavelli and Don Quixote: The Odd Couple . . . . . . . . 293
Is It Crass to Care? . . . . . . . . . . . . . . . . . . . . . . . . . . . . . 294
Dreams vs Pipe Dreams . . . . . . . . . . . . . . . . . . . . . . . . . 295
Guidelines for Success . . . . . . . . . . . . . . . . . . . . . . . . . . 296
Your Own Guidelines . . . . . . . . . . . . . . . . . . . . . . . . . . . 304
Caveats, Codicils, and Conundrums about
  Leaders and Leadership . . . . . . . . . . . . . . . . . . . . . . . . . 306

*Notes*　　　　　　　　　　　　　　　　　　　　309
*Index*　　　　　　　　　　　　　　　　　　　　319
*Biographies*　　　　　　　　　　　　　　　　　323
*To Our Readers*　　　　　　　　　　　　　　　　325

# Preface

**WHY THIS BOOK?**

The last thing our profession needs is yet another textbook on educational administration. There are already hundreds of them. They all deal with specific aspects of administration and leadership. The hundreds of thousands of students of educational administration who have read these books and who have taken these courses have certainly read *about* administration and about leadership. Obviously, many of them have even become "certified" administrators and are practicing administrators today.

Yet, few students of educational administration became "street wise" from either the countless textbooks or from the countless courses which attempt to deal with the subject. Such wisdom, which is so vital for the survival and advancement of anyone in this field, cannot be learned from books. Such knowledge is gained from the "school of hard knocks"—from years of experience, of collecting scars, of learning from past mistakes. Go to any convention, meeting, party, etc., where educational administrators are in attendance, and you will hear countless war stories.

What price have these survivors paid for their successes? What price have their families paid? And how many potentially excellent would-be-administrators never make it because none of the books or the courses in administration ever taught them how to survive? Nothing in their training addressed the fact that once classroom teachers cross the threshold of their classroom doors and leave the classroom for administration, they all but leave the field of education and enter a new field altogether—the field of politics.

Those qualities which led to success as a classroom teacher may have little or no bearing on their new profession; they may even be a hindrance! The rules of the game are different and, for the most part, *are unwritten.*

Throughout the annals of political writings, one treatise stands out for its attempt to deal with the unwritten rules of the political arena—*The Prince,* by Machiavelli. More recently, *What They Don't Teach You at Harvard Business School,* by Mark H. McCormack, has made its debut. McCormack's book attempts to fill in many of the gaps—the gaps between a business school education and the street knowledge that comes from the day-to-day experience of running a business and managing people. Similarly, our book attempts to address those aspects of the political arena of educational administration and leadership which are necessary for survival itself.

This book is based on the contributions of countless veteran administrators who have read the textbooks and taken the courses in educational administration but, more importantly, who have *survived.*

This book, then, should be read by students of educational administration, as well as by practicing school administrators. Like all other textbooks on educational administration which preceded it, it is about leadership and administration. Like *NO* other book on this subject ever written before, it is about swimming with sharks—and surviving!

J.A.B.   Northport, New York

F.W.E.   Bethlehem, Pennsylvania

# Acknowledgements

**A PERSONAL WORD FROM THE AUTHORS**

This is a passionate book. It represents our passions for what schools do *to* and *with* people, teachers, and students. It is not a scholarly work based on codified procedures and standard measures. It is a book based on our lives and experiences with schools and school people.

We met most of them in our travels. In the course of changing jobs and moving from state to state we've met gentlemen, con artists, playboys, imposters, princes, queens, and our share of bastards. They were on boards of education, in the administrative ranks, and on faculties. They populated PTA's and booster groups. We've battled with them, fought them, and been hurt by them. But through the years we've learned from them.

Both of us have been hired and fired. We've won jobs we were proud of and lost jobs we loved. We've lived through the frustrations and bitterness. We've learned who our friends really were. We've become better people and, most importantly, better administrators because of our wounds and bruises in the organizational battles in which we found ourselves.

We've come to view our schools not as holy places or shrines of learning, but as social–political marketplaces where good guys don't always win and educational priorities are debauched by the crassest kind of political pork-barreling possible in a democratic society.

We've been ambushed and we've been *had* because we believed schools were ethical places. Nobody told us any differently. Not when we were students or teachers, and certainly not in our educational preparatory colleges. In the process of fighting the good fight, we've taken off the blinders and looked again. Schools are enshrined with noble purposes, but they act like all other human organizations. And they are peopled with every kind of human being there is.

To this end we've decided to deal with the schools as we've experienced them—not as we wish they would be or thought they were, *but as they are.* No more and no less.

Yes, we've been warned about this book. Friends have cautioned us. "It could ruin your careers," we've been told. You should "soften" this or "change" that. Through it all we listened and made changes where we thought they were right. In the end, we had to look inside ourselves and decide what we really wanted to say and how best to say it. For the most part we stuck to what felt right in our guts. We wrote what we believed best represented that which we encountered, not what others might want us to have encountered. And we stuck with the words of the language that conveyed our passions, even when they were from the vernacular. So be it.

Most of all we took heart from a few kindred souls through history: Machiavelli, the first scientist of human behavior in organizational life, and people like Tom Paine, Patrick Henry, and Saul Alinsky, the radicals who acted on what they believed in spite of the consequences.

We believe as Alinsky wrote:

> Life is an adventure of passion, risk, danger, laughter, beauty, love, a burning curiosity to go with the action to see what it is all about, to search for a pattern of meaning, to burn one's bridges because you're never going to go back anyway, and to live to the end.
> *Reveille for Radicals*
> New York, Vintage Books (1946, 1969)

This book is a combination of so much of Alinsky's definition. It is passion, laughter, an itching to search for the meanings of our experiences, a compelling re-examination of what we've done and what we were after, *and love.* It expresses love for the profession we so deeply respect and on whose behalf we've spent our lives. It is a gesture of deepest love to our students and colleagues, who stood with us in our times of need.

To them we say thank you. And to our enemies we grudgingly give not respect, but acknowledgement of the lessons learned. And mostly to our fathers, Nicholas Black and Melvin English, who would wish of their sons the courage of their convictions in a life of frequent ambiguity. And to the continuing search. . . .

# Power and the Context of School Administration

## CHAPTER 1

# Power and Politics

"I like making money. I'm not telling you I'm Robin Hood. The poor widows of this world aren't my responsibility." Relaxing by his pool, corporate raider Carl Icahn reflected on his strategy to take over TWA.[1]

"I'm tough, ambitious, and I know exactly what I want," confessed rock megastar Madonna.[2]

Educators find these words hard. Education *is different*. The cruel world of high finance or show business is not what schools are about. Schools are different places and the administrators who run them are more humane and caring.

Nowhere is the mythology of power more pervasive than in educational administration. Our critics see us one way. We *see ourselves* as clean and pure, ennobled by our "higher calling" rather than degraded by crass money-grabbing in a material world.

Whether male or female, too many educators are uncomfortable about their own motivations towards power. Mary Cunningham observed that women are still their own worst enemy when it comes to power. She noted, "They have been made to feel almost afraid of power. Women are still embarrassed to admit that they have power and to embrace its energy as something that can be very positive if implemented with a conscience."[3] We would expand that to include males.

People who enter educational administration *want power*. They may deceive themselves as to *why* they want it, but they want it. Our observations indicate that a hard look at the real reasons for wanting to be school administrators should be part of any program of licensing future school leaders. The self-deception that muddies what school administrators do and why they do it is rampant in the literature that prepares school administrators. Hopefully we have not contributed to it in the past, and this book is an attempt to move in the *opposite direction* in the future.

Glossing over what actually motivates people to be school administrators does the business of schooling a disservice by:

- making us more vulnerable to our critics than we need be;
- insulating us from the real world of running schools;
- detracting from our ability to exert effective leadership with teachers and parents.

Our view is that school administrators should always be students of human behavior, *beginning with their own*. School administration is a dynamic, complex, and demanding occupation. It is made infinitely more difficult when the administrator is not honest about why he/she wants the job in the first place.

Our pasts are filled with memories of colleagues, friends, bosses, and enemies. We remember:

- *the little Hitlers,* mostly male but a few females too, who went into school administration to "fill up" their own barren personal lives. Power was ambrosia. It took the place of their own psychic sterility. They lived for power. There was never enough of it. We call them "power-hungry-deprived" or "ph.d's" with a little *P* to distinguish them from holders of the academic degree, though there are academicians with the same problems as well.

  Working for these bosses is hell. They are jealous of encroachment on their prerogatives and perquisites. Take their parking spot and you've insulted them in much the same way as if you slapped their faces with a glove signifying you desired a duel in the parking lot at noon. They're anxious to add staff, increase the size of the budget, and have more equipment and teachers to order around. Kids have nothing to do with it. The size of the school is proportional to the size of the ego. One is a reflection of the other.

  Then there are the central office types who nit-pick memos. Every sentence is an invitation to search for grammatical nuances to be bounced back with red circles. They can be compulsive rule-followers who make no exceptions, even when children suffer and the organization becomes less effective and humane. Protected from the front lines and situated above the battle on the perches of the organizational table, they wade through the coffee breaks and work through the paper in the "in box" until quitting time.

  We've worked in central offices and even run one or two. A central office is a haven for the power-hungry-deprived of the educational world. What matters to ph.d's is the kind of office they have and the view from the window. Wars are fought and lost on the turf of the central office over whether one has a rug or a potted palm near the light switch. Little Hitlers suffer from chronic "status hiatus." It is a malady that haunts all downtown hierarchies. It is as addictive as heroin.

- *the people puppeteers,* those administrators who enjoy controlling and manipulating others. They are different from the first type in that they are not so much sterile as manipulative. They take great delight in gumming up the works and walking away like kids who drop firecrackers into trashcans and stand "innocently" around feigning propriety.

  People puppeteers work through memos and telephone conversations where one can't see their verbal expressions. They give double messages. Words take on special meanings, often far beyond what was intended. Word games go on and on. We know one superintendent who would invariably start many conferences by looking up in his dictionary the meaning of some word he found in a memo, and he would take great delight in iterating so many meanings that his subordinates got befuddled and forgot what they really had intended to say. He took pleasure in mental intimidation. Instead of viewing meetings as places to unify and clarify, he used them to play with people and put them down. His meetings were despised by his staff who felt like gladiators fighting in the pits before the Roman Emperor.

- *the power conservatives,* the tightwads within the administrative cadre. The only reason they want power is to keep others from having it. They are afraid to let go because they know they can stop things from happening. They are lovers of the past and put the brakes on the present. Each decision they make is relegated to the SQQ leveler, i.e., the "status quo quotient."

  Power conservatives are the fodder of giant bureaucracies. They breed indifference and antipathy to change. They give most organizations a bad case of constipation.

- *the good sports,* those who entered administration because life in the classroom got boring. They look on the affairs of the schools as a golf or tennis match. They don't take much seriously except their fringe benefits, vacations, lunches, and conventions.

Getting a commitment from the good sports that involves
more than a 9:00 A.M. to 3:00 P.M. lifestyle is often difficult
unless it involves a free lunch. Finding them can be impossible. We know of one who is continuously "in the field."
Most of his time is spent driving between meetings, if one
could judge by his mileage account. We are reminded of a
cartoon which showed a "good sport" being chastised by his
boss. The caption read something like, "Benchley, as soon as
I figure out what you do around here you're fired."

The good sports take the view that life and tasks within
the educational hierarchy is a play and the best way to survive is to be "scenery." You can't get in trouble if you aren't
seen, except on payday of course.

If you find yourself becoming annoyed, perhaps it is because you
too have bumped into one or more of the wrong people in school
administration. Maybe you are one. There *are* good people in school
administration. Some of them are still in the schools and central offices of the land. Some have turned sour, gone cynical with the ebb
and flow of human affairs and follies. That we may rid the offices
and schools of the wrong ones, those that alienate teachers and colleagues, is one of our purposes. To arm the good ones so that they
understand what must be done is what this book aims to do. What
earning an education degree does *not* do, this book intends to do:
make these persons "street smart." They must not only survive, *they
must make a difference.*

The problem is that we don't ask people in schools of education
why they want power. We don't make people examine themselves
and their own motivations or intentions in seeking administrative
posts in the schools. To do so would be to intrude on the "private
lives" of degree-seeking candidates. Psychiatric exams are pro-
hibited for school principals but are necessary in the training of
airline pilots. The masters of our teachers remain inscrutable!

As long as school administration is conceived as a "bag of tricks,"
of skills connected to certification as such, the elements of leadership will be sacrificed for behavioral modules aimed at technical
competence. We will and do trade wisdom for wizardry. So, the
wrong people will continue to get certified as school administrators.
With their state supported and issued "hunting license" they can
shoot at anything that moves in the schools, including creative
teachers and students' inquisitive minds. As long as that condition
prevails, there will be a need for this book.

## JFK, STALIN, CHURCHILL, AND IACOCCA—WHO WOULD MAKE IT AS A SCHOOL ADMINISTRATOR?

John F. Kennedy, Josef Stalin, Winston Churchill, and Lee Iacocca have much in common. Each was a leader. Each was considered powerful. How successful would they be in the schools?

To know that is to ponder the correct situations in which they could be successful. But let's look closer.

The contrasts seem apparent. Stalin used raw power to move to the top of a totalitarian system. Quality-circles and sensitivity-training would be of little use to him within the context of his situation. Once, when informed that the Pope had spoken out against one of his actions, he remarked, "How many armies does the Pope have?" Force of arms and fear were Stalin's main weapons.

But the situations and systems in which John F. Kennedy and Winston Churchill operated were quite different. Here, the use of raw power would not have led to their rise up the ladder of their systems.

Kennedy's wit, charm, intelligence, and appeal were definite assets, as was his mastery of the processes of consensus behind the scenes of democratic politics. Churchill's oratorical skills were what the British needed to inspire them to persevere during their struggle against the Nazis.

Then there is Iacocca, the street smart engineer turned salesman, who made it up the corporate ladder of Ford with stunning successes, such as the Mustang that produced a very fat "bottom line" for the company.

But Iacocca knew how to "kick ass" when he had to. And if one can believe his autobiography, he had to at Chrysler to turn the company around. Because public (and many private) school systems in America are supposed to operate within the context of a democracy, perhaps Stalin would find it most difficult, if not perplexing, to be in school administration. Our view is that even the old iron-fisted superintendents of the early nineteenth century couldn't have approached the track record of a Stalin despite being labeled as dictators by their critics.

Lee Iacocca, who relied heavily upon the "power of the pink slip" to rid Chrysler of a top-heavy and ineffective administration, could not do so in any school district where employees in question were tenured. Iaccoca would have to relearn personnel strategies, which would no doubt be frustrating, if not intolerable, to him.

Certainly, Winston Churchill or John F. Kennedy would be more at home as school administrators. Their use of persuasion, diplomacy, and statesmanship would facilitate dealing with the people around them, and school administration is most definitely a "people job." They seemed comfortable with power and dealing with the powerful, yet neither seemed "power hungry" for power's sake.

Would either of them be equally successful as superintendents? Probably not. That would depend upon the makeup and needs of the board of education, among other factors. But their essentially democratic styles would at least not throw a school district into culture shock.

School administration involves knowing the territory. The territory of the profession in general has attracted many persons who have sought security (tenure) and safety, individuals who place a high premium on predicting their futures (i.e., steps and columns on salary grids, retirement pension formulas, etc.). The risk-takers often take their chances in the open marketplace of talent and ideas, a marketplace which offers no salary grids and columns projecting twenty years into the future and no job security or tenure.

The traditions of the schools are its territory. Understanding that *tradition is the territory* is the first job of a radical who wants to change any organization and the way it functions, according to the well-known modern radical, Saul Alinsky. Alinsky brought the rich and powerful to their knees by understanding traditions. "The opposition is always stronger than you are and so his own strength must be used against him. I have repeatedly said that the status quo is your best ally if properly goaded and guided."[4]

Alinsky began organizational change by making sure he understood how organizations worked on their own territory. He then could use their superior force against them. He called it "Alinsky style mass ju-jitsu."[5]

School administrators can come to the same understanding. But they will have to shed self-deceptions about power and why they want it. We propose that these ideas about power are more correct than older notions.

**IDEAS ABOUT POWER: THE BIG "P" OR WHO HAS IT AND WHO DOESN'T**

*Power Is Not a Thing or a State, It Is a Perception of a Relationship*

Power is not something one has or doesn't. It isn't something one can put into the bank. A person twice up on the hierarchical organizational ladder is not *twice as powerful* as the person below that office. Power is neither ordinal nor neat.

Power is a perception about a relationship between people. In the early stages of the second Reagan Administration there were some bad stumbles. Noted one insider, "The perception of power becomes the reality of power, and if your power is eroding—as ours has been— the perception erodes exponentially. The reverse is also true, though."[6]

*Power is* as power is *perceived.* The secret to power is not in the person who may choose to use it, but how people perceive its use. That's what Saul Alinsky discovered. The key to power is in the eyes of the beholder.

### Power Diminishes with Use

The more power is used, the *less powerful* it becomes. Since the power of power lies in the perception of it, the more it is used the less effective it is. Take a classroom example. If the teacher threatens to send a child to see the principal when he or she misbehaves and then does so as a measure of last resort, it may prevent other children from doing the same thing. However, the more the punishment is used with more children the less effective the threat, simply because the use of power has been weathered. Now what? What else is there in the arsenal?

In the words of an old basketball coach, "If the coach makes every game a matter of life and death he is in trouble. For one thing he will be dead a lot."[7]

The most powerful people rarely use power indiscriminately. People will invariably give an opponent more power than he or she may really have since our enemies take on our worst and most feared attributes. Once enemies are revealed as weaker than we perceived them to be, they are by definition less powerful. They have been stripped of something we gave them, not what they had to begin with. The trick is to maintain power by shielding it, so that it never has to be displayed totally. Implied power is always more threatening than power used in the light of day.

### Paper Power Is Not Real Power

"Management by memo" is a favorite game of some administrators. Intimidation by memorandum, veiled threats, high-handed bluffing, intellectual jousting, and potshots by footnotes and authorities are the weapons of the paper-pushers. Sometimes "memo wars" get started and, like flames in the California canyons in the summer, burn out whole sections of organizations.

Real power is not paper power. Midgets engage in memo wars because they have no real power to wield. The great "mini-minds" of the bureaucracy resort to paper attacks because they have no other weapons. Universities are famous for paper wars, and file cabinets bulge with the results of raids and battles over rank, status, budgets, titles, territories, and perquisites. Real power is always *eyeball to eyeball*. There is no other kind in human transactional currency. That is why power involves direct confrontation one way or another. Power is what people are about. Power isn't something you write about, it's something you do. Power is never third person, it's first person.

The school administrator who understands this principle of power never gets sucked into "memo wars." (S)he confronts, preferably on the other person's turf, the matter at hand, nose to nose.

Once an administrator gets a reputation for confrontations, he or she will have fewer and fewer of them because most people will walk a country mile to avoid one.

An international arms expert once explained why, during the period when duels were fought, only 1,000 were held, but 100,000 people owned dueling pistols. Having been bought and practiced with, the dueling set was prominently displayed in the house to tell potential adversaries that its owner was ready. It meant not to mess around unless one was serious. Apparently most people got the word.

For this reason the school administrator is a "people person." It's the source of his or her power. Good administrators feel comfortable and easy with people—all people of all ages, occupations, and educational backgrounds. But more importantly the school administrator knows how to deal with power positively, to develop unity and strength, and to move to and *with* people towards common goals.

Very little of a school administrator's power is derived from his/her title. Probably no one who works within a school building today in America can be told, "Clear your desk by 12:00 noon and collect two weeks severance pay on your way out." Yet, Lee Iacocca fired thirty-three out of thirty-five vice-presidents during a three year period at Chrysler Motor Corporation. Few school districts could afford the legal fees they would incur for the due process hearings necessary before that many tenured teachers or civil service employees could be removed, no matter how desirable the removal.

Therefore, a school administrator's use of power is more subtle, more internal. He or she must be able to *win* people rather than *force* people.

## POWER PLAYS, POLITICS, AND POLITICIANS

We suggest that the main goals of the school administrator are to nurture and help shape a department, building, or a district into the best functioning outfit it can be. Such a person should have the confidence that (s)he will be able to make a difference for the better. Power to such a person is a means to that goal, not something to be sized up as a prize in and of itself.

With this in mind the actual power of the administrator is very limited. Yet what little there is of it makes a difference. To enhance power and thus the energy behind change, the school administrator engages in power plays and politics. If one has power, others will attempt to influence one's use of it, and still others will try to curb or take it away. That's simply the way it works.

Unions, school boards, and the courts have all but totally removed the coercive power of school administrators. Power these days is attained by example, persuasion, charisma, or negotiation.

Power plays consist of adding to the perception that what you have to negotiate is important because of the coalition you have built around you. Coalitions are groups of people who are allied with you and with whom you have exchanged support for common goals.

A power play happens when your side makes a move or responds to a move from some other side in the organization. What must one know? Listen to the advice of experts in the case of the hostage crisis in Lebanon in 1985:

> You have to understand what is behind the rhetoric—what is essential for them and what is rhetorical. And you have to know when they have to save face. You have to know when they are too sure, too confident of themselves. You have to know what the negotiator on the other side is going through.[8]

The other sides in organizational conflict talk and they act. Mostly they talk just like you. They aren't anxious to lay their cards down until the last hand and then only if they have to. There is a lot of jockeying, little feints here and there—shadow boxing.

In the case of the hostage crisis, one must find out where the locus of power lies.[9] The person talking is not necessarily the person with the power. Locating the actual power is part of the shadow boxing. It requires *teasing out of the situation* that cast of characters who are the leaders and then determining their motives. What do they want? Where is the line of exchange, the *quid pro quo? Patience* is the major prerequisite for the school administrator engaged in internal power plays.

## THE ZERO SUM GAME AS ORGANIZATIONAL POKER PLAYING

At the base of most organizational power plays is the fact that resources are finite. The three major resources are people, time, and materials such as buildings, books, buses. All of these can be represented in a budget. It is true that conflict is caused by personality clashes or ideological differences, but these are usually only the wrappings on the *real cause.*

People and groups *compete* for the resources within organizations. The acquisition of those resources represents the winnings of the collective poker game played by the participants. Most educators don't think of building a school budget as akin to a poker game, but indeed it is.

The basis of the arithmetic is the same in poker as in the school budget. The concept is "the zero sum game." Simply put, this means what one player wins, some other player must lose. The number of chips is set. The game redistributes the chips. The chips in schools are represented by staff, facilities, materials. The bigger a department's budget, the more chips it has. In order for one department to get more staff, facilities, or materials it must "win" at some other department's expense.

This dynamic forces all of the people in organizations to form coalitions. There is always an uneasy peace in them for this reason. There will always be a certain amount of tension because of the competition for the limited resources within the budget.

School administrators must become adept at playing organizational poker. They must learn to recognize the signs of the players, when they have "the cards" and when they are "bluffing." Simply put, "to have the cards" means that when it comes to a showdown and a player must reveal his cards (his source of power), he or she has *got* the winning hand.

To have a winning hand, an administrator must have friends. These friends provide assurances, i.e., *support* when it comes to divvying up the pot or slicing up the budget pie. Friends are aces and kings. They may be the budget manager, the superintendent, other principals, the teacher's union, parents, or booster clubs.

To give the reader an example. Burt King was principal of Martha Washington High School. The school desperately required a new football stadium. In fact, it was condemned to be torn down. Burt needed about $250,000 for the stadium. He didn't have it. The school district didn't have it.

Burt went out in the community and knocked on some influential doors. In short time he had financial commitments for the stadium. Then he got a bulldozer and knocked the stadium down himself.

When the superintendent found out, he was furious. Burt had never asked permission. What did he mean knocking down the stadium? But the superintendent was loath to make a public discussion of the problem for fear of alienating the community. So he privately stewed about it. The new stadium was built.

The following year the other high school, John Adams, put into the budget monies for a new football stadium. The request was granted. Burt was outraged. He had worked for it and now the other school just got it without having to do the door knocking routine. So Burt went to the superintendent and said his people were really put out about it. He said that an equivalent amount should be spent on a new outdoor track to placate his community. The superintendent screamed but consented. The money was put into the budget for the new track at Martha Washington. Where did the funds come from? Three junior high schools' science rooms were to be refurbished. They were moved back one year for the new track.

In the poker game just played, Burt King used the superintendent as an "ace." He needed that ace to insure that his priorities were met at Washington. It didn't matter about the three science rooms. He had his people to fight for because they were his support in the poker game. The superintendent was a reluctant "ace," and Burt had to continually watch to shore up the strength of the superintendent's commitment to the track.

This kind of infighting goes on all the time. Nobody in school administration is surprised by it. The problem of finite resources causes people to engage in competitive activities for those scarce resources. Everyone is a player even if they are not at the table. For example, parents in Burt's community were unseen support but counted when Burt was "called" by other forces within the school system.

Surely one could not equate an outdoor track with three science rooms? Logically it would be hard to argue the case. However, organizations are not logical. Choices are made by political consensus in a power poker game. Look across the land and find numerous examples of green football fields and shabby science labs. There are plenty around. The same game accounts for these facts, as in the example we cite.

And school systems aren't the only ones who do it. Congress is the extreme example. The Grace Commission which examined government waste found that fully 16 percent of federal support was pure waste. The Commission identified $424.4 billion that it avers the government "burns" every three years.

According to the Grace Commission the day to day operations of the government "are 'micromanaged' by 535 Congressmen and Senators who are vastly more concerned with the near-term good will of the folks back home than with the long-term welfare of the nation."[10] The same Commission cited scores of examples of how Congress had blocked plan after plan for reducing waste and improving services. Why? *Patronage. Power. Poker.*

We can't defend the system; we can only tell a rookie how it works. If you don't know it, you can get burned. Kids are not the name of the poker game, and academic priorities can only become priorities when the power forces are lined up to redistribute the "chips" in a more sensible fashion.

The most probable recourse would be for the three junior high school principals to band together to corral some "aces" of their own for the next budget round. You can bet Burt will be back, perhaps for a request for a new gym floor. The three principals can cultivate support from a variety of groups. If they wanted to play nasty, they might try several tactics. The first would be to get the labs condemned as unsafe by somebody or some agency. They could try getting someone from the State Department of Education to come down and inspect the labs. They could try the regional accrediting agency and see if some standards could be violated. This outside "ace" would be powerful leverage in the budget poker wars. Even Burt would find it difficult to argue his case against pupil safety in the science labs.

Given the processes just described, it is not difficult to arrive at the conclusion that organizations are essentially *amoral*, i.e., they are not concerned with some ultimate "right conduct." They are not preoccupied with ethics. They are neither moral nor immoral. They don't set out to do anybody in or to usurp their overall mission. Like a careless hunter they may shoot themselves in the foot, but they never meant to.

Only people are moral. Only individuals decide to be moral. Sometimes groups can be moral, but the more they become diverse and represent broad interests, the more amoral they become. Diplomats and labor mediators are amoral. They don't make judgments about friends or enemies. They just want an agreement or a pact.

Rather than bemoan the fact that organizations lack ethics, which in turn makes every good administrator a prostitute, we believe that this dilemma sets administrators free *to become moral.* We like Saul Alinsky's comment that:

> . . . the late Justice Learned Hand's statement that "the mark of a free man is that ever-gnawing inner uncertainty as to whether or not he is right." Having no fixed truth he has no final answers, no dogma, no formula, no panacea. The consequence is that he is ever on the hunt for

the causes of man's plight and the general propositions that help make sense out of man's irrational world. He is constantly examining life, including his own, to get some idea of what it means.[11]

It is the amorality of school districts, like other human organizations, that makes them vulnerable to attack both internally and externally, but that at the same time presents choices to administrators as to how to behave.

We don't suggest administrators become Don Quixotes, jousting at windmills in the name of honor. We do suggest that administrators know how the system works and why it works the way it does. It never meant to screw you—it just did. As Alinsky says, "Through experience you learn to see people not as sellouts and betrayers of moral principles, but as the result of ongoing processes."[12] It's the ongoing process that this book is about.

### BUILDING COALITIONS: THE CHESS GAME

To do just about anything in schools and school systems the school administrator must increase his/her clout at the table. To do this requires understanding the game. Our analogy takes us from the poker game, as it reflects the budgetary processes, to the political processes at work. To do this requires a more sophisticated and complex game. The ideal game is chess.

Learning the game of chess requires understanding not only what each individual piece can do, it requires knowledge of how to use pieces collectively, in tandem, and in groups. Pieces can be weak or strong based on their relation to other players opposing the "enemy."

So it is with the players and their combinations that prove winning strategies. But remember the other players are in the same game too. They will be counting on you to hoist their banners. There is an old Russian proverb to sum up your dilemma, "In this world, not everyone with a long knife is a cook."[13]

So be careful when choosing allies. The same set of Russian proverbs warns, "Be friends with the wolf, but keep one hand on your ax."[14] To form coalitions there has to be something in it for *both* parties. You want something and they want something. Be sure you can give what they want, *if* they want it. Be sure they can give what you want, *when you want it.*

Let's provide an example. Charles Hauck is the director of the gifted program. He faces a lot of hostility from principals who are jealous that he is taking away the "bright kids" from their schools. He faces some antipathy from the central office personnel who don't like the idea of "elites" being formed in the school district because administration is difficult enough without an elite parent group.

Hauck needs more teachers and supplies. He desperately needs to expand his program to continue momentum established earlier. Faced with this dilemma he initiates a three-pronged attack. First he goes to the superintendent and proposes an objective study of the gifted program. He sells it on the basis that this may quell some criticism of it by friends and foe alike.

Next he handpicks the consultants who will do the study and knows what their attitudes about gifted education are beforehand. Then he goes out to recruit a principal on whom to try new ideas by promising more resources for the total school. Finally he contacts two board members with students in the gifted program and tells them about the study to get their backing financially on a board vote. Hauck knows that the two members (of five) plus the superintendent and the forthcoming recommendations will provide both the recommendations and the impetus to act on the study. He knows that the resources he has promised to the principal will most likely be there if needed.

What Hauck has done is to piece together an agenda like a patchwork quilt in which, no matter what the motivations of the persons involved, they will agree to at least one of the moves to get where he wants to go. In tandem, it is a do-able strategy. Hauck knows that the board members are really in it because they want to keep their kids labeled "gifted" and brag about it at cocktail parties. He knows the superintendent would really like to keep a lid on the program via the consultant's work and so has agreed to the study, but he has checked the superintendent's probable move by handpicking consultants with a known track record. Finally, he has blunted the possibility of a principal boycott of program expansion by finding a principal who will agree to allow the program to be expanded because he wants more resources for the teachers and students at his school. Thus the power of the principals to outgun Hauck at the budget table or administrative council has been bypassed.

When building these kinds of coalitions it is good to remember that you don't make judgments about why your allies are with you, i.e., *their motivations*. One can't control that. You should know what they are, but don't force them to be with you for *your reasons*. It's *their agenda* that counts when enlisting their support. You must show how your agenda and theirs are *compatible*.

Such coalitions are very temporary, almost ad hoc. It's harder to maintain such coalitions when the time line becomes so long that payoffs for all parties become more risky. Short-term payoffs can work. Long-term coalitions are only possible for very emotional issues or life threatening ones. When a lot of teachers may be laid off because of an administrative action, then coalition-building aimed at restoring them may be forced onto a longer time line. Holding the coalition together also becomes harder over time because the more diverse the group, the more it finds it difficult to keep some center ground common to all. Time has a way of whittling away at consensus and emphasizing the differences rather than the commonalities.

The key to building coalitions is to understand that in every organization there is a momentum going someplace with groups tugging and pulling, but being swept along. It's not a matter of forcing your momentum on anybody or any group. It is finding out what the momentum is and who it involves, and then hitching your wagon to it. Played right you can end up at the front of the group, but it doesn't matter. What matters is that you understand the crosscurrents of life inside schools.

## IS SCHOOL ADMINISTRATION FOR YOU?

Whether just beginning or somewhere along the administrative career ladder, one should take stock. Is this for me? A major reason why some of our colleagues fail in educational administration is that they chose the field for the wrong reasons. Almost all school administrators start out as classroom teachers. They chose to become classroom teachers for a variety of reasons. Some may be:

- enjoying working closely with children and young adults;
- preferring a nine month work calendar;
- feeling completely autonomous (independent) in the classroom;
- seeing direct results with children and sensing its importance;
- having the security of tenure;
- being able to teach the subject one loves;
- being a member of a helping profession;
- enjoying the colleagiality of fellow professionals;
- being respected in the community;
- being a "born teacher";
- being able to structure and control one's time.

As the years go on, many classroom teachers, like anyone else, become bored with what they're doing. Many look for a change. Others look for a challenge. Some look for money or prestige. And still others begin to see titles in the administrative hierarchy as being rungs on a career ladder.

Before taking any steps which lead away from the classroom, teachers should ask themselves:

- What am I getting from my present job (the good and the bad)?
- How much of the good will I be able to keep on the "next rung" and how much will I have to leave behind? How much of the bad or unpleasant things can I leave behind?
- What are the new goods and bads I can expect on my new job?

For example, the higher up the administrative career ladder one climbs, the less daily contact one has with students, and the contact itself becomes different. While a classroom teacher often plays the role of counselor, friend, mentor, etc., an administrator is most usually in the role of disciplinarian. And most school superintendents don't relate to kids at all!

In addition to their changing and declining relationships with kids, school administrators deal with adults, parents, teachers, custodians, bus drivers, teachers' aides, cafeteria, and clerical staff. A "hot-shot" teacher is not necessarily a sure-fire winner as a school administrator.

The higher up on the administrative career ladder one goes, the more the administrator deals with *groups*—PTA's, boards of education, unions, advisory committees. A course in adolescent psychology isn't nearly as useful to a school superintendent as is an understanding of group dynamics, organizational behavior or abnormal psychology!

Another necessary adaptation upon entering the world of school administration is a lengthening of the work day and work year— usually directly proportional to the height of the rung on the ladder (i.e., the higher the title, the longer the hours). Often building administrators are the first to arrive and the last to leave the building. All successful administrators spend many evenings at meetings, school and district functions, etc. Plenty of time with the family is a fringe benefit one must give up as an administrator.

Autonomy is another myth attributed to school administrators, usually by teachers. What most teachers do not know is that no administrator enjoys the autonomy of classroom teachers within the four walls of the classroom! No one in education is pulled in more directions and is accountable to more people than school administrators. Understanding that the board of education is just one group to whom an administrator is accountable is not imagined by those without experience as administrators.

Seeing direct results and having a direct impact on the learning process of children is another fringe benefit of the classroom teacher which must often be left at the classroom door. While a principal may work sixty hours a week, often the feeling, "Just what am I accomplishing?" is a prevalent perception. And if test scores rise or vandalism decreases, a full moon is more apt to get the credit than an exhausted principal.

While tenure is enjoyed by many administrators in some states, superintendents generally do not receive tenure, and job security for administrators is more tenuous than for teachers because administrators are more vulnerable to public pressures and board caprice than teachers who enjoy the protection of the unions and the courts.

Finally, classroom teachers enjoy an incredible amount of control over their workday. For the school administrator, one irate parent, one faculty member with a crisis, one student with a severe problem can blow the plans of a whole day, sometimes many days. Once an administrator shows up for work anything can happen—and usually does—with little regard for the administrator's time or plans.

So who would make a good school administrator? First, we believe someone who has come to terms with his or her own ego needs. If they are being met in the classroom, then why leave it? But if they are not being met or if they have changed over the years, then school administration may offer a possibility.

Once administration is entered upon as a career, one is into power and politics. The sanctuary of the classroom is left behind. This is the rough and tumble world of dealing with other human beings whose motives are as endless as the plots in mystery thrillers.

Like it or not, administrators are *power brokers*. Administrators generally have more power than classroom teachers. They can do things that classroom teachers cannot do. They can make things happen that classroom teachers cannot.

Power is the essential ingredient of any prognosis for the success of a practicing school administrator. Ask yourself these questions:

- What is your attitude toward power? Does it interest you? Does it embarrass you?
- Are you comfortable with power?
- Can you handle power? (Many people can't.)
- How do you react to powerful people? Do they intimidate you? Do you begrudge them their power?

What is the price of power? Listen to those who've been there:

You have so many things coming at you that are divisive, that involve disputes. You have to be able to hear people out and to roll with the punches. Ninety percent of the job involves saying no. And you must be able to do so agreeably.

JAMES BAKER, *Secretary of the Treasury*[15]

Public officials today are so exposed that they're subjected to continuous criticism . . . and a lot of it tends to be ad hominem—so a thick skin is an absolute prerequisite.

ZBIGNIEW BREZINSKI, *Former National Security Advisor*[16]

Is it worth it?

Edward Koch, the mayor of New York City, once observed:

The unique compensation for all of this is that you have an impact on life that will live on long after you have left office. It is this power to change things for the better that is awesome and at the same time so challenging that it brings out the best in the best and makes it all worthwhile.[17]

We would agree. But let's all know the price *before* going into the game, not after we've been in it.

## CAVEATS, CODICILS, AND CONUNDRUMS ABOUT POWER AND POLITICS

- Despite their exalted function, schools are not much different in terms of the people in them than most other organizations.
- Most school administrators are afraid to admit they like the power of the office and that it's one of the attractions for them to be in administration.
- Most administrative training programs at colleges and universities are aimed at the development of technical skills. Sometimes they end up training the bastards and making them worse (better?).
- Being successful in school administration means knowing what situation you are in and which ones you are *not in*.
- Power diminishes with use.
- Real power is face to face. There is no other kind in human transactional currency.
- One must be able to win people and not force people.
- The person talking is not necessarily the person with the power.
- People and groups compete for the resources within school and school systems.
- School administrators must become adept at ''organizational poker.''

- Schools are essentially amoral places; only people individually are moral.
- "In this world, not everyone with a long knife is a cook" (Russian proverb).
- "Be friends with the wolf, but keep one hand on your ax" (Russian proverb).
- Every organization has its own momentum. Hitch your wagon to it.
- Teachers may need courses in adolescent psychology. Administrators need one in abnormal psychology.
- An administrator's tenure is tenuous.
- The notion that an excellent teacher will make an excellent administrator is excellent—as a *notion*.
- The most concrete daily plan an administrator can make is showing up for work.
- Becoming an administrator is a career change.
- Administrators are power brokers.
- In school administration the power is NOT in the title.
- School administrators do not have pink slips.
- Making a difference is the goal; power is the vehicle.
- Administrators must be good chess players.
- Only risk-takers can cope with vulnerability as an occupational hazard.
- Administration is the road less traveled.

## CHAPTER 2

# Are You Ready to Play the Game?

## THE GAME, THE PLAYERS, THE STAKES, AND THE RULES

Anyone who decides to become a school administrator must clear his or her mind of the many lofty theories of leadership packed into education course books. Such persons must develop a proper mental set: the one that it takes *to play the game.*

School administration is a GAME, and don't forget it. As with any game, a sense of humor and a sense of balance are critical. If you take the game too seriously, you can take one loss too hard. Once, after the USC Trojans had lost a particularly bitter football game to a rival by a lopsided score, the coach, John McKay, told his players, "There are still over sixty million Chinese who don't care if we won or lost."

And if you can't tell the players without a score card, better get your score card in order. While school administrators usually relate to the players as individuals, your score card should help you identify them as members of cluster groups:

- superiors
- subordinates
- PTA
- faculty
- students
- unions
- alumni groups
- religious groups
- senior citizens

- reform groups

- vigilante groups

- non-certified staff
- board of education
- the media
- taxpayers groups
- business groups
- ethnic or racial groups
- advisory boards
- special interest groups
- residents WITH children in the district
- residents WITH NO children in the district
- assassins, crazies, kooks

The list of players and player clusters is endless, unique to each school district, and always in a state of flux. Each player is somewhat like one of the blind men groping around a part of the proverbial elephant—each convinced that by feeling a part of it, he "sees" the whole picture. And since most of the players within a cluster see it pretty much the same way, why, five million Frenchmen can't be wrong!

Of course, the school administrator is one of the players and, we hope, an active one. Don't take the game too seriously as many of our colleagues have done, ending up with heart problems, alcoholism, ulcers. Remember that you're a player, not a saviour. Players win one day, lose another, but they have to come back to play again. Martyrs don't have another chance.

As in any game, there are stakes and the stakes are simple. The title of a song popular a year ago was "Everybody Wants to Rule the World." The ultimate stakes are the kids—the ones who grow up to be President, or senator, judges, army generals, and, hopefully, sound citizens. Since the game is being played in arenas throughout the U.S., the result is the future of America and perhaps the world.

Like most games the rules are the key. Most of the rules are *unwritten*. They're learned from experience. So school administrators, especially during the early years, have to endure a trial by fire. It's somewhat like being forced to walk through a mine field. You learn by stepping on one or two.

If one remembers that one is playing a game, one can get an "intuitive feel" for the rules the way a dog can detect explosives by scent. One comes to realize that like national, state, and local politics, the educational political wheel is oiled by compromises and its rim strengthened by the spokes of strong coalitions.

### THE NATURE OF SCHOOL ADMINISTRATION

A school administrator's power is his/her ability to influence and persuade. That makes one a politician, and school administration is politics. Does that mean that school administrators are not educators and that educators can be found only in the classrooms? Not at all. But we do mean that school administration is political first and educational second. To think otherwise is asking to become disillusioned and bitter later. Any reading of the life stories of some of the early public education heroes like Horace Mann or Henry Barnard will amply illustrate the art of politics in establishing public education in the nation. Both educational leaders were astute politicians in the finest sense of the word.

The school administrator builds bases of support—slowly, knowing that if he/she is too good too fast, some of the players may leave the game or choose to end it. Without players there is no game. The game must go on if education is to go on. And there will always be a game. The players that left the table will start a new one. Don't be left out. The schools can't afford to be left out.

The nature of school administration reflects the very nature of the school district pyramid itself. At the top is a group of board of education members elected by the residents of the district usually because those who vote for them think that the board will give them what they want. The board then hires a superintendent whom it feels will give them what they want. A superintendent will hire an administrative staff that he feels will give him/her what he/she wants. The administrative staff will hire teachers who they feel will give them what they want. And teachers will go into classrooms and try to get kids to do what they want.

Often this leads to what we call "domino paranoia." The kids are afraid of the teachers; the teachers are afraid of the principal; the principal is afraid of the central office administration; the central office administration is afraid of the superintendent; the superintendent is afraid of the board. The board is afraid of the people. The people are afraid of the entire system and don't trust anybody. They just want good teachers to care about their kids.

Into this climate of anxiety treads the school administrator. The players are both enemies and friends. You can beat them in a hand, and if you're really good, they won't even know. But you must never defeat them. They'll get you for that, and then the game will be over for you. They'll keep playing without you.

## WINNING, LOSING, WINNERS, AND LOSERS

As in most games the object in school administration is to win. But unlike most games, in school administration, YOU CAN LOSE BY WINNING TOO MUCH TOO OFTEN! A school superintendent who is too popular with the teachers has to be "in bed" with the teacher's union. And while all boards of education profess a desire for a strong educational leader when screening for a superintendent, in reality, they get scared to death when they meet one in the flesh. A strong, dynamic, charismatic, intelligent educational leader in any position in school administration is at risk because he/she probably is a threat to those who see this power as their impotence.

So in this game, always keep in mind that WINNING IS NOT JUST GETTING YOUR WAY AND ACCOMPLISHING YOUR OBJECTIVES, IT'S MAINTAINING YOUR COALITIONS. Sometimes a school administrator even has to lose one for the system to win. It's the old "win the battle but lose the war" situation.

Some school administrators go to great lengths to avoid even appearing too much as winners. One superintendent we know offered this advice to one of his young elementary principals who drove a new car, belonged to the community yacht club, and lived in a high priced house in one of the most expensive parts of the district.

"Linda," he said, "let me tell you a story about an old friend of mine, a fellow superintendent. This guy would always 'low-key' it in everything he did. He'd never wear expensive clothes. He'd always drive old jalopies. His home was modest by any standard. Then he retired. His last day of work was on Wednesday. And do you know what he did on the very next day, Thursday? He walked right into a Cadillac showroom and bought a brand new Caddy right off the showroom floor. He drove that sucker right down the main street that same afternoon."

The superintendent's young administrator could see why he had so identified with his friend. The superintendent had a reputation for being cheap. Nothing about him or his wife was the least bit lavish. No one would ever guess from his observable life-style that he was the most highly paid school superintendent in that part of the state.

Yet the elementary school principal was saddened by the story. After all, both her boss and her boss's friend were doctors in their own right (Ph.D.'s). They each commanded budgets, physical plants, and employees whose numbers rivaled those in many moderate corporations. Why shouldn't they live like corporation presidents or chairpersons of the board? Yet in order to remain winners, both superintendents felt they had to appear as less than successful.

You see, some superintendents really take the term "public servant" literally. They probably worked for school boards who saw educators as a kind of domestic help. Some still do. Of course, posing as a loser in order to be a winner remains an option, and it is an option that is used by many players—sometimes even subconsciously. But we have to admit that it is not a very attractive option to either of us for a number of reasons. First, we think most school executives are worth far more than many of their corporate comrades because school administrators can't get rid of the deadheads and smart asses on the spot or at least as readily as their corporate counterparts do.

Secondly, school administrators deal with real people and what they become and make of their lives. Certainly that is as important a concern as the medical doctors who save lives. Yet few MD's fear for their practice if they drive a Porsche. Woe be it to the superintendent who drives one to work. And why shouldn't a high school principal make more money than the vice-president of a paper company? Finally, we don't advocate posing as someone else as a game strategy because it's dangerous. Kurt Vonnegut said it best when he wrote, "We are what we pretend to be, so we must be careful about what we pretend to be."

While we don't advocate rubbing your boss's nose in your material possessions (or your lust for them), we do believe that in general, any job that diminishes one's life-style isn't worth having. Any boss or board of education that can't deal with that isn't worth working for—and there are plenty of them out there who aren't.

But wealth is just one way to turn off a coalition of support. We know of a superintendent in the Midwest who is one of a kind. His administrators would follow him anywhere. The teachers in the district adore him. He is responsible for the relatively high morale within the district in spite of the fact that administrators have been working for two years without a contract and teachers have been without a contract for over a year.

Our hero's reward is that his own contract will not be renewed at the end of this school year. The teachers and administrators are at a loss. They can't understand the reason. They simply say, "He's too good for them." In a way, they're right.

As it turns out, the president of the board is ego-maniacal. He craves the affection the superintendent gets. He perceives the publicity and adoration of the superintendent as a loss for him.

The bitter superintendent sees the situation this way: "Those bastards didn't want anybody with conviction. They wanted a 'yes-man.' Well, screw 'em. I'm no yes-man. I did it my way."

In the three years he had served as superintendent of schools he had won many battles. As a matter of record, he had won just about _every battle_. But he lost the war—perhaps because he had won every battle. A better politician would possibly have made that school board president into an ally, a person who felt _enhanced_ by the superintendent's being there rather than feeling diminished by the superintendent. Doing it "your way" is fine as long as you can keep doing it. But what the hell is such a big deal about doing it your way if there are thirty days left to your three year contract and the school board isn't going to renew it?

There are sensitivities present in every community. If one's life-style is such that living in a town will be considered a topic of conversation over many dinners and cocktail parties, live somewhere else if possible. If the boss's life-style is too conservative, don't insult the life-style by offering a sharp contrast.

The elementary principal we cited never lived closer than ONE

TOLL CALL FROM THE DISTRICT. She maintained a separation of her private and professional lives through geography.

## The Winners and Losers Grid

We offer the following simple grid as a way to cope with the problem.

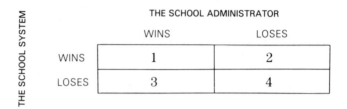

There are two entities in our grid. The first is the school administrator. The second is the school system. The "cells" are as follows:

(1)  In this case the administrator "wins" and the system "wins."
(2)  The school administrator loses but the system gains.
(3)  The school administrator wins, the system loses.
(4)  The administrator loses and the system loses.

The best situation is where the administrator wins and the system wins. This can only occur if the goals of the system are compatible with the administrator or vice versa. One example might be where the administrator puts in a new curriculum which in turn improves pupil achievement. Everybody wins.

One example of a "type two" situation is where the building principal loses his or her fight to install new auditorium seats, but the elementary schools put in a gifted and talented program which silences community critics and results in a positive editorial in the local paper.

A "type three" situation prevails where the school administrator wins something, but the result is that the overall system is lessened because of it. This is where the actions of an administrator result in more resources going his/her way, but where everyone else suffers. Thus, the total system is worse as a result of one person winning.

Finally, the last situation, the "type four" is where everybody loses. One example occurred in one school district where the superintendent insisted on putting in covered walkways between schools in a state known for sunshine. The taxpayers used this as an excuse to torpedo a complete bond issue in which critically needed classrooms were also lost. Clearly, the superintendent lost, and the system and children did as well.

In the case of the charismatic superintendent whose contract was not renewed, both the administrator and the system lost. The system lost an outstanding administrator who would have inspired the district's personnel to continue to do good things with and for kids. The administrator lost his job—and the right to continue the game.

The "type-four" situation is the most wasteful because everybody is a loser.


## JOCKS, JIVE, AND JOKERS

One phenomenon in school administration that occurs so frequently is the number of school administrators who were physical education teachers and/or coaches of athletic teams. One often heard explanation of this phenomenon is that it occurs because P.E. teachers, unlike their colleagues in academic areas, had no papers to correct or school work to prepare for at home, thus giving them the time to take courses in school administration and become certified.

In general, coaches put in more time after hours and on weekends than anyone else in any given school building—including the principal. So that's not the reason.

If school administration is a game, who in education is more skilled at playing games than coaches? They can see that it's a game, and they're at home playing games. They have spent years dealing with strategies, ploys, plots, parents, and politics. Any coach worth his or her salt has to be good at public relations, moving easily among members of a potentially lethal parent "booster" club, speaking at sports banquets, lobbying for a bigger share of the school budget, inspiring and motivating their teams, arbitrating conflicts of interests between teachers' demands on students and students' commitment to the team, placating parents who constantly second-guess the coach or have their noses out of joint because their kids aren't playing enough. Coaches are naturals as school administrators. They can move from one job to the next easily.

Therefore, what most jocks know about school administration almost intuitively is of vital importance for everyone else to learn. But, of course, jocks need to learn about other things that go along with the job as well, such as curriculum and content assessment. And if they're smart, they'll waste no time learning about them.

Unfortunately, what many jocks do is to surround themselves with other jocks who spin yarns about sports anecdotes and "jock talk" each other from morning until evening. The most sinister kind of network referred to these days is the "good ole boy" network. These are usually former jocks who are decidedly anti-intellectual and approach each problem with either a pep talk, a joke, or a pat on the rump. Few things will cause more resentment among a school faculty than a jock administration which treats them all as high school athletes who need praise or criticism, as if they were at halftime waiting to follow the band back onto the field.

### Jive

"Jive" refers to the special term in music that means "swing." It is also the talk of "hipsters." It means for us a kind of sweet talk that is governed by a realistic appraisal of the situation covered over by adroit use of language.

One example that comes to mind is the famous wit of the Canadian Ambassador's spouse, Sondra Gotlieb. Instead of shrinking into a tea cup and Washington gossip, Sondra Gotlieb emerged as a powerful intellectual asset to her husband in representing Canadian interests in Washington.

A former novelist, Sondra invented a new language to describe the milieux of Washington. The nation's capital is known as "Powertown." A very high cabinet official is known as "Mr. Secretary." A former aide to someone powerful is called "a Used-To-Be-Close-To." An over zealous puffed-up official is called "a Powerful Job," and his wife, "a Wife of."[1]

Sondra's husband, Allan Gotlieb, has broken past patterns in dealing in "Powertown." Canadian officials spread out and work many fronts in many agencies. This new approach has increased Canadian visibility in Powertown.

> "I am practicing a diplomacy that is thoroughly modern. It is different from traditional diplomacy. It is not in any books. It is not widely understood. And it is not practiced in any other country," says Gotlieb.[2]

Gotlieb's approach is getting close to powerful people. It works for management in dealing with less powerful but just as important people. When examining how Japanese management acts with American employees, one report noted that the Japanese don't believe in big consultants or senior people making much of a contribution to excellence. They believe in rolling up their sleeves and working with their people on the assembly line. They wear the same uniform as the employees.

> The Japanese have a strong belief in the "little brain theory. . . ." They see the worker as an extraordinary resource that, properly motivated, can find little ways each day to do the job better.[3]

We think of the lesson learned in wooing Hispanic voters by the Reagan people. First they tried using familiar symbols to woo Latins such as the Statue of Liberty. Previous President Gerald Ford committed the unpardonable sin of eating the corn husk that a tamale was packed in, thus demonstrating his lack of understanding to all Hispanics.[4] Chicago's Mayor Jane Byrne also ran aground of Hispanic sensitivities when she referred to a late conference as running on "Latino time."[5]

When the Reagan campaign shifted to the language Hispanics understood, they used Hispanics speaking to the President's "fuerte," or "strength." The advertisements stressed traditional Latin virtues of hard work, family values, and patriotism.[6]

In conversing with teachers, the sensitive educator avoids alluding to the "top" and "bottom" of the bureaucratic hierarchy. The reason is evident. For too long, teachers were positioned near the base of the administrative pyramid, and "bottom" had come to connote "of lesser importance."

Other sensitivities will help the staff understand that one practices curricular congruence not to produce "uniformity" but to achieve better "coordination." "Uniformity" to most teachers means assembly line production models with impersonal relationships to "things." "Coordination" means working more closely together to improve teaching for kids.

In other closely related situations one does not talk about "teaching to the test," but rather making sure that our children are taught what we test because it is unfair for them to be placed in a situation where they may fail because of our inattention.

"Jive" means learning the language of the people you work with and learning what words mean to them. It means respecting them and being observant of their feelings.

World famous singer Julio Iglesias once commented on his approach to courting women. Said the international crooner, "If the lady is a dentist, talk about teeth. Don't bring her into your world. Enter hers."[7] We think that is fairly sound advice to cover all situations.

## Jokers

Jokers are those individuals who want to embarrass the school administrator any way they can, but usually in public at board meetings. These frustrated souls are some of the "regulars" at board meetings in most towns and cities. For whatever reason, they become "board junkies." Most have axes to grind. Most hate administrators. Many are unhappy at home or at their jobs.

We call them "jokers" because they can ruin any good hand you may have set up or spoil almost anything if you let them. After jousting with them for years, in public and private, we've developed a general kind of strategy for dealing with them.

First, never put them down in public. The more outrageous they get, the better. Ignore them. It will drive them crazy. Most of all they want you to lose your cool. They want your blood on the floor, not theirs. They want to provoke you. Never get into a fight with a skunk. Even if you win, you lose. Everybody smells bad. Force them to play their little games in the public arena.

You will have to endure some endless evenings of tirades, maundering, nonsense. The more they talk the more unflappable you become. Answer them in detail if you can. Always straightforwardly. Never a tone of annoyance in your voice. The people around you will become annoyed. The audience will become a group of vigilantes. They will hang the joker with the rope he had spun for you. We've seen it happen time and time again. But it is a game of patience. We've seen audiences critical of us turn on a "joker" who was so outrageous that they ended up defending us. One can almost see the body language. People move away to different seats. They frown. They turn away. Social ostracism takes care of most "jokers." It will do it more effectively than anything you could do or say. Don't be sucked into this kind of battle. It's a "lose–lose" situation.

### CAVEATS, CODICILS, AND CONUNDRUMS ABOUT PLAYING THE GAME

- School administration is a game; that's why coaches are naturals.
- There's just no future in martyrdom.
- The rules of school administration are unwritten.
- The "big guns" of the school administrator: influence and persuasion.

- In school administration, conflict is a way of life; if you can't accept this, don't become the boss.
- You can beat your opponents, but you must never defeat them.
- Winning too much too often can make you lose.
- Winning is not just getting your objectives, but maintaining your coalitions.
- The green-eyed monster is a formidable foe.
- "We are what we pretend to be so we must be careful what we pretend to be."—Kurt Vonnegut, Jr.
- Any job that diminishes one's life-style isn't worth having.
- Doing it your way is fine as long as you can keep doing it.
- Enhance a stranger, you've made a friend; diminish anyone and you've made a mistake.
- Never get into a fight with a skunk; even if you win, you lose.
- When an administrator wins and the system loses, the administrator also has lost—he/she just doesn't know it.
- "Jive" means learning the language of the people you work with and learning what words mean to them.

## CHAPTER 3

# Bureaucracies, Babus, and Baksheesh

## VACUUMS, INERTIA, AND ADMINISTRIVIA

The problem of bureaucracies confronts civilized people all over the world. It makes no difference whether a society is capitalistic, socialistic, or communistic, none has been able to rid itself of these organizational dinosaurs. Our daily routines and thinking are pervasively influenced by bureaucracies.

The word *bureaucracy* was coined by the German sociologist Max Weber. He indicated, among other things, that bureaucracies were distinguished by these features:

- neatly prescribed roles/jobs which were tied to examination systems;
- roles/jobs set into patterns following a superior/subordinate relationship;
- career ladders in which qualified people could move "up" within the organization on the basis of performance/merit or, at least, qualifications;
- permanent roles not dependent upon finances nor influence.

School administrators work in bureaucracies. School systems are examples of bureaucratic organizations in that they possess all of the features of the classic Weberian organization. Indeed, school administrators are *bureaucrats*. We use the word descriptively and not pejoratively.

Learning how to function in a bureaucracy is not only a matter of survival, but of success. Bureaucracies have rules of their own. Once a bureaucracy gets going, it is difficult, perhaps impossible, to dismantle it. President Reagan often referred to Washington bureaucracies as the "puzzle palaces on the Potomac."[1] Indeed, while bureaucracies have some redeeming features (most notably per-

*35*

manency), it is their inefficiencies that have made them famous. We cite a few examples:

- From *Pravda,* the world famous Russian newspaper, comes the story of the lost freight train. It seems that in June of 1983 a twenty-eight-car freight train was lost by the Russian Rail Ministry.[2] Noted the paper, "Even Sherlock Holmes from Baker Street in London could have lost his way in the paper labyrinth."[3]
- When Admiral Turner took over the CIA and was asked by President Carter for some overhead photography of a war in the Third World, it took many weeks to deliver the goods of a "Mickey Mouse War."[4]
- When a prize-winning Miami newspaper photographer was killed in an operation because of accidental injection of glutaraldehyde instead of cerebrospinal fluid in the removal of a cancerous eye, a Miami malpractice lawyer noted, "The problem is not the competency of the staff but the bureaucratic system in many hospitals. Everybody is so concerned about their own narrow niche that no one is worried about the total picture. The National Center for Health Statistics in Bethesda, Maryland, reports that more than 2,000 patients a year die as a result of medical accidents."[5]
- The IRS (Internal Revenue Service) was accused of shredding 63,000 letters in order to ease the workload of the agency that was caused by a breakdown in a new $103 million computer that was supposed to help the agency become more efficient.[6]
- When the U.S. Commerce Department agreed to give a West German firm permission to make bulletproof garments for the Syrian military, the Pentagon discovered that some of the garments would wind up in the hands of Islamic terrorists. The Pentagon then had to pay $12 million for 11,000 flak jackets and limb protectors it never wanted in the first place.[7]
- The U.S. Post Office finally abandoned a new electronic mail system tabbed as ECOM after blowing $99 million on the system. At last reading they were looking for a buyer. No takers were to be found.

The slowness of bureaucracy to move in any direction at all is well known. John Ashworth, a member of Great Britain's Central Policy Review staff and now vice chancellor at the University of Salford commented on the technology race the British were running against the Americans and the Japanese. Noted Professor Ashworth in commenting upon efforts the British were making to "catch" the competition:

> They're spitting in the wind. By their nature, all these cooperative ventures are bureaucratic. How could they not be? . . . As I see it, the chances of success are far better if bureaucratic programs are directed at heroic areas like space.[8]

It is the battle of the bureaucracy that is the supreme test for any new political leader. New Indian Prime Minister Rajiv Gandhi's acid test will be his ability to move sixteen million lower level civil servants known as *babus*. India is in the troglodyte grasp of the babus. One story mentioned is that when a *babu* demands a bribe for performing his service (normally a stamp on paper) and is told by an Indian that Rajiv Gandhi no longer permits *baksheesh*, the babu responds, "Then get your license from Rajiv Gandhi," and throws away the application in the round file.[9]

*Baksheesh*, the practice of paying for routine services, is known throughout the world. In an Indian railroad station, a gaggle of bureaucrats moves paper from desk to desk, each move carrying with it the need to pay the person to stamp the paper and move it to the next desk.

Even the new Russian Premier, Mikhail S. Gorbachev, was given high marks for consolidating his power in the Soviet Union, but a low chance of upgrading the entrenched and conservative middle level Soviet bureaucracy.[10]

So bureaucracy is stifling. It cares little about the services it provides. It is more interested in its own self-interests than the clients its services are aimed at. It is a self-perpetuating form of organizational behavior which is suspicious of change and interested only in maintaining the status quo.

The costs of bureaucracy are enormous. We are told that in one state government office in the U.S. dealing with rehabilitative services, it took four weeks to process forty-two separate pieces of $8 \times 10$ sheets in twenty-one different forms to obtain an $80.00 pair of eyeglasses for the person to work. The "file" was kept in a six-ply folder in which the person signed his name forty-two separate times.

The overriding objectives of bureaucracies and the *babus* in them is security and stability at any cost. The purpose of the bureaucracy is not to serve *but to be served*. Therefore, a preoccupation with administrivia, forms, procedure, regularity, and routine is the dominant value of bureaucracies. Decisions can only be made if they "fit" the forms and procedures.

*Babus* despise vacuums. A vacuum is an invitation to deviate from protocol. Babus rush in to create *structured inertia* so that the bureaucracy can continue to function in "business as usual" methods. Bureaucracies create mazes to slow things up, to routinize problems, and to remain comfortable at all costs.

The school administrator confronting life in a bureaucracy must run a curious and dangerous "double life" of conformist and spy, loyalist and traitor, to the well trod paths of bureaucratic happiness. One team of authors has described a successful school principal as one who engages in "creative insubordination" with downtown superiors.[11]

After spending many years in the corridors and offices of school bureaucracies we pass on these tips for beating the system.

### COMPETENCY AND POTENCY

Being competent is not enough to make it in school bureaucracies. We know lots of competent people trapped in bureaucracies who make the ultimate peace with the organization and settle for a life of comfort in rules and paper flowcharts.

To be potent requires knowing how to keep the bureaucracy off one's back, i.e., from becoming oppressive and grinding one down, and to take the "end run" around the bureaucracy to get things done. Keeping the bureaucracy off your back and the babus out of your life is the first "street smart" lesson for the school administrator.

### Rule 1: Don't Be the Exception

Bureaucracies run on "management by exception." The routinized is rarely questioned. What is different is questioned. Exceptions require a decision. Decisions are risky, even routine ones. Non-routine decisions are impossible. So whatever you do, avoid being the exception, the case that requires the formation of a committee, or an appeal to some high level bureaucrat. Take any action to appear "routine."

James H. Boren, President of the International Association of Professional Bureaucrats, puts out a number of words that capture the idea of being routine:

| | | | |
|---|---|---|---|
| fuzzify | oozify | intervoid | laserize |
| mushify | tincturize | thunderate | delegate |
| loopify | hunkerfy | drivelate | oopsify |

All of these words signify the need to paint reality with the well-worn hues of bureaucratic camouflage, to stretch the problem to fit the channels, to stay within the chain of command, to avoid being singled out. Remember, bureaucrats don't like to make decisions. Rather they are gatekeepers. They don't manage or motivate. They merely move things along. Their favorite word would be to "facilitate" things. A facilitator is not a decision maker. Just what a facilitator does is unknown. That's the way bureaucrats like it to be— *mushy.*

## Rule 2: Keep Paper Moving

Paper that sits too long on desks and in your "in box" can get you in trouble. There are always deadlines for it to be returned. Have your secretary classify it by sorting it into stacks by deadline. Forget what is important. What is important is what must be returned. The content is almost irrelevant. In one's drive not to be the exception deadlines must be met.

## Rule 3: Fill in the Blanks

Blanks are symbolic vacuums. Bureaucrats find blanks disturbing, a sign of a deviant, a question mark, a threat. For this reason fill in all of the blanks. It doesn't make any difference what goes in some of them. We know of one school principal who had learned this lesson but forgot it. Her boss was one of those prone to anxiety attacks of ambiguity in his sleep. For this reason he scanned the returned forms only for blanks. He didn't have time for anything else. The principal had submitted an employment form for a custodian. In it, a blank was left where it asked the reason for leaving high school. Now it didn't really matter since the person was going to be a custodian. But the principal's boss bounced the form back with a notation.

The principal waited for a time, then resubmitted the form. She filled in the blank as "abducted by space aliens." It sailed through with no problems. *Bureaucracies are mindless.* Only channels count! *Guidelines must be met.* Substance always takes a backseat to form. Form and timeliness are what count.

## Rule 4: Paper Is Reality

To a seasoned bureaucrat paper is not a symbol of reality: *it is reality.* Numbers come to be real things that can be added, subtracted, multiplied, and divided, and power is to manipulate numbers in a variety of reports and forms. Bureaucrats get to feel powerful. They come to believe they are running things by shifting numbers and columns. It is a game of self-deception. Many bureaucrats never come to believe in number magic. Thus, when former U.S. Budget Director David Stockman told the *Atlantic* magazine in 1981 that "none of us really understands what's going on with all these numbers," he was not criticized for being truthful but for saying it in public![12]

According to the Grace Commission on Government waste, the federal bureaucracy utilizes four times all of the office space in America's ten biggest cities. "In fact, the government doesn't know exactly how much office space it has, or where it is, or how much it is paying for it."[13]

It is easy to be seduced into believing that paper is reality when that is all one sees or knows. Paper is never reality. The Chief of the Internal Revenue Service put the matter into perspective when he told the American Bar Association that the IRS "put far too much emphasis on the numbers game" and too little on how well the work was done. Said the IRS Chief, "We have to start reminding ourselves more forcibly of what we're about, which is service to the taxpaying public."[14]

Reality in schools is the interaction between teachers and students and the results produced in that dynamic partnership. Anything else is window dressing, and the paper that describes it is too often not even a shadow of its quality.

Administrators must know the game and the players, but not be seduced into believing that paper trails and paper games are real. Lord Chancellor Edward Thurlow said it best when he said, "Did you ever expect a corporation to have a conscience, when it has no soul to be damned and no body to be kicked?"[15] The bureaucracy is always blamed, but it is the administrators in it who are responsible. *They decide to play the game,* knowing what rules pertain. The consciousness of the school system rests in that decision which is at the same time an *acceptance of the system.* Blame begins there.

### ROCKING IN THE BOAT VS ROCKING THE BOAT

Bureaucracies deal with the hackneyed. Change can be sneaked in by bureaucrats only if the words used to describe it are painted over with old language or nebulous non-threatening language. Most of all, the language must fit the forms and appear in the same place. Job titles match the forms. Messing with the forms means tinkering with one's territory and security. Nothing will get the dander of a bureaucrat up more than a threat to his or her job. This is rocking *the boat*. Rocking *in the boat* means fitting change or innovation into the symbols and signs of the tried and true. New wine must always be in the same old bottles. Although it is unknown, the authors are willing to bet that some of the objections raised by loyalists when Coca-Cola changed its ninety-nine-year-old formula were bureaucrats. It didn't matter that blind taste tests always favored the "new Coke." What mattered was the *form*, hence Coca-Cola profited from old wine in old bottles with Classic Coke, a marketing coup.[16]

Other examples abound. The battle over how much money to spend on defense has many arguing. However, pumping the unemployment problem with old Democratic programs isn't popular. It has been observed by Senator Ted Stevens, who is Chairman of the Appropriations Subcommittee on Defense, that the military budget is mainly "a jobs bill."

What he meant is that some members of Congress wanted $57 million for constructing twenty-four planes the navy said it didn't need. Another Congressman worked hard for a $75 million naval berthing pier. Universities struggled to obtain $175 million for research under "defense." The bottom line was about $4.5 billion on such projects that would have been cut under old or new titles in disfavor. Under "defense" such requests sailed right through.[17]

We think of an educational example. When one elementary principal learned about the concept of "curriculum alignment," she determined to make sure the staff accepted it. Alignment refers to the accepted but somewhat new practice of making test content congruent with classroom curriculum. This increases the potential of the teacher's work for improving test scores.

Rather than strive to acquaint the staff with curriculum alignment, she merely inserted both scores and curriculum content, as referenced in the textbooks used by the staff, into the faculty handbook without the proper titles. She labeled it "strengths" and "areas needing improvement." Then she reviewed it at the beginning of each school year. Not only have test scores improved, but there has been nary a whit of commotion about "curriculum alignment."

## BEATING THE SYSTEM VS BEING BEATEN BY THE SYSTEM

The system can beat you down. It can erect obstacles and construct endless paper procedures with elaborate checkoff and counter checks. It can be frustrating and insensitive. Yet, every day, hundreds of school administrators in thousands of school systems make it work. They have learned how to "beat" the system rather than being beaten down by it. From our own experiences and shared notes with many of our industrious colleagues we offer these points.

### Understand the Informal Organizational Structure

The "chain of command" refers to the formal, adopted table of organization and the boxes on them. This is the "official" blueprint of the school district. However, few organizations really run that way. In every organization there is the underbelly, the soft side, the real side. This is the structure that really makes the organization tick. You won't find it described anywhere. It won't be written down on anything, nor will there be any "policy" or "regulation" that creates it or rules it.

The informal organization consists of a potpourri of officers, secretaries, line and staff, superiors and subordinates, influential outsiders, insiders, and intruders. It's all quite loose. If you want to find out how it works, you can either ask someone who has been around a long time about it, or do your own observation and discern and discover it.

Questions like "Who do you really see about this problem?" will help in approaching an old timer. Another is, "If I heard a nasty rumor, who would really know if it were true or not?" Seasoned administrators have cultivated friendships in most of the downtown offices. They know secretaries and clerks. They know custodians and bus drivers and nurses. They know longtime teachers. They have developed a "network" of friends and allies. These friendships and associations exist in all organizations. They form around breaks, recreational interests, social events, clubs, and children's activities like Little League. Such networks carry over into work.

The official communication tool of the underbelly of the school district is the *grapevine*. Some studies of the grapevine indicate that about 80 percent of what is on the grapevine is true, but that it is only about 50 percent of the truth![18]

The grapevine can be your DEW line, an "early defense" that something is up. It can also be used to send messages to key people *through other people*. Perhaps this sounds devious. So be it. Complex and large organizations present almost implacable opposition to change or even performing their services to fit their clients. Rather than being manipulated by the system we prefer to manipulate the system for the betterment of children. Dozens of our colleagues have made the same decision.

Through the informal organization, much of the "work" of the organization gets done. By knowing whom to call and what to say, problems can be solved. Supplies can arrive on time. Films will be ready to be shown as teachers designed them—to reinforce classroom learning. Buildings will be painted and maintained. Morale will be good. We think it is worth it.

## Split the Opposition

Experienced school administrators facing a unique situation "shop around" for a decision maker who will give them approval if they require it. In all school districts there will be officers who are more dynamic and who take greater risks than others. Because lines of authority are rarely "clean" and most problems will fit one or more bureaucratic channels, it is possible to be selective in referring a problem for a decision.

Based on a personal knowledge of the biases and leadership styles of various central office personnel, school principals often "shop" for a decision maker to give them the green light. If the problem and the necessary decision happen to "fit" the preferences or biases of one administrator, send your problem there. Be sure, however, that the person has the "clout" to work your problem through the system. The "shopper" must know who has real power and who has paper power. This knowledge is usually based on personal experience and observation.

## Check the Anti's

For every action there is a counter action. This is as true in human dynamics as physics. The street smart administrator knows that if he or she initiates an action to solve a problem, someone may take exception to it. Thus the initiative may be blocked by a "higher up" in the pyramid.

Just as the administrator shops for a decision maker, so must that same administrator be on the lookout for a power to "check" or "block" the antibodies working against the change.

Rarely are these moves taken overtly. All of it happens mostly behind the scenes, and it can be quite subtle. A favorite gambit of the "anti's" is to make the request for a decision seem like an "exception." This must then be studied. A recommendation is made to form a committee. Place enough diversity on the committee and whatever happens there will be effectively stymied. The change is allowed to die slowly with the passage of time.

In this strategy, the opposition never is blatant. Nobody was really *against* your idea or proposal. It just had to be properly studied. Street wise administrators are on guard against this ploy. *Keep proposals away from committees!* Keep them close to the "line" authority of the organization. Massage problems until they "look like" the familiar. If your request might be stalled on a bureaucrat's desk, create your own SWAT team to rescue it.

The SWAT team may consist of a secretary who pulls it off the stack and sends it somewhere else before the boss has a chance to see it. The SWAT team may be a colleague of the person who reclassifies the problem into his domain. The SWAT team may be a superior who is befriended and snatches your proposal from the jaws of a veto by requesting to review it *with* the person who has your proposal.

Working a proposal "through" the tunnels of the bureaucracy is an art form. It is as tricky as maneuvering for a takeover or merger in the business world. And despite the best of intentions and finesse, the bureaucracy blocks, kills, stonewalls, and dissects most serious change before it is through. The failure rate is high. This is usually one set of records that the system doesn't keep.

### Know How High the Stakes Are

Working the system means understanding what is important and what isn't. A school administrator who "calls in all of his or her chips" for a bucket of paint is playing "overkill." Every proposal is not of equal value or importance. One never plays an ace unless an ace is required to take the trick. The degree of urgency or priority must be thoroughly understood prior to launching an attack on the bureaucracy.

The human network is an interesting phenomenon. It can't be overworked. If overused, your people just stop listening. They become progressively more unresponsive over time. Everything can't be an emergency. The school administrator must use the system only when the stakes are high and the result is critical for success.

### BLUNDERS AND BUSINESS ACUMEN

Now and then we read about a school administrator who was tempted in the bureaucracy to steal some money or use his or her position for personal gain. We know of the case of a superintendent of schools who lost his job for gold-plated plumbing in his beach house. He used a "dummy" class at a high school for which to order the plumbing equipment. A special slush fund was used to purchase the stuff.

We know of a state commissioner of education who created a fake bank account in the Bahamas into which contractors could dump "kickbacks." He went to jail.

Before one gets tempted to take advantage of his or her position in the bureaucracy, we offer some advice about it.

*If You're Going to Steal, Take a Lot*

We don't advocate stealing, but if you are going to do it anyway *take a lot.* Anything much less than half a million cold cash isn't worth it. The more you steal, the more the chances are improved that, if you are caught, you won't even be prosecuted. First, the system is mighty embarrassed that you could take that much and may decide it can't stand the publicity. You may have to repay the money if you haven't found a foreign country without an extradition treaty with the U.S. And you can always afford a high-priced lawyer who can search for loopholes or help you plea bargain.

Only extreme examples of white-collar crime get the public's eye.

Of the 9,900 white-collar offenders sentenced last year, 60% received no prison term. Those sent to jail typically serve one year or less.[19]

Perhaps one example is the E.F. Hutton case in which over three years the company cashed checks for more than one billion dollars than it had in various accounts at 400 banks. The daily overdraft scam, called "check kiting," meant that Hutton had the use of millions of dollars of interest-free loans.[20] The nation's fifth largest brokerage firm denied that its top leaders knew of or condoned the plan.

Despite the fact that evidence was emerging that the brokerage firm's auditor questioned the overdrafts at the highest levels of management and therefore they had to have knowledge of the mechanics, and despite the fact that House Representative Bill McCollum said that the auditor's questions should have "raised a big red flag" in front of the corporate moguls, there have as yet been no indictments and no convictions of anyone at Hutton.[21] The firm was fined $2 million.

Now consider the case of the father of the nuclear navy, Hyman Rickover. While the Admiral was building the nuclear navy, it seemed that he hit up the defense contractor, General Dynamics, for periodic gifts and trinkets and other gratuities. Admiral Rickover was reprimanded by Navy Secretary John Lehman for demanding and accepting $68,703 worth of gifts that included payment for cleaning bills, chauffeur charges for 504 trips, dinners, and thirty to fifty pounds of fresh fish at the launching of each new sub in the nuclear navy.[22]

At the same time that General Dynamics was kowtowing to Rickover, it was charging U.S. taxpayers for its submarines with over-padded bills and directing the charges of its executives for country club dues and kennel privileges for the executives' dogs.[23] In the midst of the uproar General Dynamics' chairman, David Lewis, resigned. To date, nary a single General Dynamics executive has gone to jail.

At one time nine of the top defense firms in the U.S. were under criminal investigation for such unsavory practices as falsification of performance records, defective pricing, labor mischarging, unallow-able claims, and duplicate billings. The firms read like the *Who's Who* of America's corporate kingpins: Boeing, Litton, Ford Motor Company, Grumman, Westinghouse, Honeywell, Rockwell International, Martin Marietta, Lockheed, and General Electric.[24]

Only in the case of General Electric were indictments given to GE officials when that Fortune 500 company pleaded guilty to defrauding the U.S. of more than $800,000 in the production of Minuteman missiles.[25]

Any case you know of in schools pales in comparison to the big ripoffs in business. We don't see a lot of business folks going to jail except an occasional Jake Butcher or Paul Thayer. We do know of a few school administrators who spent some petty cash on redecorating their offices, or who double charged for airline tickets or padded their expense accounts. Our advice is: *don't do it*. The smaller the crime, the more likely you will get caught and get hit with the big one. Petty thieves are a dime a dozen (no pun intended).

## The Board Is Always Right Even When It's Wrong

It may be possible for business leaders to argue with their boards of trustees, but in schools, it's *sudden death*. Whether elected or appointed, boards of education are the bosses of the business.

Boards of education are probably one of the few grassroots, democratic vestiges held over from the nation's dim past. As such, one can find the best and the worst in dealing with boards. For every "rose," there is a big weed. For every clear thinking honest citizen, there is a bastard who's in it for his or her ego and who really wants to be superintendent and meddle in administration.

As the tenure of superintendents has become shortened, so has the average tenure for board members. Experienced superintendents have told us that whereas in the past people came to boards with the "good of the district" uppermost in their minds, that nowadays people come to boards with special interests as their motive for being on the board. Board members come *for* gifted education, or *against* sex education. This narrow perspective makes governing hard because a board's stock in trade is its ability to provide a workable consensus for the school administration.

Our experience tells us that often teachers and medical doctors make the worst board members. Teachers, contrary to popular wisdom, don't come to boards with a total perspective. Most come with an anti-administration bias and view the system from the isolation of their self-contained classroom. Many don't respect and are ignorant of what administrators do, and most teachers feel administrators are overpaid at best.

Many medical doctors can't handle the "give and take" of board sessions. Doctors talk only to God on their jobs (except for an occasional malpractice attorney). Doctors can't usually work on a board and treat garden variety people as equals. On the other hand, social workers, professors, housewives, union leaders, lawyers, and corporate exec's make pretty decent board members. They are used to the rough and tumble of argumentation and compromise. One rule about lawyers: while one is good, *two is not better!* Two lawyers on a board is bad. It follows that one lawyer equals one brain and two lawyers equal half a brain.

Some school districts have established themselves as a kind of "meat grinder" for school superintendents. The culprit is the board. Normally it means that the board cannot work together and that the community has not found the political means to elect people who can work for the good of the common cause in improving schools. The lack of a community political consensus means that there won't be anyone on the board to sustain much change. The lack of support means that the school administration must continually work to build a consensus, issue by issue, instead of towards a common set of goals or objectives. It is in this arena that school administrators make enemies quicker and lose their base of support.

## Loyalty Has No Status in School Administration

Typically, board loyalty extends only so far as the next meeting of the board. Boards are amoral and therefore they cannot give loyalty to anybody. We know of many school superintendents buried on boot hill who believed their boards when they said, "Do it and we'll back you.'' They watched the votes fade away when the heat was on and the board used the superintendent as a public scapegoat.

We know of one superintendent who was told by his board to "get tough" with the teachers even if it meant taking a strike. When the teachers struck, the board wilted and blamed the superintendent. They served notice that his contract would not be renewed while the man was in the hospital being examined for a possible heart attack!

Business has long ago come to view loyalty as a vice and not a virtue. "The sleepy solid citizen who stays with the company for thirty years isn't loyal," said Rosabeth Kanter at the Yale School of Management. "He is simply viewed as having nowhere else to go."[26] Loyalty won't get you much of anything, perhaps not even ninety days to look for another job.

Seasoned superintendents who are veterans keep their resumes up to date and their bags partially packed. Some who take over perilous jobs live in house trailers. Like the old Western marshalls who often moved from town to town, superintendents are modern educational nomads who stay only as long as their support lasts. It isn't *if* "they" get you, it's *when*. The opposition is always out there, and it's only a matter of time. In big city superintendencies, nine years in the same job is considered highly unusual.[27]

Bureaucracy is a powerful self-perpetuating political machine. It can grind up and spit out the boat rockers as easily as it can wear down the idealistic thinkers until they become semi-conscious bureaucrats. It would be no surprise to us if the quote from Woody Allen which follows came from any retired superintendent:

> My teachers loathed me. I never did homework. I am amazed they expected me to work on those sleazy projects. To this day I wake up in the morning, clutch onto the bed and thank God I don't have to go to school.[28]

### CAVEATS, CODICILS, AND CONUNDRUMS ABOUT
### BUREAUCRACIES, BABUS, AND BAKSHEESH

- Bureaucracies are the plague of civilized people no matter what form of government they prefer: capitalism, socialism, or communism.
- Babus are bureaucrats in India. They have relatives everywhere.
- All bureaucracies run on a kind of baksheesh or at least a quid pro quo.
- The purpose of bureaucracy is not to serve but to be served.

- A vacuum is an invitation to deviate from protocol; it is therefore a threat to a bureaucrat.
- Exceptions are the bane of bureaucracies.
- Keep paper moving and fill in the blanks.
- Paper is reality in a paper world.
- The grapevine is the soft underbelly of the school system.
- Keep real proposals away from committees; organize your own SWAT team.
- If you're going to steal, take a lot or it isn't worth it.
- The smaller the crime, the more likely it is you will get caught.
- The school board is always right even if it's wrong.
- Medical doctors and school teachers make the worst board members as a rule.
- Loyalty is the sign of a dull mind and a person with nothing to sell.

# *Connections*

## CHAPTER 4

# The Community

The community is a posse waiting to be formed to "assist" the administrator out of town. Remember when you came in? You came alone. You'll go out alone too. It's only a matter of time.

We like the words of Abraham Lincoln when he was asked in his first term how it "felt" to be President. In his usual jocular way, Lincoln commented, "I feel like the guy who was tarred and feathered and taken out of town on a rail. When they asked *him* how he felt he said, 'If it wasn't for the honor of the thing I'd just as soon as forgotten about it.' "

The community is a force waiting to be *galvanized*. It can work for or against you. Knowing something about this entity is a key to your survival.

## THE "COMMUNITY" IS A MIRAGE

Like a vision on the desert, the community is not really there at all. It is a mirage. The reality is that there is never *one community*. There are many smaller communities *in one*. In whatever terms people identify themselves: race, religion, ethnic background, position, geography, common interests, there are *communities*. There may be a minority community. There may be many minority communities: black, Chicano, Chinese, Vietnamese. There may be *many* majority communities: Italian, English, Irish, German, Swedish, or Polish.

Rarely does the community act as a single entity. Rather it reacts to events. There are crosscurrents, tensions, feuding, compromises, and battles. Often the crosscurrents are felt strongest at city hall and in the public schools. Administrators are therefore a first line of defense or obstacle, depending on how one looks at it, in the act of influencing what goes on in the schools.

The community rarely speaks with one voice: There are many voices. It is hard to distinguish the majority and the minority if one were to simply make a determination at a board of education meeting.

A vociferous minority can sound like a majority at a board meeting. Remembering that there are many communities "out there" helps avoid being stampeded by such minorities.

One of the best sources to help identify your community is the U.S. Census. Census data will identify people by racial background, age, type of homes, and many other indicators of wealth. Data about who owns phones can be obtained from the phone company. Data about the community can come from any other public or private agency serving your community. Utilities normally have a lot of information about the communities in your community.

Once you know what is in your community, then it is a matter of figuring out who the people are who are the leaders in your various sub-communities.

### TAPPING THE POWER BASES OF THE COMMUNITIES

First, the board of education may not be truly representative of all of your sub-communities. For a long time boards of education have been over-represented by white male business leaders with a protestant background. Such boards were overwhelmingly conservative in defining and approaching problems. Perhaps only in the cities has this type of over-representation been corrected. In the other 16,000 school districts the trend largely continues a sexist and economic bias towards upper-middle-class males.

So the board is not necessarily a good place to look towards really finding out the community's power structure. The *power structure* of a community refers to its informal and formal network of citizens who are influential in making things happen. One must be quite careful in looking for the power structure. The obvious is not always obvious.

Let's take a case of a dentist who works in town and belongs to the Rotary. He may even be president of the Rotary Club. He belongs because his office is in the community. He knows a lot of people. But he doesn't *live* in the community. His kids go to some other school system. His support may not count for much, even if he is president of the Rotary. He may not be an influential member of the community.

An influential leader is one whom other people look toward to see "what" they should do about something. There are hundreds of such leaders all over the community. They may not belong to any clubs. They may not have any official titles. But they are leaders nonetheless. Finding them isn't hard. It is a matter of time. If you ask someone about something which requires a decision, as in a vote, he or she may say, "I will have to see what Joe Jabonlski thinks about it."

If you never heard of Joe Jabonlski, you may ask who he is. You may be shocked. Joe may work for you. Joe might be the head custodian, or in buildings and grounds, or in maintenance. Joe might gas the buses in the morning or be cutting grass in the late afternoon. Chances are you never thought much about it.

We've found that a lot of informal community leaders who are true leaders already work for the schools, and not usually in a professional capacity. In fact, a large majority of most districts' classified staff usually live in the community, as opposed to the professional staff, who may not.

The people who often pass bond issues are not the teachers, but the secretaries, bus drivers, custodians, maintenance workers, cafeteria staff, and aides. These are the people with a vested interest in the community and the schools.

The formal organizations of a community may have some community leaders in them and in leadership posts. But don't be fooled. They may not have as many as you might think. We've found that the community groups that usually do have the real leaders in them are the "anti's." The "anti's" are the taxpayer watchdog groups, conservative causes or clubs, or other groups largely negative towards the schools. This is because issue-specific groups are usually run by indigenous local leadership. Their strength is that they tap the actual power base of the group which is complaining.

This stands in stark contrast to the usual, more "pro" groups such as PTA, Rotary, Kiwanis, Lions, Chamber of Commerce who have non-issue-specific stands and are composed of people without specific "axes" to grind. School administrators often belong to these types of groups. If these groups are non-representative of the actual power base of the community, an administrator can be duped into believing that his or her time is being spent cultivating the community when it just isn't so.

## SPOTTING THE PEOPLE IN POWER—THE INFORMAL NETWORK

Perhaps one of the first ways to spot some of the informal networking of a community is with the "board watchers." This group of people are regular attendees of board meetings.

It takes a special interest to come to board meetings. Most board members wouldn't come if they didn't have to. And you can believe that most administrators wouldn't be there either. As one experienced superintendent once remarked about his board, "This is the only place I know of where the inmates are in control."

So don't come to the board meeting to watch the board, unless there is nothing better to do than watch the cars rust on a Tuesday night. Come to watch the people *who watch the board.* Notice:

- who sits with whom;
- who usually says what and how does the audience (not the board) react;
- who the regulars are, i.e., "the board junkies";
- to which larger or other groups these board watchers belong.

We will provide you with some examples. Let's take the regular Tuesday night meeting of the Topnotch School District, Topnotch, USA.

In the front row are the "twins," Perla Twitch and her friend Paula Partoon. Perla and Paula are the officers of the Gulf Gate Elementary School PTA. They come to be ready to speak to any issue that would endanger the closing of Gulf Gate. They are influential in the Gulf Gate PTA and in the wider community. Because of this influence they can be "powerful" on that issue. Otherwise they usually spend most board meetings giggling and passing notes about some of the idiocy and pomposity that goes on about them.

Then we have Twila Twitterspoon, the grand duchess of the Fifth Avenue crowd. Twila comes to all the board meetings. She speaks on anything and everything. She hails herself as a spokesperson, but nobody takes her too seriously despite her barbed tongue and her ability to be amusing on occasion. She sits alone and goes through the board packet leaving pages scattered all around her chair.

Carl Peabody is Mr. Nasty. He always comes late and sometimes stands in the back of the board room slouching on a large table there. He serves on one or two committees the board forms from time to time. His comments are always negative, his tone always condemnatory. He sounds like the prosecutor at the Watergate hearings most nights. He always begins with an insinuation that the administration is cheating the taxpayers out of something. Although Carl would dearly like to be a leader in anybody's eyes, he is a malcontent and a monk of misery. The only reason he comes to board meetings is to have somebody other than himself recognize him as important. Once in a while, he gets quoted in the local weekly, when there is coverage of the board meeting. Carl speaks for no one. He lives for a line in the press.

Robert Missal, on the other hand, comes to board meetings and rarely speaks. When he does, the room becomes silent. He is unusually well informed. He has his facts straight. Sometimes he gives a prepared statement to the board. They read it without any prompting.

Sometimes they have been known to adopt his prepared statement as a motion. Robert heads up the local Little League. By day he is a brick contractor. On occasion he has been eloquent. He speaks roughly at every four board meetings. He sits with his friend Chad, the guy across the street. The tentacles of Little League stretch all over the community. Robert is a natural, indigenous leader of Topnotch. He has friends everywhere, including the school system.

Twice in three years the board meeting has been graced with the presence of Beverly Buffer. Beverly *is* the grand duchess. She has lived in the community thirty years. She tracks the board through her "stooges," Rita Boop and Patty Birp, who are usually there at every meeting. Boop and Birp report by phone to Beverly. Beverly runs a dry cleaning establishment on Main Street. Her husband Fred used to be on the board. Fred has been dead a decade, but Beverly knows everybody because they come to her establishment regularly. She is a key player in any matter of great importance in the city or the schools. Her three sons all attended Topnotch High School. They are all successful and graduated, two from prestigious colleges.

Beverly plays a key role in board elections. She is the "queen maker." She encourages people to run for the board. When she doesn't like a board member, she can run them off in one election. Mostly, though, she is never heard at the board meeting. Boop and Birp don't say much either, but they take a lot of notes. Once in a while they ask questions to clarify something. That's all.

One other regular, Jacques Pedigree, only comes to board meetings at budget time. He is very concerned about taxes. Throughout the board meetings he sits with his slide rule checking and rechecking figures and columns. He delights in finding an error. He checks the tax rate over and over. Jacques usually alienates the audience. He is such a nit-picker that both the audience and the board tire early from his bombastic tirades. He has no sense of humor and usually has to be cut off from the floor before relinquishing the public rostrum. He is irritating but harmless. Nobody identifies with Jacques. He can't be a leader.

Most board regulars are not the power structure of Topnotch. The power structure is out there. Sometimes it is kept informed as in the case of Beverly Buffer by friends. The real power in a community tends to be "irregulars" at board meetings. The exception is Robert Missal.

Board "groupies" are not usually dangerous, but they can goad the unwitting administrator into skirmishes and fights where some blood may be drawn. Blood attracts the big fish. A fight is always fun, and it is always reported in the press. Our advice most of the time is not to rise to the bait. Board "groupies" may be obnoxious and ego tripping on your time, but you have to be there anyway, so let them talk, *not you*. Besides, it isn't the administration's meeting, it's a meeting of the board. You're there as a guest. So watch your manners.

Another way for the administrator to spot the power bases is just to wait for them to emerge. Power bases appear in many ways. Sometimes a member of the community will just call up and want to meet you.

At one time, one of the co-authors received such a formal invitation from a civic association in the community. According to the invitation, the purpose of the meeting was to "welcome the two new junior high school principals to the community." Since the other junior high school principal had already served for one year without being so welcomed and since the civic association was based in the other junior high school's community, the newer principal tried to get out of the evening meeting. Since he could not do so graciously, he attended the meeting, albeit reluctantly.

Lucky for him that he did. To his surprise he noticed that, although blacks throughout the district numbered only approximately 20 percent, 100 percent of all the persons attending that meeting were black (well over fifty). Clearly, this was actually the community's black caucus under the name of Fairfield Avenue Civic Association. And the pointed and politically charged questions asked by members of the group after initial pleasantries were exchanged confirmed the principal's suspicions that he had stumbled upon a major power base.

The group had made it clear that they expected both principals to report to their superiors that "the community" was concerned that "their" junior high school not be closed (at the time there was discussion of closing schools). Their point was that there was only one school building located in the black part of the district and that it was heavily used by that part of the community for meetings, indoor sports, community group activities, etc. If that building were closed— no matter how much sense its closing made on paper—the black community would be the only segment of the district with no building of its own in which to carry on community activities. This would make them most unhappy, we were told.

Their point was well taken, and the way they made it was very effective. They didn't scream and carry on at board meetings. They didn't set their homes on fire or overturn automobiles. They saw school closings coming up as an issue that could affect them a year before all the screaming at board of education meetings began. They invited two power brokers who had access to other power brokers (i.e., central office staff, superintendent of schools, etc.) and gave them the message to pass on—which they did. No doubt they approached selected board members similarly. One thing is certain; a year later when the board presented the findings of several separate studies detailing many options and combinations of different schools to close, closing the junior high school located in the Fairfield Avenue Civic Association's neighborhood was not one of them. At the stormy board hearings before the actual decision was made, the president of the Civic Association got up and gave a very understated and polite *reminder* that the community represented by the Civic Association would be most upset if their junior high school were to close. He didn't have to scream and carry on like many of the others who spoke, because his message had already been given to those who needed to hear it, most effectively *before*. A polite reminder was all that was needed.

Watch who goes to the powerful and to whom the powerful go, and you will better understand where the power bases are. And if you are one of those people whose attitude is, "I just do my job and mind my own business; I'm just too busy doing my job to concern myself with politics," then you're too busy. At least you're too busy to be an administrator in our opinion, based upon our many experiences. If that's your attitude—and it is a legitimate one—better consider getting back to the classroom or never leaving it in the first place.

The fact is that the most politically astute administrator will never know everything about all the power bases—including where they are. To know this, one must know everything about who is sleeping with whom (you'd be suprised—even if you think you wouldn't be surprised—take our word for it), who drinks with the Friday afternoon crowd at Jetson's as opposed to who drinks with the payday crowd at Barney's, and who drinks at both places all the time. And speaking of drinking partners, do the superintendent and members of the board each drink alone?

Often, especially in one newspaper towns, the newspaper reporter (many times there's just one) can help you spot the power bases.

Advisory boards, if used carefully, can be a vehicle to facilitate tapping power groups. A high school principal, for example, can bring about the formation of an advisory board consisting of a microcosm of the school–community (i.e., containing a member from each community in the community). Such a group would furnish her/him with direct access to and influence of groups represented by each member of the advisory board. Administrators must give advisory boards true, useful functions if they are to continue. But they must always be on guard against the "tail wagging the dog." Sometimes, dealing with advisory groups can be like making love to a gorilla. You can't stop until *it's* finished.

Building principals have a unique, yet natural way of tapping various power bases within the community. A principal can develop an intimate relationship with the parents of his/her youngsters through a monthly newsletter written in the first person and called "The Principal's Newsletter." By keeping the families of his/her students (natural constituents) informed of their accomplishments and activities, as well as those of the faculty, the administrator establishes an involvement or relationship with his readers in the same way other authors do with their readers. And if organizations such as the PTA are given space upon request to advertise their special events, the Newsletter continues to become a vehicle whereby the administrator taps various power bases within the community.

In some districts, organizations such as the PTA or community service groups even contribute the funds necessary to defray the cost of paper, printing, and postage. In addition, we know of schools where PTA members come into the building once a month to collate and otherwise prepare these newsletters for mailing.

In any event, to the extent that the Newsletter becomes a vehicle which brings about *active involvement* of individuals and groups with the school, such a newsletter will be a great asset to the administrator in his/her attempt to tap various power bases within the communities.

Certainly, school superintendents have discovered the power of the printed word a long time ago. It is a rare superintendent who does not rely upon some kind of district newsletter—whatever the name—in order to achieve the same purpose. Public relations and good communication are important aspects of the job of an administrator. But they are also very powerful and effective strategies.

Power bases can be tapped. Being able to reach out, to communicate, being easy and comfortable with people is essential. Genuinely being a "people person," genuinely liking people are important qualities of an administrator. Administrators who are extroverted, who "have a way with people," who attract people, and who are attracted by them are "naturals" for the job.

**USING THE POWER BASES OF A COMMUNITY**

Administrators do not always have to be out in front leading every battle. As a matter of fact, they shouldn't be. One little-known powerful arithmetic axiom is: "The best way to multiply power is to divide it." Said another way, the best way to possess power is to give it away.

Power bases in communities can be used to improve the system and, in fact, *want* to be used. No one becomes powerful and influential for the sake of having power and influence. Until that power and influence are actually *used* for something, they may as well not even exist.

The key to using power bases is to let those who comprise them know they are important, valued, have the ability to make significant contributions to you, the administrator, and to the system, and that their contributions will be acknowledged. These are tangible payoffs for wise and appropriate *uses* of power. Another payoff— perhaps the most important one—is *enhancement*. After using his power, a powerful person or group of persons want to feel ENHANCED personally or as a group, or both. In the absence of this important ingredient, the person or group will feel *used*, and once this happens, will no longer be available to the administrator as a potential power base or supportive coalition.

It is upon the bases of the many "communities" that an administrator must function. Juggling different interests and conflicts among the sub-groups can be dangerous over the long haul. That few superintendents last long in communities at war with themselves is a fact of life. Sooner or later the superintendent will take a fall, lose his or her base of support, and be washed away. If he/she doesn't leave town, he/she will be carried out of town.

Competent administrators will survive longer than those who believe in the myth of the "community." One experienced urban superintendent, a writer, scholar, and now professor, noted after his demise, "There are fall, summer, spring, and winter superintendents—but none for all seasons."[1] The nature of school communities is such that the chief for all seasons is also a myth. Know that fact riding into town, and the ride out is a lot less painful. It can also prevent you from ending up on boot hill. Walking out under your own steam and preferably to a better job is much better. Laugh all the way to the bank.

## CAVEATS, CODICILS, AND CONUNDRUMS ABOUT THE COMMUNITY

- The "community" is a mirage; what you see, you don't get.
- The power structure of a community refers to its formal and informal networks and the people in them that make things happen.

- Leaders within a community who are in "pro" organizations that are not issue-specific may not represent the actual sub-communities in the larger community.
- "Anti" groups often have the best indigenous local leadership.
- Come to the board meetings not to watch the board but to watch those watching the board—you'll learn a lot more about community politics.
- If you're too busy doing your job to worry about politics, you're not doing your job.
- The local newspaper reporter can give you more than the news.
- Involvement is disarming.
- The board meeting is not your meeting, it's the board's; you're a guest.
- The best way to multiply power is to divide it. The best way to possess it is to give it away.

## CHAPTER 5

# The PTA

## WHAT THE PTA IS NOT: TEACHERS AND MEN

The PTA is supposed to stand for The Parents and Teachers Association. However, most PTA's either have token teacher representation or no teacher representation whatsoever on their executive boards. The reasons are not hard to discern. If PTA meetings are held during the day, teachers can't attend because they are teaching. If they are held at night, most teachers either won't want another night out or can't do so because of family or professional commitments. And then there is the customary lack of faculty interest in the PTA. Teachers don't stand in line to serve on PTA executive boards, and they don't attend PTA meetings either.

Another species you won't find in abundance on PTA's in general and on PTA executive boards in particular is *males*. There probably are historical reasons for this. When PTA's first emerged in this country, male/female roles were rigidly stereotyped. "Macho" males went to work and did "macho" things, while their demure and docile wives stayed home and minded the PTA STORE.

PTA membership and involvement was considered "women's work" like so many other things and not a legitimate function for men. Among the early activities and purposes of the PTA was a drive for putting hot lunches in the schools, which began in 1912. The serving of food was part of the female "nurturing" role and was a "natural" agenda item. But females and PTA's have come a long way, baby.

PTA's now have clout, *political clout*. While the men were working, the women were *gaining power*. It is no accident that the very first organization meeting in 1897 (the founding organization), the National Congress of Mothers (see why men were excluded?), took place at the White House. It was a reception sponsored by Mrs. Grover Cleveland. Washington and White House connections have been strong ever since. Today, most PTA's are, in fact, *power bases*.

While many males do their 9:00 A.M. to 5:00 P.M. thing in the market place, their PTA women serve as effective lobbyists in Washington, have access to powerful local, state, and Congressional legislators, and, in general, often exercise influence and control over curriculum content, personnel, and other vital and absorbing school matters.

Also, for this reason, the interests and activities of PTA's often collide with the interests and activities of school administrators. School administrators have come to understand that while PTA's can be *allies*, they can also be *adversaries*.

### GOSSIP, "GOTCHAS," AND GRIPE SESSIONS

Our own experience and that of many other school administrators, male or female, indicates that too many PTA meetings revolve around gossip, gouging school personnel directly or indirectly, and gripe sessions. If a school administrator thinks he or she is walking into a group of friends at a PTA meeting, he or she may be in for a rude shock. It may be a gang of cutthroats. More than one school administrator we know was met not with a conference, but a confrontation at a PTA Meeting.

Such confabs have a tendency to get mired down in the mundane. PTA meetings are not places where lofty goals are discussed in the abstract. They are more often than not elaborate probings of the nitty-gritty operations of the school or school district. PTA's are concerned about why buses don't run on time, why tacos are not served on Thursday instead of Monday, whether to spend another $12.00 on balloons at the carnival, donating $20.00 to send a child to summer camp, the Tuesday cake and cookie sale, and endless reports of committees. The PTA is a social organization first and foremost that has its purposes centered *around school* but not necessarily *on school*.

PTA members can be separated into three camps: friends, critics, and assassins. All three engage in gossip. All three gripe. They gripe about teachers, curriculum, homework assignments, grouping, scheduling, report cards, administrators, and administrative behavior. However, friends and critics want to improve the school or district. *Assassins want to kill.* They gripe to discredit the administrator, erode confidence in the administration, embarass a particular administrator. All of this occurs under the guise of "helping." In a group meeting, assassins can work under the protection of the umbrella of the overall purpose of PTA. They smile but they jab, jab, jab, jab, all the time. If one even watches their faces, one might forget the pain of the incessant slices and cuts of the verbal rapiers at work. A slice is known as a "gotcha."

It's this atmosphere of personal carnage that repels teachers because so much of the griping is *about them* or directed *at them*. They vote with their feet. They don't and won't attend such pickings. Administrators wouldn't attend either if they didn't have to. *So you're stuck.* And don't expect these women to be the liberated types either. Professional women can't meet during the day, and they have the same problems as men in getting to night meetings. So PTA's are largely dominated by non-working women who have mostly a traditional view of male and female role stereotypes. They don't promote women or back the kind of agenda endorsed by the National Organization of Women. Many are frankly antagonistic to women's issues. You won't find many PTA's pushing to have more female administrators because too many of the members really don't believe women can be administrators. The PTA has rarely been a place where women were advanced beyond the traditional teaching role at the local level in the thousands of school districts where only 16 percent of the 43,000 school principals are female and not more than 4 percent of the nation's superintendents are women.[1]

### PAYOFFS, POTHOLES, AND PARSIMONY

We are then left with why a more than likely traditional, conservative, non-working woman would join a PTA. Answer this question and one is better able to understand the motivations of the group you must work with and survive. Few people become involved with PTA's because they love going to the meetings, though it's true that home lives of some of the members may be even more boring than some of the PTA meetings.

Most of the PTA members come because most believe that schools will be better as a result of their efforts. Others are interested in socialization and want to be close to the power so as to have the "skinny" about school system politics. PTA executive board members have easy access to school administrators and board members, not enjoyed by the average citizen. They are free to push their own agendas and to gain information not readily available to the rest of the flock back on the block. They are powerful back on the block because they have access to and data about what is going on.

And, too, PTA types know that if they are perceived as powerful enough by the school administration their children will enjoy some of the payoffs for being high up in the pecking order. Put the PTA president's child in the turkey teacher's class? *Not on your life.* Not if you want to survive your first executive board meeting! It's no secret that a PTA exec's kids get preferential treatment. So part of the PTA agenda is extracting the best of the system for their kids. Working within the system offers some additional assurances that it will really happen. *That's the payoff.* Even your worst assassin will only want to wound you if you've promised her the best physics teacher in the school for her son. If you're dead, no deal.

Such "deals" are rarely overtly discussed between PTA's and administrators. It's just the way the game is played. Know the rules and you won't get shafted at the next coffee klatch.

For the PTA'ers who really want the "inside info," starve them out if they are assassins. Support for the school administration is rewarded through accessibility and open communication—especially information heard first at a PTA executive board meeting or data which is not on the "street" yet. Inaccessibility to the assassins and to some of the nastier critics will result in their being the last to know what's going on by making sure they are not the first to know. A steady starvation diet treatment over a period of time has got to make some of your enemies wonder. Once the payoffs are gone, all that's left is the work. The work is not enough to keep them coming back *without the payoffs.*

By now it should be clear that the image of the PTA as being a benign teacher-centered group with parent partners is bunk. It is one gigantic pothole. Drive in without thinking and you'll ruin your wagon's wheels. PTA's are, in fact, perfect nesting places for barracudas. Be prepared.

PTA's are political groups. They are overwhelmingly conservative. In fact they are so much so that many locals have disaffiliated with the PTA and call themselves PTO's (Parent Teacher Organizations). The assumption that your PTA is pure, that it has no axes to grind, that it is apolitical, that it is your staunchest ally and that its support is in the bag, that it represents and speaks for its own rank and file membership, and that it couldn't possibly get a principal or superintendent in trouble—all of these are potholes. Look out. Many of our naive colleagues, not to mention our own experiences, will testify otherwise.

The PTA is a bureaucracy. It is riddled with rituals, rules, and regulations. By-laws and constitutions are always in need of revisions. Endless hours are spent debating nuances of *Roberts Rules of Order.* While some PTA's break away from the regimen of tight regulation to undertake big projects and think big, it is too often the exception. Most of the PTA's we know are examples of "small think." *Small think* precludes having to think at all. One merely memorizes the questions and *the* answers. Indeed, the "experts" on PTA mumbo-jumbo are those people who have memorized more reasons why you can't do things than anybody else. They are always in positions of authority.

## VIRULENCE AT THE SECONDARY SCHOOL

Secondary school principals are faced with smaller groups of PTA members. Some secondary school PTA attendance is so bad that most of the time the same people serve as officers in various capacities year in and year out.

Secondary school principals are often left with the most virulent strains of the worst of the elementary school PTA's membership. Many members go back to school or back to work. Others tire of the harangue, intrigue, and backstabbing. *That leaves the diehards!* These members are more sophisticated, more street wise, slicker, and smarter. They have been seasoned with conventions and the art of guerilla warfare. They are professional "Contras" in the strongest sense of the word.

To prepare the administrator, we have picked out a case study of how one secondary school principal fought back. We call it the Rockville High School Case.

Casey Brown was a new high school principal. He inherited a fine school and excellent teachers. However, his PTA was run by Lucretia Logicplumer, a stickler for detail and discountenance. Her domineering discipline left the meetings in the doldrums. Casey noticed that every time he had to go to Lucretia's lambastings of arsenic and lace, he got physically ill. Sometimes it was a stomachache. Other times it was a headache. Once it was a backache.

Casey analyzed carefully in his mind what had gone on at those meetings over the past four months and discovered the reason for his hypochondria. After four months, nothing concrete or positive had come from Lucretia's lips. The PTA seemed to have no purpose except to provide a forum for the president's irritations. Lucretia had few friends on her own board. She appeared to her own members as pushing hidden agendas which revealed her own insecurities and politics. No matter how she started, the group ended up bickering and backbiting.

After taking a few "gotchas" from Lucretia's lips, Casey went to the superintendent. The superintendent, a wise administrator of many years told him, "She's a man-eater. She lives to cut up men. Put her in her place before you let her do you in. She's done it to your predecessor."

Casey had an idea. He asked each of his principal colleagues to write in one sentence what they thought was the purpose of the PTA in each of their schools. This was to be followed by a brief description of what an ideal PTA should do.

At the very next PTA meeting he shared their responses with the group and told them that he had asked his colleagues for this information because he had been confused about the purpose of his own PTA at the high school. He led the group in a discussion about the purpose of their own group. At this point Lucretia had to come into the open and put her agenda on the table in the form of demands and opinions. She no longer could be subversive and snipe.

When the group saw fully the nature of Lucretia's invective and distrust, her anti-male bias, and vituperation, she was grounded! For once, her real agenda had been laid bare. She was seen for what she was. Even she shrank from the picture she painted before her own council.

Casey got the group to adopt a rule. No gripe about an individual would be permitted unless it involved the entire group as a whole. Exceptions were to be taken up with him privately.

The meetings got better. Some days Lucretia's nose was out of joint, but Casey's hypochondria subsided. The meetings were tolerable. Some even bordered on being positive. The superintendent had been right. Deal with her openly. Flush her agenda into the open. By the end of the year the high school PTA executive board voted her out of office. A new slate of officers promised better understanding and greater school support.

We're not saying that all high school PTA's are like this. Both of us have worked with some marvelous PTA's on the high school level. But Casey Brown's experiences are certainly not unique.

### AND VIRULENCE AT THE ELEMENTARY SCHOOL

PTA virulence isn't always confined to the secondary schools. For example, we know of one excellent veteran elementary school principal, Clyde Barnes, who wound up with egg on his face because he wasn't minding his PTA store.

A group of hysterical vigilantes, none of whom had any children in the high school and some of whom had no children attending district schools at all, decided that they were going to force the district's only high school to have a closed campus and to "tighten up" its reins.

One of these hysterical-types happened to be the president of Clyde's elementary school PTA. Using her position (and without telling him) she decided to communicate with all of the parents of the children attending Clyde's elementary school. Within a single day, she ran off a flier addressed to "All Parents of Thornwood Avenue Elementary School" from "The Concerned Citizens for Closing Baywood High School's Campus." The document called for all "caring" parents to attend a special meeting of the board of education about this topic after an impassioned (albeit illogical) editorial on the subject. To add insult to injury, the flier was then sent home through the children!

Of course, some of the parents of these kids didn't bother to read the flier. Others no doubt read it and didn't know what was going on or didn't care. And others must have read it and agreed with its message and were glad to have received it. But you had better believe that some parents were outraged because they believed in the educational philosophy of Baywood High School. Others were outraged because they felt that this flier should not have been printed at Thornwood Avenue Elementary School at District expense and that most of all, their children should not have been USED to hand deliver that propaganda. They demanded to know why the principal didn't seem to know what was going on in his own school and why he didn't have much control over his own PTA.

Of course, the principal of Baywood High School, who had been battling to maintain his school's policies, was less than thrilled with his elementary school counterpart for making his job even more difficult.

So Clyde Barnes, ace principal, gets zapped by his ace PTA president, Petunia Mettlesome (albeit unwittingly). Sometimes, even the good guys can get you into trouble if you're not minding the store— or, et tu Petunia?

We don't believe that all the problems of PTA's can be solved by achieving a better balance between males and females in their ranks. However, it would be a good starting place. Males ought to join PTA executive boards. True liberation of women from stereotyped sex roles has, as a by-product, resulted in similar liberation of men from stereotyped sex roles.

Just as cooking and house cleaning are no longer the sole provinces of females, so too, the responsibility of educating and raising children is a shared responsibility in many American homes. As a matter of fact, in many single parent homes it is solely a male responsibility. Males actually deprive themselves of experiencing these new freedoms from stereotyped roles by sticking to the old roles.

To underscore our point we reprint an account of a male PTA member of an executive board who served as president of his elementary school PTA. Help your own PTA create a sense of purpose, a sense which seems to be missing from so many meetings we've attended. Share with them a vision, a dream for their kids. Let them experience the power of making those dreams come true by putting them in touch with their own magnificence. Then ask for their help and watch them work with you to *do it*. They might even come to your rescue should you need it. It sure beats dodging the barracudas.

---

BACK TO SCHOOL

## A Male Gets Truly Involved in the PTA[2]

BY CURT LADER

*Teacher, Northport High School*

For two years in a row, I've been elected president of the Dogwood Elementary School PTA in Smithtown, which is unusual because I'm a male and have been the only man on the PTA's executive board for the past five years. Fortunately, more men *are* getting involved in their Parent-Teacher Associations (Marvin Fretwell was recently elected the first male president of the State PTA), but if the PTA is to have more influence on the education of our children, even greater numbers must get involved.

Men have shied away from PTA elective office. They fear endless meetings with debates over trivial items not related to educational issues. The image of PTA fund-raising activities and cake-baking intimidates most men. However, this does not necessarily have to occur.

It's very simple for men to get active in a local PTA unit. First, join your local unit and attend an executive board meeting. (If they are held only during the day, suggest they alternate meetings between day and evening.) At the meeting, volunteer to join a committee or hold a position that interests you. Those range from PTA representative at school board meetings to hospitality committees. There also are program committees that plan informational meetings for the entire membership.

If more men get involved in the PTA, there would be a greater diversity of ideas. Educators would be impressed by a PTA unit with a mixed membership. The expert background that many men have in running other organizations would certainly be a plus. Programs that are sponsored by a PTA consisting of men and women would generate greater involvement from the entire educational community. For example, our unit has run informational meetings on:

- How to be an effective parent.
- Getting to know the school board president and vice president.
- Sex education.
- Curriculum offerings.

State and national PTAs have legislative concerns and were instrumental in achieving stronger DWI laws. Locally, units pioneered fingerprinting for children as a means of identifying them if they are missing.

Once involved in PTA affairs myself, I quickly discovered that even though I am an educator (a teacher in a neighboring district), I must play a different role as a PTA president. As a man, I found a double standard among some people in the educational community: They would treat women PTA leaders in an almost condescending manner, but they gave me respect. In addition, I found that just by identifying myself as "President," doors that were usually closed to me as a parent immediately opened.

Reactions to my presidency have varied. At meetings attended by a vast majority of women, the chairwoman kept on speaking to "ladies." Other PTA members automatically assumed that as a man, I would not get involved in such fundraising activities as a fashion show. In fact, I insisted that I model and the event was expanded to include males modeling tuxedos.

There have been times when I would come home from work and regret that I have another meeting to attend. However, realizing that the PTA has a positive impact on my child's education makes it well worth it.

---

Straightening out gossip with facts, turning gripe sessions into positive action meetings and avoiding getting stung by the "gotchas" through being honest and forthright should be parts of an administrator's agenda at every PTA meeting. This group, primarily the parents of the youngsters who attend our schools, are our greatest natural allies. But we must constantly remind them that their children are the real agenda items and the common bond between the PTA as a group and us.

### CAVEATS, CODICILS, AND CONUMDRUMS ABOUT PTA's

- Females and PTA's have come a long way, baby.
- Have you hugged your Senator or Congressman lately? Chances are a PTA lady has!
- Watch out for benign groups; some are malignant.
- Once the payoffs are gone, all that's left is the work.
- The PTA is a social organization first and foremost.
- PTA members are three types: friends, critics, and assassins.
- A slice is known as a "gotcha."
- Secondary PTA'ers are the "Contras" of the organization.
- The missing ingredient in *Robert's Rules of Order* is purpose.
- Share with the PTA your vision: it sure beats dodging the barracudas.
- The real agenda items and the common bond between the PTA and us are the kids.

## CHAPTER 6

# The Staff

There are *three* resources that make a quality school:

(1) The Staff
(2) The Staff
(3) The Staff

There are *three* kinds of major problems at schools:

(1) People
(2) People
(3) People

There are *three* fundamental solutions to major problems:

(1) People
(2) People
(3) People

Education is a labor-intensive business, and it is *big business.* The costs of schools (including higher education) were approximately $240 billion. In 1984 3.1 million people were employed as teachers with 300,000 as administrators or other staff members. Public elementary and secondary schools cost approximately $134.5 billion with an additional $10 billion going to private elementary and secondary schools. With 70 percent to 80 percent of most school budgets in people, one can easily see that schools are about *people.*

## THE STAFF VS THE FACULTY

The staff is *everybody.* The faculty refers to *teachers.* The staff includes secretaries, custodians, cafeteria workers, nurses, speech therapists, crossing guards, and hall monitors. Most school administrators have been teachers. Very few have occupied other types of positions in the schools.

It's easy to forget the many "little people" that make schools go.

It's easy to concentrate only on the teachers. Teachers constitute perhaps 60–80 percent of the total staff of many schools. Add up the other people and you will have a sizeable number. *They all count.*

Let's take the school nurse. We've worked with a lot of them over the years. Hardy women. They've heard every excuse there is about why kids can't come to school. They've seen just about everything there is to see in a school, from measles to rare and exotic strains of microbes that would make some medical researchers envious. They have tended to sick kids and picked up dead kids. Most of the ones we know are totally dedicated to kids and to the health of the school. In many schools, the nurse knows more kids than anyone else and she knows more about the families of more of the kids than anyone else. The nurse is a V.I.P. to anybody in school administration with half a brain.

And there are the bus drivers, nowadays mostly women in many districts. These staff members see kids like nobody else sees them. They watch them a lot in rearview mirrors. They see them when they're fresh in the morning and when they are ready to kill in the afternoon. Most would swear kids were combinations of Jekyll and Hyde, or at least that would be the names of their parents.

The cafeteria ladies also get a glimpse of kids when they're grumpy and hungry. They know who eats what and what kids like and don't. Kids don't have to explain why they don't want to eat a "federal lunch" with spinach or turnips. They just don't eat it. Cafeteria ladies often pretend they don't care if the kids don't like what they cook. *But don't believe it.* Watch their faces when they get to cook pizza or tacos. When the kids are happy, they are happy.

Secretaries and custodians are so important to the principal that we've spent an entire chapter on them. All the people are important. The staff is there to handle all aspects of making a school function. A school administrator who focuses only on teachers is making an error in estimating what it will take to make him or her successful. Focusing only on teachers means that the rest "only work there." That attitude in anybody in your school or school system means that all complaints will have to go to you because you're the only person that matters, unless you only work there too, in which case the superintendent should fire you.

> "I only work here," means "I don't really care if I work here or not; one job is as good—and as meaningless—as another one to me."[1]

That administrator who doesn't consider the staff an entity, as deserving as the faculty, deserves the ulcers and hemorrhoids and high blood pressure that come along with getting dinged by the support staff in hundreds of little ways that add up to one message, "Don't complain to us about this school, we only work here. Talk to the principal."

## THE FACULTY: SUPERSTARS, SUPERCHARGERS, TURKEYS, STOOL PIGEONS, AND WIMPS

Seasoned school administrators come to recognize early that they are, at least in part, psychiatrists without residence or training, for the faculty. The faculty is the teachers. As far as the educational program of a school is concerned, the quality of the faculty is the only benchmark for a school and its instructional character.

Most administrators have been teachers. Unfortunately, most were not the best ones because the skills of teaching have not been the basis for promotion into administration. Only recently with the emphasis on the effective schools research movement have there been solid expectations of principals to be able to lead teachers in instruction.

The faculty is made up of individuals. Sometimes it acts cohesively and sometimes (most of the time) it doesn't. For many generations teaching was a first choice occupation for women and a second or third choice occupation for men.[2] The bulk of most elementary school faculties are women. At least 40–50 percent of most secondary school staffs are female. So teaching is largely a feminized occupation. It therefore behaves that way in some situations.

Teachers are highly sensitive about status differentials. They are highly resistant to change. They are suspicious of authority. They are politically conservative.[3] They are not an easy group to lead, govern, congeal, motivate, or cajole. They are, however, easily insulted, provoked, intimidated, or angered. Great teachers are always prima donnas with their principals and sometimes with their students.

It should be remembered that administrators deal with teachers as adults. However, teachers are most used to dealing with students. They often have a terrible time dealing with other adults and especially with persons in authority. Some teachers are just awful adults. Administrators soon learn that a super teacher is not necessarily a terrific adult. We've known more than one teacher who was great with the kids but had acerbic staff/colleague relationships and an almost adversarial relationship with his or her administrator.

The bottom line with a faculty is to try and get *synergy*. This concept means that by getting individuals to work as a team, they are more than the simple sum of each: they become larger than the sum, or $2 + 2 = 5$. To do that, one must understand some of the cast of characters which normally inhabit school faculties. We'll start with the *Superstars*.

## The Superstars

There are very few Christa McAuliffe's, i.e, the first "teacher-naut," on school faculties. Sometimes there aren't any. The ones we know come in all shapes and sizes, male or female, black, white, yellow, brown, fat, and thin.

Great teachers have not necessarily been a roaring success in any other aspect of life. Sometimes they have been miserable failures. The skills of instructing the young and the ability to motivate and inspire do not necessarily transfer to other occupations or vice versa.

One superstar is Chuck Nog. Chuck was a part-time actor, a bit player of sorts. He never acted in anything major. He was an English major in school, specializing in obscure English poets. He finds the lives of obscure poets interesting. He has the knack of transferring his interests through witty, insightful, and often sardonic lectures to his Advanced Placement English section. He is frustrated because he never received a doctorate. While he often gives excuses, he didn't really do all that well in administrative courses.

Chuck's students fall all over him. The more able and bright idolize him. Chuck works his students very hard. They read shelves of books at a rapid pace. Chuck is a "bear" about deadlines. He won't tolerate anything arriving late. Some students have been known to drive to his house to deliver a late paper prior to a midnight deadline. Chuck's students delight in the comments he writes on their papers. Sometimes they are downright insulting, but always the petards are humorous.

Chuck loves to be adored by his students. He takes great delight in their growth and in their ability to use the language. His former students have attended some of the best Ivy League schools and done very well. They will often correspond with him because he has related to students as persons. Chuck has been a high school teacher for over twenty years. Once he served as department chairman but gave it up when the rest of his colleagues rebelled at his often high-handed decision-making style and his satiric probing of their faults, personal and otherwise. So he was dethroned and Patricia Etwing installed. Patricia is less charismatic but more practical than Chuck. She can run a good department meeting and the rest of the teachers feel she is fair. Chuck goes merrily on, forever the ham, forever the unemployed actor.

Chuck Nog's eccentricities and his ego trips on the remainder of the faculty or occasionally on a class are forgiven. His principal understands the frailties of talent. So do Chuck's colleagues. Chuck is tolerated because he is not only competent, he is a *master teacher*. The title is never bestowed by anyone, except by the fact Chuck doesn't take much guff from others, including the principal or Pat Etwing. He does his business and he does it superbly. With a Chuck Nog you take the good with the rest. He is a rare breed.

Great teachers (not just good ones nor even outstanding ones) have always been in *short supply*. They always will be. Just as it has been said that great athletes are genetic "freaks," so are *great teachers human freaks*. They operate above whatever milieux in which they may be functioning. They live to interact with their students because it is from them that they receive the rewards that keep their psyches going. The satisfaction of teaching is in the dynamic interchange and there is nothing else like it. No merit pay plan will mean anything to Chuck because he would do what he does without pay. He has endured several superintendents, countless idiotic board dicta and innumerable board meddlings in this and that, at least four chairpersons, and two high school principals. He's seen them all come and go. The fire that lights his lamp comes from none of the switches in offices or politics. Chuck is still in love with learning after all these years. He is still able to light that internal fire in most of his students. It is the gift of a lifetime. Every parent should wish that his or her child would be touched by a Chuck Nog just once in thirteen years of their educational lives.

And then there's Eileen Bender who, in a brief period of time, took a Latin program that was near extinction and brought it back into the national limelight. Eileen Bender was a former parochial school teacher who finally certified for public school teaching. She came late to teaching. Her love of the Latin classics permeates her classes. In three years Latin enrollment went from 21 to over 250 students. Latin is an elective. Eileen is the only teacher. She drives her classes mercilessly. She is a task master in a game show outfit. She has "words" for the day. She has students create pictures and read, read, read. She promotes Latin competitions. She spots students and gets behind them. From her own pocket she buys books for her students. The gift is always a "quid pro quo" and accompanied by a comment, "By Friday you will have read *all* twelve chapters."

There are toga parties and bus trips around the state to Latin competitions. In a few short years Eileen Bender's students have won top honors. Finally, in national competition they brought home national honors to Woodbury High School. Eileen is twice named teacher of the year. She is quoted in *Time* magazine. She makes the editorial page of a prestigious national newspaper for being cited as an outstanding teacher.

Her classroom? A modest wooden structure set apart from the rest of the school. She has low seniority for a regular classroom. Instead of moaning about it, she used the place as a tool to motivate students to decorate it inside and out with pictures of Rome and turn it into an ancient and revered place of learning about antiquity.

Several of Eileen's students make the national Latin Hall of Fame as participants in highly competitive team contests in which they joust over the intricacies of Roman mythology and daily living, history, and language. The depth of knowledge of her students astounds friends and foes. Students spend endless hours reading Latin works and authors and debating the meanings and nuances.

What motivates Eileen Bender? Anyone close to the scene knows her personal life was tragic. Two marriages. Deep personal tragedies with her own children. Yet in school Eileen Bender is superwoman. Eileen Bender wasn't motivated by any career ladder enacted by a state legislature. She isn't even a department chairperson. She has no designs for any administrative position, but she won't tolerate any administrator standing in the way of her kids and her program. Eileen's staff relations aren't super either. Other teachers are envious of the publicity but wouldn't work her long hours. And Eileen isn't a proud union card carrier. From her viewpoint as a former parochial school teacher, public school teachers have an easy life and unions protect the laggards.

The great teachers are always iconoclasts. But then most of the greats in other fields are the same way. We were amazed to find in the business page an item about Phillip Estridge of IBM. Estridge was killed in the Delta plane crash at Dallas-Fort Worth in 1985. He was a maverick that put the PC (personal computer) into the forefront for IBM. Estridge's employees worshipped him. His division alone would rank as the third-largest computer maker. Yet Estridge was described as "a wild duck who didn't fly in formation. IBM needs more like him."[4]

The schools need more Chuck Nogs and Eileen Benders. No matter what the walk of life, they are always a rare and precious human talent. The "wild ducks" of the faculty are always a breed apart. They are never more than 1 percent or *less* of any educational institution. In sports they would be known as franchise players, i.e., their presence in the lineup makes or breaks the entire franchise. They stand in sharp contrast to the "turkeys" of the faculty.

## The Superchargers

The Superchargers are the better than average teachers who are more dependent upon the "atta boys" or "atta girls" provided by colleagues and administrators. If career ladders work at all, these are the teachers they were designed for. The Superchargers are the faculty overachievers. If pure hard work means much, they will give it their all. But in contrast to the "wild ducks," the Superchargers can lose their volts over time. If not tended to, these teachers can burn out and become disillusioned.

Superchargers are an institution's bread and butter "good" teachers, the best of the bunch. They need a lot of TLC (tender loving care) to keep putting out the same energy level year in and year out.

Let's take Kathy Edwards, third grade teacher. Kathy loves school and teaching. She always wanted to be a teacher. She puts in long hours in her room, changing bulletin boards, learning centers, planning, correcting students' work. Kathy works on weekends, holidays, and evenings. Her room is alive and vital. She always has kids around her. She is very sensitive to the views of her principal, Maria Meyer. Maria is very visible in the building and gets to most classrooms once a week. Maria has given Kathy several written notes of appreciation for an excellent educational program, in addition to the feedback from her students. Kathy will keep putting in long hours.

## Turkeys, Stool Pigeons, and Wimps

The remainder of the faculty comes from the pages of *Mad Magazine*. They are the *turkeys*, the absolute "pits" for instructors. These folks consist of the turned off, disenchanted, jilted, deadbeats, and child haters. These "bored" people only "work" in schools. They put in their time and little else. They complain a lot. They grump and gritch. They act like teachers, but all semblance to good teachers ends there.

They are the masters of mediocrity, the fodder of too many years of rotten low pay and too little prestige for the teaching profession. Most have never worked anywhere else but school, so have little idea of the real world outside of their insulated cells and bells environment.

The turkeys are interested first in security, and second, stability. While they sleep and muddle around, they want their paychecks rolling in. Their motivation is to find a home in the rock and watch the clock. The kids in their classes do a lot of clock watching too. That's the only thing that won't get stolen in their classes because there's too many eyes fixed on it most of the time.

Arnie Ordinare is a *turkey*. Over the years Arnie has hardened into a cynical coot. He delights in nit-picking kids, their work, their dress, their slang, and everything else. The disciplinary referrals from Arnie's classes constitute fully 48 percent of all such referrals to the assistant principal at the junior high which Arnie calls home.

The only thing at school Arnie finds inspirational is payday. Friday is the only day he can stand. The rest of the time he comes to class at the last minute with no lesson plans and shoots from the hip. This means he thumbs through the pages of the math book to find some exercises and assigns the kids the problems to do. He then slouches back in his chair and reads the newspaper, growling if a kid has a question.

In the last eight to nine years he has found a lot of trouble with eighth grade girls who defy him, some openly. He shoves the blame for their hostility on their permissive parents, corrupt morals, and "patty cake" administrators who refuse to swat kids anymore and keep good discipline so he can teach.

Arnie is critical of everybody: the administration, the board, the union, kids, and colleagues. He sits in the faculty room most days drinking coffee in an old beat up mug while reading the *Daily Racing Form*.

Myrna Brown is a *turkey*. A nice lady with a soft voice and two master's degrees, Myrna manages to kill every program she has taught in. Myrna is absolutely tepid about everything including teaching. Discipline in her class is marginal at best. She has outstanding lesson plans. She just can't execute them. She is kind and unassuming. She sets no standards and the students soon see she has none. Three former principals have all tried hard to "save" Myrna. They've sent her to advanced training workshops, conventions, classes at night, therapy, had her observe competent colleagues and she's been observed by dozens of supervisors and administrators. Myrna is B-O-R-I-N-G! Any elective she touches dies the following year for lack of interest. When she teaches required classes, and the parents find out Myrna is going to be the teacher, there is a squawk. Complaints run from the bizarre to the sublime:

> Tall women give my son an inferiority complex. It reminds him of his Aunt Clara who tried to cook him when he was a baby.

I think my daughter is definitely allergic to her deoderant, whatever it is.

She speaks so slowly that it gives my son a headache. He's too used to watching *Hill St. Blues.*

Myrna loves teaching but her ardor would belie her claims.

Fred is a *stool pigeon.* He listens to the gossip and the grapevine and the bitching and sniping in the faculty room and, when no one is looking, ducks into the principal's office to spill the beans. He takes immense pleasure in ratting on his "friends." He believes it keeps him invaluable to the administrator.

Fred will tell you (if you listen) that Jim Bates, the science teacher, lost his key to the assembly seating—that's why his class sat in Alice Gaun's seats at the last assembly; that Doug Wartle is preaching about Jesus again in his algebra class; that Susan Pickering is trying to get pregnant but isn't married; that Moe Rafferty broke the ditto machine; that Will Banks said your plan for the curriculum committee was BS; that Janet Willover has a discipline problem and winks at ninth grade boys; and Wretha Fine was the one who threw away the state tests nobody could find last week.

There are at least two or three stool pigeons on every faculty. Before you decide to listen to them or use them to carry your message or have them be your "ears" around the place, remember that if the faculty as a whole finds out, you and your pigeon are dead. As in the spy business, pigeons can be set up, used both ways as unwitting "double agents." When given false information, the tables can turn rather quickly.

One very crooked principal was informed by his pigeon that the faculty was planning a surprise birthday party for him. However, it was to be at an odd hour on a Sunday night at a beer hall in a not-so-great part of town. The unusual location was to throw off any suspicions of a party.

The principal was called with a plea to help an old friend who had car trouble. When the principal arrived, he was chased by a couple of hefty muggers around winos and other derelicts and ladies of the night. The faculty room crowd is laughing up their sleeves at the principal's egotistical gullibility. Both he and his pigeon have been put in their places.

Kurt Butrex is a *wimp.* Wimps are the whiners. They always feel they have no clout and are asking the administrator to give them "muscles" that will make them feel powerful. Instead of developing their own biceps and triceps with practice, they "borrow" them from the boss and hold it over the kids. Wimps want the administrator to deal with rough kids, discipline their kids, talk to problem parents for them, and make them feel like Charles Atlas at the beach. Wimps come in both sexes.

## MORALE AND NETWORKING

Morale is always going down. Morale was always better last year. These are the only truisms we know about morale. Morale is a state of mind. It refers to the zeal people have for their work. When people don't like your actions, they threaten you with "lower morale."

We've visited hundreds of schools in forty-nine of the fifty states. Never once were we greeted with the cheer, "Morale here is off the wall. I've never seen it so good." Morale can only be viewed in *retrospect* since it is impossible to know what it will be tomorrow. Therefore, *by definition,* it could have been better. Morale suffers from the 20–20 syndrome. Since humans are rarely perfect, their tomorrows are rarely perfect either. Morale is the name of a small town you know only after you've been through it.

Networking refers to the idea of weaving channels of influence and communication among the staff, support people, and teachers to create a caring human environment. In this environment it is okay for people to fail. We like the story of the President of IBM, Tom Watson, who once called in an employee to inform him that his mistake cost the company $10 million.

After the conference, the sorry employee says, "I guess you're going to fire me." Watson responds, "How can I fire you now that I've just spent $10 million educating you?"[5] That kind of environment will result in trust and esprit de corps. It will help you build synergy.

## PEDAGOGUES, POKER GAMES, AND PRIVIES:
### FACULTY ROOM DYNAMICS

Nowhere are faculty dynamics more revealed than the faculty room. The usual faculty room we could construct for a theater set by memory. There are four walls, old furniture with the padding hanging out, ashtrays with cigarette butts, dirty coffee cups, an old manual typewriter, a ditto machine, a wheezing refrigerator that makes odd sounds, and perhaps an old version of a microwave with food scraps from moldy cheese sandwiches inside.

Last week's newspapers are everywhere with last month's magazines. On the bulletin board are bell schedules, a sign to join the union, or an announcement about the bowling league.

The faculty room is the jumping off place for the classroom. Here teachers wind up, hunker down, calm down, scramble for lessons and time stuffers, grade papers, and bitch. The faculty room is the great resource center of life. The closest thing to it outside school is a bar. In some places it is called the "faculty lounge," but that has caused some resentment. Nobody in the community likes to think that teachers have a place to "lounge." So it has been renamed "faculty work room." That's better. The protestant work ethic triumphs again!

While most faculty rooms look like a scene from "The Bowery Boys on Skid Row," we would offer the most sage advice about them after years of experience in schools, elementary and secondary. *Stay out of them.* The faculty room is the safety valve for the staff. They must have a place to let off steam, to get away from being watched by students, to step off their pedestals and be just people. There has to be a place for the jokers to gag it up, where teachers find some gallows humor in what they do trudging down the corridors of time fighting boredom without the tools of a billion dollar entertainment industry. There has to be a place to gather oneself up and hurl oneself one more day at split infinitives, the Pythagorean theorem, the priests at Pythia, and the wonders of pyrophosphoric acid mixed from water.

The smart administrator treats the faculty room like the embassy of a foreign country on home soil, and all persons in there are diplomats with immunity! Nothing counts in the faculty room and anything goes. The faculty room is the teacher's place. It is a sanctuary amidst the rules and regulations. It is "home sweet home." It is backstage at the Bijou in the days of vaudeville. It is an oasis. Don't ruin it. As long as there are schools, there will be faculty rooms. Respecting the faculty means protecting their place from intrusion, outsiders, and do-gooders. When teachers stop bitching in the faculty room, they've taken to the streets. The wise administrator insures that their territory is protected for his or her own protection.

Into this menagerie steps the fearless administrator without pistol or whip. Armed only with a baton and a sense of humor, he or she must turn this poised cacophony into the sound of music.

## CAVEATS, CODICILS, AND CONUNDRUMS ABOUT THE STAFF

- There are three kinds of problems and three solutions to those problems in schools: (1) people, (2) people, (3) people.
- If most people "only work" at your school, you're working too hard doing their work.

- $2 + 2 = 5$ is the bottom line for faculty growth as *synergy*.
- Great teachers are human freaks. They are "wild ducks" who won't fly in anyone's formation, yours or the union's.
- Great teachers are the "franchise players" of any school.
- Wimps want to borrow the boss' biceps to pretend to be Charles Atlas.
- Morale is the name of a small town you know only after you've been through it.
- When people don't like what your actions are, they threaten you with "lower morale."
- The faculty room is the great "resource center of life."
- The faculty room should be treated like the embassy of a foreign country on home soil, and all persons in it should be diplomats with immunity.
- When teachers stop bitching, they've taken to the streets.

## CHAPTER 7

# The Media

## THE TRUTH NEVER GETS IN THE WAY OF A GOOD STORY

Show us an experienced school administrator and we will show you the scars of past lessons learned from the media. Media people are amoral. They don't make judgments. They don't sell the truth. *They sell newspapers.*

Any school administrator who believes media people sell the "truth" or are even remotely interested in the truth has a lot to learn. Reporters from the papers are the proctologists of print. They are a little like career assistant principals who have done nothing but deal with discipline for too long. If all one sees are the thieves, turkeys, charlatans, and other dregs of humanity, it's easy to put all of the rest of us in the same boat.

Listen to the words from an interview with one of the most famous political cartoonists of our times, Pat Oliphant of the *Washington Post.* Oliphant's sketches have won him fame and fortune. Nothing is sacred. Once he penned a cartoon of an overweight Elizabeth Taylor, arms spread-eagled, being ridden over a brick wall by her ex-husband, Virginia Senator John Warner. The caption read, "Tally-ho, A Virginia Hunt Scene."

When asked, "Do you care about these people at all?" Oliphant shot back, "People in the public eye are public figures. They're fair game." When asked if his work was good for the country, he responded, "I don't want anything for the good of the country. That's no good for a cartoonist. . . . I need villains."[1]

We know dozens of reporters, TV journalists, radio news commentators, and editorial writers who feel the same way. The good news is boring. The bad news sells papers. So when achievement test scores remain the same or go up slightly: "big deal." But let them drop, and a front page bar-graph depicting the "slide" will be spread across eight columns with a picture of the glum superintendent announcing the Fall of the Roman Empire.

A school administrator is a public figure. We know of many who have been tried and hung on the front pages of the nation's press without a trial and without a jury. We've had our share of misquotes taken out of context and played with fanfare in a different song than the one we sang when interviewed. We've heard all the typical reporter's replies too:

> "Sorry, I don't write the headlines, just the story. The headline writer is responsible for that."

> "Isn't that what you said? I'll try and review my notes."

> "My editor cut out that second part where you qualified that opinion, but you did say the State Superintendent flubbed the report on test scores."

> "The deadline wouldn't let me deal with it in the same level of detail as you went into when we talked."

Media people want *easy generalizations*. They want "good copy." Good copy means:

- something easily understood by the person on the street with a sixth grade education (the level of the *Reader's Digest*);
- a simple story line that can be captured in about four to five simple paragraphs;
- some content-rich quotes that "flavor" the story and provide a character reference for the reader;
- something that will provide a "hook" for an eye-catching headline.

The last thing the media people want is a highly complex problem, interlaced with a lot of ambiguity (controversy is okay because one can write about it without having to understand the real nature of the controversy), which takes a lot of space to explain or be understood by the person on the street. That kind of stuff doesn't make it to the front page. It won't even get a box in the obituary section.

If the media people would just go away, the school administrator would be okay. At least a lot of our colleagues seem to feel that way. But there are always problems. There are walkouts and strikes, budget problems, taxpayer resistance, curriculum controversies like sex education or values education,[2] a teacher caught ripping somebody off or in a compromising posture,[3] a student who won't salute the flag,[4] or feuds between the state department and local administrators.[5]

In order to "cover the news" reporters can be pushy and overbearing. We think of President John Quincy Adams who, while taking a dip in the Potomac in the nude one morning, was met by reporter Anne Royall who sat on his clothes until he gave her an exclusive interview.[6] Adams wasn't the first public figure nor the last to be cornered in a compromising situation by an aggressive "space bandit," a slang term used to describe reporters in show biz. It happens all the time.

Public figures are human. *Only too human.* It is their frailties that usually end up in the headlines, not the strengths or virtues of the administrator. And public figures can be vilified. They are easy prey. Second-guessing is a way of life in the press. The media is always dealing with an event *after it happens.* School administrators have no such luxury. They handle problems when they blow up. Clarity of vision in the dust and grime of the pits often obscures the "best" decision. In many instances the "data" wasn't all there when a decision had to be made. After the fact, the media has all the data. Then the chickens come home to roost with the Monday morning quarterbacking corps in full pursuit.

Learning how to deal with the press is a survival skill. We've gathered these gems from the dusty pages of our scrapbooks at points where we most often wince with embarrassment.

## STROKING THE PRESS

Dealing with the press is a matter of posture and practice. One must be perceived as open and not fearful. Always return phone calls to reporters within a short period of time. They may be facing deadlines and it is in your best interests to quash rumors or deal with factual inaccuracies *before* they hit the press rather than after. Being quoted after something has appeared in the press *always* puts you behind the ball. No matter what, it's a strike! As in baseball a batter must anticipate the ball and often swing ahead of the time he thinks the ball will arrive. Remember that. You can't duck the press.

When you get the interview, whether in person or on the telephone, follow these rules:

### (1) Keep Your Answers Simple and Talk Slowly

It is far better to oversimplify a problem than to go into complexities and run the risk of a serious misquote. Avoid highly technical or sesquipedalian vocabulary. The latter refers to the practice of using very long words. Reporters will always shorten them. A misquote can result from the translation process. We show an example on the following page:

| REPORTER | WRONG RESPONSE | BETTER RESPONSE |
|---|---|---|
| *Question:* "The test scores are down, what's wrong?" | "It was probably a fluctuation caused by irregularities in certain abnormal responses in the distribution of the total scores. We detected that in the standard deviations we examined." | "Based on our review of the actual results we don't think it's a serious problem." |

If the reporter is with you, watch him or her write your response. Pace your answer to his or her writing speed. Go as slow as necessary to be correctly quoted *word for word.* If you say something and the reporter writes only one or two words, chances are you are talking way too fast. Slow up. Repeat your statement.

## (2) Don't Appear to Be Defensive, Even If You Feel That Way

A defensive person is a target to investigate. Reporters already believe that many, if not most, public officials hide things. So don't give them any ammunition or excuses to go hunting or take potshots at you.

| REPORTER | WRONG RESPONSE | BETTER RESPONSE |
|---|---|---|
| *Question:* "Why didn't you know that state aid would be down next year?" | "I didn't say that, I mean we just didn't know, who could know? We tried to get the data, we really did." | "We knew what the state knew. When they told us our aid ratio we changed the budget estimate the same day." |

## (3) Don't Volunteer Anything, Just Answer the Question

Most of the time reporters frame simple questions because they want simple answers. Don't reframe the question to a more complex level so that you can answer it. It isn't your comfort level that is important, *it's the reporter's.* If the reporter is satisfied with your answer, *wait.* If the reporter is not, he/she will ask you another question. *Wait for it.* Look like that's all there is to it. Nothing more. Many times reporters are on a "fishing trip," i.e., they don't know what they are asking or have not thought through a line of questions very well. Some say the first thing that pops into their heads. If you jump in, then off you go down a path you really should not have opened up in the first place.

| REPORTER | WRONG RESPONSE | BETTER RESPONSE |
|---|---|---|
| *Question:* What's that painting on the wall? | "You like that? I only paid $1500.00 for it." | "A British hunt scene." |
| *Next question:* "You used school funds to redecorate your office?" | | |

In the example above the reporter was curious. *Now he or she has a story.* No matter that you didn't use school funds to buy it (we hope not). What matters is that a $1500.00 painting is in the administrator's office. *That's news.* Most administrators talk too much. If you can get away with a "yes" or "no," it's all the better.

## (4) Duck Two-Edged Questions That Can Get You into Trouble

Reporters who have been around the block start a conference with a loaded question. Often it's one that no matter how it is answered you're in trouble. These are the "When did you stop kicking your cat?" type. On these, *duck.* Force the reporter to reframe the question.

| REPORTER | WRONG RESPONSE | BETTER RESPONSE |
|---|---|---|
| *Question:* When are you going to correct the problem at the high school about dropouts? | (1) "Well, pretty soon." <br> (2) "We won't until the spring." <br> (3) "We've always been working on it." <br> (4) "What problem?" | "There are many problems to be solved in the district, some old, some new." |

The reporter's *next* question:

FOR RESPONSE (1)  "Why haven't you started before this?"
FOR RESPONSE (2)  "Why are you still waiting?"
FOR RESPONSE (3)  "And you mean you haven't solved it yet?"
FOR RESPONSE (4)  "You mean you're going to continue to ignore it?"

The best response is a response that *says nothing.* Watch an experienced politician being interviewed by seasoned reporters on TV. Without batting an eye, they answer every question with firmness and finality and say little. It's an art. Your answer should shoot *above* the question. The tone of your voice, as well as all of your body language, should indicate it has been answered. If the reporter is going to pursue the line of questions, let it take on another form where each can be answered with a simple declarative sentence without your being trapped in the response. If he/she persists, simply say, "I've already answered that."

## (5) Don't Make Yourself Available Too Long

Unless it is an emergency, reporters should have to make appointments. Tell your secretary to schedule you tightly. Instruct her to let the reporters know that you're on a cramped schedule but you will fit them in. In that way, they get to the point and get out. Reporters can't go snooping if they have no time for it. In this way the administrator is actually keeping a lid on what reporters can do.

### DEVELOPING A MEDIA "PRESENCE" THAT SELLS

*Handling the TV Types*

Many school administrators panic when the first TV crew shows up to do a "spot" program. What they fail to notice is that almost all of the "news" is rehearsed. That's why it flows so well on the camera.

When the TV crew shows up, here's how to handle the situation. As they are setting up the camera and working out angles and lighting, ask the anchorperson, "What are we going to talk about?" In almost all cases the anchorperson will review briefly the questions he or she intends to ask. That enables one to know what data will have to be available, if any. It also gives the administrator a chance to organize his or her thoughts beforehand. No surprises before the camera. The last thing you want to look like is a segment from "Candid Camera." Reporters who play games in front of the camera are not long for the world because their sources and subjects dry up fast.

*On Camera*

Once the lights go on and the camera is whirring, the anchorperson asks the first question. Concentrate on the question. Answer it very simply and in a straightforward manner. Look at the reporter asking the question or slightly over the top of the camera so as not to be distracted by a reflection from the lens or have to shade your eyes from the light. This makes you look rattle-brained and caught off guard.

After you've finished answering the question, once again, wait. Since the film is rolling, the anchorperson will step right in and ask the next question. Most often, they don't even listen to your response. What they listen for is the intonation in your voice that cues them you're finished. While you're talking, they're thinking about the next question. You only have to wait. *And wait!* Don't feel in the least obliged to fill in the silence or the spaces. That is the TV person's job. It's his or her film that is being shot. The next question will come fast. Answer it. No matter how complicated the question, you should finish your response with not more than five sentences. Your facial expression must convey the clear message that *in your mind the question was answered.* No doubt about it. All questions answered. Of course, some may be answered more specifically than others. That's not your problem. Reporters can always ask more questions. Just answer them. We don't remember yet a reporter saying after an answer, "Yuk, can you folks believe that persiflage?" That would be editorializing about the news. It won't happen. *Leave 'em blinking!*

## TURNING BAD NEWS INTO GOOD NEWS:
## BEING YOUR OWN PRESS AGENT

On this item we are reminded of the reporter who came back from his first national educational convention who wrote that, "the schools are failing so badly that half the students are now below average." How one sees something is not only a matter of perspective, but how it is stated.

We know of several school districts that have asked for external reviews of their educational programs. They are called educational performance audits. One superintendent wanted a report that was a straight shot of the truth. "Tell it like it is," he said. "I'll handle the press." When the educational auditor came to town, he was interviewed on the TV. Before the auditor was through, he was interviewed "at exit" by a reporter. Of course, the auditor kept the findings general until words were put to paper.

When the report was finished, sure enough there were some glaring "holes" in the educational program. How did the superintendent handle it? He called a press conference and handed out the audit. He said, "We didn't bring this guy in from 2000 miles away and pay him the bucks to give us a pat on the back. We wanted the straight stuff. Here it is."

Then he walked the reporters through a carefully worded press release which highlighted the recommendations of the auditor rather than the findings. The district garnered all kinds of praise for being open and interested in program improvement. The "bad" news was buried by the candor of the administration, which was the "good news" and not the news itself, i.e., the content of the audit. The press can be finessed because it too is human after all.

Being your own press agent means taking the initiative to call the press or to write something for them. Such "releases" must be professionally prepared and ready to be used in a story. Many local papers will use copy as you wrote it if prepared well. They neither have the staff nor the money for many personal interviews. That is left to the dailies, where school districts are small potatoes unless there is a scandal or a tragedy.

We would also recommend developing your own arsenal of newsletters that are well prepared and are mailed to your entire community at least four times per year giving the good news and plenty of it.

## TWO SOURCES OF INFORMATION ABOUT THE SCHOOLS YOU SHOULD KNOW

There are two bonafide sources of news about your schools you should know about. The first are real estate agents. The real news about the schools is carried by real estate agents who make it their business to know how good the schools are. They get asked all the time. After buying and selling many houses in six states, we have yet to be disappointed by a real estate agent who, with little prompting, will tell you the best school districts and the best schools in the best districts. How do they know? They read the papers. They talk to people. They listen. Smart administrators have a luncheon for them every year and give them brochures about the school district. Many districts have initiated an aggressive campaign to keep children coming into a school district in the face of declining enrollment by courting the real estate agents.

The other source of information about your schools happens every night. It occurs when Johnny's mom says, "What did you do in school today?" An administrator who has never thought about Johnny as a reporter knows that Johnny will say, "nothing."

The school superintendent who knows Johnny will talk enthusiastically about what happened at school today is the same one who was asked by a reporter, "Of a $125 million budget, how much do you spend on public relations?" The superintendent answered, "$125 million."

The entire school budget is spent on PR every year. Some districts never thought about it that way. Neither did their administrators. The press are the civilized carrion crows of our society. Rather than be their victims you can be the victors. Knowing them for what they are helps. Reporters are the used car dealers of the information society. If you don't want to be misquoted or have any more problems than necessary, know how to deal with them. With some notable exceptions, we know that they are not purveyors of truth. Diogenes is dead.

Bobby Knight, Indiana University's flamboyant and controversial basketball coach, the subject of more than one newspaper headline, put it this way, "Absolute silence—that's the one thing a sportswriter can quote accurately."[7]

## CAVEATS, CODICILS, AND CONUNDRUMS ABOUT THE MEDIA

- Media people don't sell the truth, they sell newspapers.
- Reporters are the proctologists of the print world.
- Media people want easy generalizations. They want "good" copy.
- President John Quincy Adams learned about the naked truth from the first "space bandit."
- Avoid sesquipedalian responses and you won't be misquoted.
- It isn't your comfort level with the reporter that is important; it is the reporter's that is important.
- Reporters can't go snooping if there is no time for it.
- The press are the civilized carrion crows of our society.
- Reporters are the used car dealers of the information society.
- Learning how to deal with the press is a survival skill.

## CHAPTER 8

# Students

## THE PAWNS AND THE POWERFUL

After the last school bus rolled out on the last day of school and the building was empty of students, a teacher was heard to remark, "You know, if it were not for the kids, this would be a damn good job." The sad thing was that she was serious.

We also know of a few school administrators who feel the same way, but not many. Students are the administrator's most important connection to the reason the office exists. Students are the reason for schools, not teachers.

We believe that successful school principals practice a kind of faith that is operationalized in pointing schools toward students and learning. What we see is that *the primary responsibility of the school administrator is to ensure that every situation in that building becomes a learning situation to the greatest extent possible.*

Principals used to be called "principal teachers." Somewhere in our past we lost that designation. Now we have just principals. While some principals put the "teacher" back into their titles by their actions, many do not since some of them left the classroom because they got tired of kids. They just jumped from the frying pan into the fire.

The principal is always a teacher, just on a new level. One principal refers to his school as a "teaching hospital." According to his analogy, in regular hospitals, brain surgeons do operations and leave. But in a teaching hospital, they have to teach while they perform their operations, even the most routine. That adds an extra special responsibility for everything that is done. Every situation in a teaching hospital may be a learning situation for a medical student. We view schools in the same vein. They should be places where every situation in the building becomes a learning situation to the degree it is possible.

An interesting phenomenon is that school administrators often

*95*

create problems with students by their own views of them. For example, if one believes students are evil devils who will not work unless prodded, will steal one blind if you trust them, take advantage of you, cheat, lie, and generally enjoy a life of sloth if permitted, the rules of the school begin to be aimed at putting an end to such notions. However, in the process of trying to cope with these "problems," one can create a self-fulfilling prophecy. Students come to believe that "if that's what they expect me to do, then I'll become that."

### A STUDENT-CENTERED VALUE SYSTEM

A student-centered value system that is focused on kids maximizes the development of human beings. By doing so, the effectiveness of the school is maximized. The response of a student-centered value system towards change or conflict is open and adapting. Competency is simultaneously defined and related to the ability of students to solve real problems, not merely to gain authority or role-occupation.

The student-centered value system recognizes the legitimacy and worth of conflict in arriving at a more open climate and as a real opportunity for involving students in their school and helping solve common problems. Before administrators can involve their students in a meaningful way, they must first share certain beliefs about them. They should believe that kids are basically decent, intelligent, and willing to take responsibility. If given the opportunity, they will solve problems and make their schools better places for everyone.

Administrators with an optimistic view of kids will make all the difference in the world regarding the kinds of schools they will run and ultimately whether the students will become their allies or their adversaries, whether the students will become powerful as people, or whether they will become surly pawns waiting to turn into queens to wreak havoc on schools. They become powerful adversaries, serfs waiting to revolt, who engage in hit and run guerilla raids on bathrooms, walls, classrooms, and windows.

We believe as Sara Lawrence Lightfoot observed in her classic book *The Good High School* that good schools are characterized by a "fearless and empathetic regard of students."[1] What this means is that "good schools are places where students are seen as people worthy of respect."[2]

When kids are involved and motivated in this kind of environment, they become turned on in general—to the school, to one another, and to their community and this carries over into the classroom. They bring that enthusiasm, that charged energy, into their classrooms. You have handed your teachers a ripe audience on a silver platter and facilitated the enrichment of the teaching process. What else is a school administrator supposed to do—shuffle papers?

But human beings are makers of meanings. If something has no meaning, it is not worth knowing about—or being involved with. We don't become involved with people or ideas or schools that mean nothing to us. Meaning motivates. Meaning involves. Meaning connects.

So school administrators have got to involve kids with their schools—and if schools automatically practiced what they preach, that should be easy—even natural. But often this is not the case.

Once your students are galvanized, energized, turned on, you have accomplished something else as well. You have given them power and thereby created yet another power base for yourself as a by-product. We say as a "by-product" because student power is not just there for any administrator for the taking. It is there for only those administrators who genuinely love and respect students. Respect breeds respect.

You've heard the saying, "You can't BS a BS'er," but we don't believe it. We are sure about one thing. You can't BS the kids. Their innate detection system for BS is still with them in school. While much of education tries to stamp out this ingrown antibody to artificiality, most kids still have much of it left even at high school. They can spot a *phony* a mile away.

So if the principal is a warden, you've got a prison. If the principal is a despot, you have a police state. If the principal is loveable and fun, but has no expectations, you have a beach party. If the principal is a wimp, you have chaos.

The principal doesn't "buddy up" with the kids, use slang that is in vogue, tell off-color jokes, or horse play with kids. A leader of kids doesn't act like a kid. So the principal isn't "the Kid of Kids." The principal is an adult. The principal is somebody who cares and deeply believes in the potential for kids to become competent, caring human beings. That is displayed every day. It colors every action he or she takes.

It's no lie that kids have a different view of the principal, that is, as warden. To get sent to "the principal's office" for most kids means they are in deep trouble. It's also no wonder that, saddled with the responsibility of being a warden, principals command little public respect. In a recent poll, public school principals were ranked *below* doctors, clergy, college professors, lawyers, business executives, and public school teachers in the degree of prestige of their jobs and the extent to which such jobs were demanding.[3] Public school principals were ranked ahead only of local politicians and realtors. Yet so much of the research about effective schools places the principal in a commanding and pivotal position to construct a learning environment that works.[4,5] Why aren't principals perceived as more important in the schools in the public's eye? We suggest that generations of kids, now adults out there in society, remember (or maybe don't remember) their principals. They remember their teachers, the good ones and the terrible ones. But the principal was someone to be feared, someone no one in their right mind wanted to spend time with. Principals and punishment went together like peanut butter and jelly.

No matter what, students are powerful by their presence. Adults are either intimidated and fearful of them, or feel friendly and empathetic towards them. Empathy doesn't mean one is a pushover, has no standards, and accepts all the things kids will do in growing up. Empathy means drawing boundaries because kids need boundaries while growing up. It means being firm, fair, and flexible.

### STUDENTS AS A POWER GROUP

Students must be willing to come to school, go to class, and do other civil things for schools even to run reasonably well. That willingness is partly a matter of believing it is in their best interests to do so, partly a matter of knowing there may be immediate repercussions if they don't. There is some coercion involved in all of schooling. But in the best schools it is gentle. It is more of a hospital kind of caring rather than a jailhouse mentality.

Back in the Vietnam war days the power of students was more visible. In those days students at college and secondary schools demonstrated. They had sit-ins. They protested. They wore black armbands in schools resulting in a U.S. Supreme Court decision that extended the Constitutional protections normally reserved for adults in open society. Schools were no longer places where students had no rights. They were only special corners of society where learning occurred, and where the Bill of Rights definitely ruled.[6]

This legal emancipation of students in schools forever changed what students could and could not do. Dress codes went out the window. Strict rules about haircuts and grooming went by the boards as it was impossible to show a relationship between the precise length of a student's locks and an exact amount of learning. Courses reserved for the academically elite were opened to anybody who wanted in. Entry standards were bypassed. Students could no longer be suspended indefinitely. There had to be a hearing where due process rights were extended.

Recently, even the school's ability to govern its extracurricular programs such as band and athletics has been challenged in the courts when boards and legislatures began requiring passing work in all academic classes to play sports or toot in the band.[7]

We see a trend beginning in the Vietnam days of stripping away from school administrators almost all of the raw coercive power to compel things to happen in schools and to enforce them with the most arbitrary and harsh measures imaginable. No one has a precise idea of what to replace them with. There is a lot of uncertainty about it.

We believe that these characteristics are important in tapping the power of students to improve a school. We offer them in the guise of a vignette.

## Student Apathy at Rathbone High

Doug White began his principalship at Rathbone with a legacy of principal turnover in front of him. His predecessor had been Godzilla reincarnated. He treated the students as suitcases in a recent ad for airline luggage. He abused them verbally. Sometimes he gave swats. He treated teachers about the same, only the "swats" were verbal and in their evaluations, when he managed to do a few. In the end, "Godzilla" retreated to his inner office where he barricaded himself behind closed doors most of the time and talked to his plants.

The superintendent had recommended "Godzilla" for tenure, but the staff had completely rebelled and protested and as a quid pro quo, after tenure he left. As White moved into his office, he found an old pair of gym socks draped over the sink in the principal's bathroom with a couple of copies of *Playboy* and *Penthouse* thrown in the corner. What kind of place was this?

Doug replaced the art work, which consisted of a picture of some nineteenth century oarsmen on some river rowing their brains out, with pictures of kids. He moved the large oak desk away from the door to a more central position. He got some furniture so he could talk to people away from his desk and around a small coffee table. Then he set out to meet the people. Moving around the school, he found teachers in labs and work places and introduced himself. He was friendly, open, personable, approachable. He even smiled.

The first meeting with the student government was interesting. When Doug entered the room, the students paled. Some appeared angry. The body language they used indicated they were about to be chastised. Doug White began talking with them about their goals for the year. He offered some suggestions and he offered money and help. The students were shocked. They had never seen the principal except when they had a problem at a dance. His solution was to ban all dances.

When the students responded eagerly, Doug White proposed having an assembly at the beginning of the year. They were astounded. "Godzilla" had forbade assemblies. They had even lost the microphones after three years of no assemblies. After much discussion White pledged new microphones and worked with the students to have a beginning of the year assembly. However, White had to muscle his two assistant principals to have it. They were survivors of the Vietnam days when an assembly was an invitation to have a riot, defy the principal, and spit at "Godzilla." White simply said, "We're going to have one. I expect you to be there, that's all."

In this opening assembly Doug White was introduced. He launched into an upbeat presentation which indicated that he expected the students to enjoy school and the year. He talked about the promise of the athletic teams and the way he saw school spirit. His tone was infectious. The more he talked the more hushed the audience became. This was a principal? He sounded more like a cheerleader! The band played a rousing and short piece. Then the students were dismissed to homeroom. No riots, just applause. They left with smiles on their faces.

In every school there are good things to talk about. There are powerful and positive forces to be channeled and utilized. There is momentum in every human organization. It is waiting to be tapped. Doug White did not look at students as "the dark side of the force." He did not see them as criminals waiting to "make a break." He saw them as people. He saw them filled with potential. He saw people as positive. He communicated his views not so much in what he said *but in the way he said it* and what he *chose* to emphasize by not concentrating on the deviation and problems. "Godzilla" would have started by noting the assembly was late and time was wasting and read the school rules, stressed the punishments for each, warned the students, and sent them to class with an admonition not to dally. He would have been facing a nest of vipers. Such assemblies are snake pits. They were created by us, not by the kids.

Kids *react* to schools. They didn't *make* schools. Ostensibly schools were made for them. Were they? So long ago John Dewey was trying to describe what kind of desk he wanted in his laboratory school. First he didn't want a stiff place where the only thing a student could see was the back of the neck of the student in front! After spending some time listening to Dewey describing the kind of furniture he wanted, the carpenter said, "Oh, you want something in which somebody can really learn in." Dewey concurred.

We communicate to students what we expect in the way we construct a building, the way chairs are laid out in the rooms, the way the place runs, what it stresses and what it doesn't, and how people react to kids. Kids can react to most anything and *will.* What they react to is *what we put in place.* The most important thing we put in place is our expectation of them. That is communicated blatantly and subtly day in and day out. Kids don't come to school believing they are stupid. Schools give that message to kids and they get it. Is it any wonder that after thirteen years of getting the message that one is stupid, unfit, unworthy to be a member of the human species, and an animal, degraded and demeaned, that some kids take out their outrage on the place that keeps reminding them they are not human and have no dignity?

We get in the schools what we expect. The problem is not new. The Roman statesman, Seneca, wrote about the line educators must walk in the preparation of youth when he remarked about students that:

> . . . to regulate their education is difficult, because it is our duty to be careful neither to cherish a habit of anger in them, nor to blunt the edge of their spirit. This needs careful watching, for both qualities, those which are to be encouraged, and those which are to be checked, are fed by the same things; and even a careful watcher may be deceived by their likeness.[8]

What to concentrate on is the problem for the school administrator. People can be evil. People can be good. Which side is the one you will choose?

We know of one high school principal and her reaction to a situation which clearly indicated how she felt. Marla Patterson found out that a group of students who looked like motorcycle thugs and riff-raff were congregating in an area of the student center. With shaggy hair, dirty pants, sloppy shirts, they were a grubby lot. The other kids nicknamed them the "dirtbags." They didn't do any harm. They were not noisy or boisterous. They just lounged around together.

When student elections came up, one ambitious lad ran on the plank of "get rid of the dirtbags" by electing him president. Marla called the candidate in and asked him what right he had to judge the others? How exactly did he propose to rid the school of the dirtbags if he were elected? Was it on the basis of dress that he had made the judgment that they should go? How was that different from the Jewish pogroms in Europe? The boy dropped the motto from his campaign.

Marla began meeting with the "dirtbags" in twos and threes. Sometimes one on one. She spent long hours getting to know them, understanding who they were. She found out that they were the "hobos" of the school. Most had been failures all of their school careers. They didn't want to leave school. They didn't want to go to class and fail again. Their rebellion was confined to dress only.

Marla worked with them through the guidance department. She arranged for them to have alternative classes. She counseled them. She boosted them. She protected them from some of their highly critical peers.

We are struck by the chord sounded by Lightfoot when she noted in her portraits of six outstanding secondary schools:

> A final way of judging institutional goodness for students is to observe the regard and treatment of the weakest members. In each of these portraits, we see a strong institutional concern for saving lost souls and helping students who are most vulnerable.[9]

Marla clearly recognized Lightfoot's concept. She practiced it. The school was a more humane, more tolerant, and caring place because of her efforts. In too many places a strapping ex-jock vice principal would have "busted" the dirt bags, and they would have been moved to the real streets replete with all of the hard lessons to be learned there. Instead, many went back to class and began encountering success as the result of a persistent principal who believed anything was possible. People, after all, were good.

### STUDENTS AS PROBLEMS TO STUDENTS AS SOLUTIONS

At Paul Jones Junior High School, the principal, George Duffy, was concerned with the increase in boys joining fraternities at Jones. Such groups were little more than organized excuses to go roaming the streets in search of fights and mischief.

Besides vandalism, racism was also a concern at Jones Junior High School. It seemed that white students in the school (especially the boys) were fighting with blacks (who comprised approximately 15 percent of the school population) with increasing frequency.

Duffy decided to take the situation on squarely. He called the key leaders of the two fraternities he was not supposed to know existed in his school and asked them to arrange a joint meeting with all the boys in both groups and him in the gym at 8:00 P.M. on the next Friday evening. Duffy knew that Friday night was one of the times when the "frat" boys "roamed."

When Mr. Duffy arrived, he was surprised to find fifty boys sitting silently in the bleachers waiting for him. Duffy never addressed the issues of vandalism or the illegal fraternities which were "not recognized" by the district. He simply shared a school problem which was becoming worse. Racism was giving their school (a generally good school) a bad name. He wanted to organize a group to "rap" with him once a week or so about what was going on, why it was going on, and how to stop what was going on. He told the boys that he was asking for their help because he felt that they were "street wise" and therefore would be of help to him.

George Duffy struck a responsive chord in the boys, a chord which transcended color. Soon, volunteers from both groups joined Duffy and a handful of supportive staff members to initiate a student human relations committee, which the kids preferred to call "The Trouble Shooters." A more appropriate name for them would be "the Trouble Solvers." Not only has racial tension decreased since the institution of this new group, but the fraternities in general, which were initially formed for "protection," have all but disappeared.

Students can solve problems that they have actually caused in the past. If an administrator has optimistic assumptions about kids, that they are basically decent, want to contribute to make their school better, and will respond to an honest request for help, they can be among an administrator's greatest assets.

## POTS, POT, AND PETS

No section on students would be complete without citing one of the benchmarks of a safe and clean school. Bathrooms, johns, or "pots," as they are sometimes referred to, say more about a school and the students in them than most other places.

Clean, safe bathrooms are the key to student morale and conduct. There are as many ideas as problems. They range from installing sweeping TV cameras in the corners to closing them completely. Neither approach is healthy, nor will it work.

No student can relax and concentrate on his or her intellectual needs until he or she feels safe to use the bathroom without getting beaten up, ridiculed, robbed, or having to gasp for air in smoke-filled or cigarette-littered restrooms.

We know of several approaches that appear to work reasonably well. One is that of a high school, an excellent one, which permanently closed all student bathrooms except for two large "gang toilets," one for boys and one for girls on the ground floor of a two story building in the center of the school. A matron frequently checks the girls' room and a male custodian frequently checks the boys' room. The school has a reputation for having the cleanest student bathrooms in the county. No student feels unsafe in that school.

One junior high school in another district finally had to follow the lead of the senior high school within that district by removing the outer doors from all four student bathrooms. A metal wall insured privacy but the lack of outer doors made it unsafe to smoke pot, vandalize the bathroom, or intimidate students, activities which had gone on before the doors were removed. The high school within the same district had done this a decade ago.

In yet another junior high school the Maggio Plan works to keep the pots safe. The plan, named after Louie Maggio, Superintendent of buildings and grounds, is quite simple. All staff members make a habit of opening the outer doors of a student bathroom when passing it during the day and then saying "Anyone in here?" No matter what the answer, the staff member just closes the door and continues on his way. The whole procedure takes seconds. Yet, the climate created is one that makes mischief unsafe.

Whatever your methods, you must see to it that your school is safe and secure. Unsafe pots or corridors, graffiti all over the place, vandalism unrepaired are all signs that the school is out of control, that the "bad guys" are winning and are in control. So if you want to tap kids' potential, clear out their pots and the pot. Kids who aren't even plugged into themselves because pot has scrambled their brains aren't going to become plugged into one another or achieve self-esteem or realize their potential. Do the job. Go back to basics, and make your school safe for democracy and other good things.

And while we're on the subject of pots and pot, we may as well also mention a major pothole concerning kids—pets. We all have favorites. We even love our own children differently—if we're honest about it. But an administrator's pet can be as much of a problem as a "teacher's pet." The end result is the same—resentment because "only the favorites enjoy favoritism." And it won't be just the other kids who will resent you and your "pet"; you will have problems with some teachers as well. The fact is that some teachers have an insatiable, almost pathological, need to be adored by the students. We see this especially on the high school level. We call these people "King of the Kids." Any administrator who is too popular with the students in general will incur the wrath (more commonly known as jealousy) of the "King of the Kids." But special venom is reserved for administrators who have pets.

We were looking over the yearbook of a retired high school principal living somewhere in the Florida keys. Every now and then he gets it out and goes through the pages, especially in a beautiful sunset. There's one that has a special significance for him. It reads (the student's handwritten message next to her picture reads) like this:

> Thank you for making my years here that much more warm and beautiful—from the first day I knew I could grow. Thank you for letting us get close to a man who has his own office with his name on the door. Thanks for joining us on this flight of life here. You are a warm human being. Thank you from my heart you've let us smile. Enjoy, live, love.
> CYNTHIA EGGERS

The principal smiles as he remembers an entire stadium filled with students one night at a football game who all lit matches and sang to him and his family "You Light Up My Life." The sunset seems dimmer by comparison to his memory of that night.

It takes a lot to be a good administrator. It takes even more to survive. Touching kids' lives in ways few classroom teachers can without having to use "subject matter" as a vehicle or having to "cover curriculum" and having the potential of touching more of them than any classroom teacher can hope to touch make the job worth the struggle for survival because it's *their* survival you're struggling for as well, not just yours.

And who else has more time and AUTHORITY to tell kids "from the first day" that they could grow? And who else can let them—all of them—get close to a person "who has his own office with his name on the door?"

Having a hand in the development of humanity is God's work, and there will be times when you'll swear that you can feel His warm breath against the back of your neck. And you'll come to know exactly what John F. Kennedy meant when he said, "Here on Earth, God's work must truly be our own." Because you'll be doing it!

**CAVEATS, CODICILS, AND CONUNDRUMS ABOUT STUDENTS**

- The principal is always a teacher, sometimes on different levels.
- The primary responsibility of the school administrator is to see to it that every situation in that building becomes a learning situation to the degree that it is possible.
- Meaning motivates, involves, and connects.
- If the principal is a warden, you've got a prison. If the principal is a despot, you've got a police state. If the principal is loveable and fun, you have a beach party. If the principal is a wimp, you have chaos.
- Love in schools means a special kind of "disciplined caring."

- Kids didn't make schools. They react to schools.
- A more humane place for kids is a more humane place for the rest of us.
- You can BS a BS'er, but you can't BS the kids.
- Effective school administrators have faith in kids and other living things.
- If the kids aren't close to your heart, your heart's in the wrong place, or you are.
- Who else in a school can let kids get close to a person "who has his own office with his name on the door?"

# SECTION III

# *The Career Ladder*

## CHAPTER 9

# Career Planning—
# The Legend of the "Chairs"

## THE LEGEND AND THE FRATERNITY

Some legends die hard. Some never die. The one about King Arthur and Camelot is still going strong. The one about the "administrative chairs" in schools is in the same league. The "legend of the chairs" would have you believe that one must occupy each of the "chairs" for a time before one can be "worthy" of ascending to the throne of the superintendency.

This would mean starting as a classroom teacher, becoming a department chairperson or curriculum coordinator, then assistant principal, and finally principal. After this comes the first promotion to the central office as director or supervisor with district-wide responsibilities, then assistant superintendent, associate super-intendent, deputy superintendent, and finally superintendent of schools.

The absurdity of this legend would mean that to become a brain surgeon one would start as a floor nurse or perhaps as a paramedic in an ambulance *before* one could get into medical school. After gradua-tion the prospective surgeon would have to learn the ropes as a head surgical nurse and maybe take a shot at hospital manager for a while, then the residency! Such training would enable surgeons, between operations, to sweep the floor, inventory equipment, bill patients, and clean a few johns in the place.

Applied to sports it would mean that in order to become a quarter-back, a player would have to start as waterboy and graduate to backup center then starting center. After a while a turn at pulling guard, tackle, and tight end. Finally split end and maybe a slot back or blocking back. After years of toiling, the opening for quarterback would come his way. Nonsense!

Nobody runs a business by the "chairs." Who perpetrates such garbage?

*109*

## The Grand Fraternity—Omega Beta Nu (OBN)

The "chairs" are the property of the nationwide administrative fraternity, Omega Beta Nu. Membership in Omega Beta Nu is strictly exclusive. Membership in the "other" fraternities Phi Delta Kappa or Delta Kappa Gamma don't stand for anything with the grand old bachelors (GOB). The grand old bachelors mind the chairs in Omega Beta Nu. They see to it each and every administrative candidate serves "his" time (women may not be members) in them.

In order to be admitted to Omega Beta Nu one must be picked by a person already a member. Then there is an initiation rite followed by years of service and incremental elevation to the top. At each and every turn candidates are given close scrutiny so that they follow the secret codes and beliefs of the fraternity. Those who deviate or take on alien beliefs are dropped. They may never get to the top chair of Omega Beta Nu. The grand old bachelors always see to it.

These are the behaviors and beliefs of Omega Beta Nu for members in good standing. They are called the *Big Ten* by the grand old bachelors.

(1) All members must be male.

(2) All members must be ex-jocks at some level in their pasts.

(3) All members must at least once a week wear white socks with their suits on.

(4) All members must be poker players.

(5) All members must like golf, but only play with one another.

(6) All members must drink, preferably beer (a lot).

(7) All members must know at least six jokes that demean minorities, women, intellectuals, liberals, and court decisions that have protected such groups' rights in schools.

(8) All members must smoke or chew tobacco or use snuff.

(9) All members must avoid going to conferences or conventions for any other purpose except to sleep, play poker, get drunk, or carouse around town.

(10) All·members must be cynical about anybody who thinks or believes differently, especially eggheads or people who believe in anything uplifting about teaching, students, or schools.

The *men* of Omega Beta Nu are *everywhere*. They live in all of the states. They work in the statehouse, universities, and Congress. They are the Mafia of the educational workplace. They see to it we remain mediocre. Mediocrity and its perpetuation are the goal of every grand old bachelor and the supreme purpose of Omega Beta Nu. Their motto is "In Mediocrity We Trust." They have been with us since the founding of the nation. They are the epitome of the American anti-intellectual. Politically they are the manifestation of the "Do-Nothing" Party. And school administration has long been one of their favorite nesting places.

In reality Omega Beta Nu is the *Old Boy Network* (OBN). And the grand old bachelors are the *Good Ole Boys* (GOB) who live and work in the OBN. They coach and promote only those *like them.* They see to it few superintendents are black, Chinese, Mexican, Indian, or women. The statistics reveal their astounding success. The educational mafia are alive and well. It is the Good Ole Boys that want you to go through the *chairs* so that they can be sure you don't make it to the top. Too many women and intellectuals at the top will certainly weaken a commitment to mediocrity. It might mean schools would change. It might mean the difference between conformity and leadership. So the "chairs" are the equivalent of making a "hit" on a prospective change-agent. The more "hits" the Good Ole Boys get, the more they can weed out the aliens and do-gooders. Sticking to the chairs means KEEPING THEM IN POWER. Bypassing the chairs means TROUBLE.

Before you decide to tackle school administration, we suggest a realistic appraisal of your chances with the OBN. It may mean camouflaging your competence for a short time to break into the OBN. Most surely you will want to know if you have to pay the price. You will. You may have to physically move. A lot. It may mean time away from your family, shortened weekends, a long commute, and continuing night classes at a university to become certified. It's not a short happy life. It's long hours spent in pursuit of a goal. How much you want it depends upon how much you are willing to tolerate the inevitable long evenings, meetings, paper work, small talk, and the continual harrassment from the Good Ole Boys in the OBN.

**THE PLAY IS THE THING—THE DIFFERENCE BETWEEN SCENERY AND THE PLAYERS**

Getting to the top means understanding what is going on around you. Each school district provides the necessary ingredients for a play along with a cast of characters unique to that district. Each school building within the district houses a "play within a play."

When either applying for a position or assuming a new position in a new district, it is essential to learn the difference between the scenery and the players—those people who are powerful and those who aren't, those people who are well respected within a district and those who aren't, those people who can help you and those people who can hurt you.

A "search committee" for a principalship headed by a person who does not have the confidence of the superintendent is one sign that the superintendent could very well have already chosen his or her "own person" for the job and is simply letting the district's "clown" do busy work, while at the same time providing the superintendent with a perfect smoke screen of propriety.

Certainly the many boxes, lines (both solid and dotted), and arrows comprising the organizational charts of a district designed to illustrate its "chain of command" are of little help in trying to distinguish the scenery from the players.

More often, these "tables of organization" or "organizational flowcharts" will do you more harm than good. They won't tell you who is sleeping with whom, who the Friday night drinking crowd is, who the Wednesday night poker players are, or who the golf, tennis, or racketball partners are. These charts will not tell you the identities of "the Fool," the "Village Idiot," the leading men and women, the bit players (no matter how impressive their titles may sound), or the leading supporting actors and actresses. But most importantly, these charts will not distinguish between the true GODFATHERS (those people who have the power to really help you) and the GADFLIES (those people who are nothing more than ne'er-do-wells).

Time and again we've read resumes of prospective candidates for openings, who become instant "turn-offs" because they listed as references some of the biggest village idiots, fools, and good old boys that could be found in the district's cast of characters. We've also watched friends or acquaintances of these gadflies, newly arrived at the district and believing them to be true godfathers, become part of the coterie of faculty room bitch groups or goof-offs.

But what's even sadder to watch is a veteran employee, who should know better, latch on to a gadfly thinking that he's really a godfather upon whose power and influence he will ultimately be able to capitalize—power and influence which don't exist.

In order to determine whether a person is really a godfather or just a gadfly, subject him to the Nemesis Test: "What do the *real decision makers* in the district (who also have hiring and firing clout) think of the person in question?" Answer that question, and you'll know if you are dealing with a godfather or a gadfly. If the person in question is one of the decision makers, then ask yourself what that person's boss thinks of him or her, or what the superintendent of schools thinks of the person.

If you're wondering about the superintendent, ask what the board of education thinks of him or her. Even if the person is hated by everyone, yet his boss or the board likes him or her, the person still has the power and is therefore *a godfather*. (Note: even females can be godfathers in administration.) The opposite is also true. The most popular superintendent in the state is just a gadfly if the board thinks he or she is a jerk and wants to get rid of him or her.

## *A Tale of Two Characters: The Gadfly and the Godfather*

Once upon a time there lived within the same high school two assistant principals—Richard the Good and Bill the Bad. Bill the Bad was a bully and a boss. He intimidated staff members whose I.Q.'s were above 100 and weren't jocks because they threatened him. He also didn't care much for women—especially if they were bright. As long as they knew "their place" (which was definitely NOT in administration), he'd put up with them.

The odd thing about Bill was that he seemed to be popular among the staff in general. He was one of the boys, playing cards with the boys in the teachers' room many days, bowling with the boys every Wednesday afternoon, drinking with the boys every Friday afternoon.

And he was superb at patronage. "His people" got to use the telephone in his office and put their feet up on his desk or just come in for an air-conditioned coffee break on hot days. As schedule master of the high school, he saw to it that "his people" were taken care of by giving them the classes and duties they preferred, giving them common unassigned periods for the daily card games in the lounge, and seeing to it that his friends who were coaches of teams were given a "free" last period.

To a newcomer, and to a few naive veterans, Bill the Bad was a true godfather. Certainly, being one of Bill's Boys had to be a plus. But anyone who had the wisdom to subject Bill the Bad to the Nemisis Test would soon realize that the opposite was true.

THE decision makers in the district with the hiring and firing clout were the assistant superintendent, the director of secondary education, director of elementary education, and the building principals. It was a toss-up which one of these true godfathers despised Bill the Bad more—each of them for personal and professional reasons, many of which went back a decade.

Even Bill's principal, who began as Bill's fan when he assumed the principalship five years earlier (in spite of caustic warnings from others), finally shared their general disdain of him after years of being defied, defiled, and deadpanned by this man.

In that district, any candidate who either used Bill the Bad's name as a reference or who was part of his coterie or who even knew him in a friendly way was referred to by the true godfathers as "B.B.'s booby" behind closed doors. Any friend or acquaintance of his who ever got a job in the district did so in spite of their association with him. In fact, they had to be so good, that their good attributes had to overpower their friendship with him. Bill the Bad's friendship was their biggest handicap, and the irony is that to this day, neither Bill nor any of his band are aware of this situation, nor would they believe it if anyone told them.

The other assistant principal, Richard the Good, was not nearly as popular with the masses. He was not one of the boys, i.e., not a card carrying member of the OBN. He didn't drink with the boys. He didn't bowl with the boys. He didn't play poker with the boys. He didn't play golf with the boys. He didn't have anything to do with making up the schedules. Next to Bill, Richard the Good was somewhat drab. He just attended to the nuts and bolts of the daily operation of the building and did all of the minutiae and paper work that the principal had delegated to him in a quiet way. At first glance, one wouldn't think that Richard the Good had any power at all. But, once put through the Nemesis Test, Richard the Good becomes even better.

The other godfathers in the district respected the high school principal and relied heavily on his advice and his opinions, and the high school principal happened to be totally dependent upon Richard the Good for obvious reasons. Richard was totally dependable and trustworthy. He did the paperwork, which the principal dreaded, with no fuss and little fanfare. Richard was supportive of the principal, unlike Bill. His advice was normally reasoned and sound. In short, Richard the Good was an asset not a liability.

But there was another dynamic that came into play. The assistant superintendent, the directors of secondary and elementary education, and the high school principal each had something in common. Each of these four players genuinely respected the superintendent. The assistant superintendent and the director of secondary education had actually worked with him for twenty years. The high school principal, "the new kid on the block," with only five years' experience in the district admired the boss as well. And guess what? Do you know who the boss' closest personal friend in the district was? If you picked Richard the Good, you were tracking us all along. Richard the Good was a true godfather. Whom he backed, whom he "mentored," and who did a good job in his opinion carried a lot of weight downtown.

## GETTING THE POSITION YOU WANT: TWO STRATEGIES

The OBN and the GOB believe in advancement by inheritance. They believe in what we call "squatter's rights." Squatter's rights refers to the practice of just being around long enough and you will "inherit" the next position. The OBN fosters inbreeding and conformity. Longevity is the key to advancement. OBN superintendents are therefore carefully groomed for the job by the district's drones. They may be passed over several times for the CEO's position and finally inherit it after "serving" some twenty years without distinction.

If you choose to play this game we advise keeping yourself in good health because you will have to live a long time. Then there is always the possibility that a new board election will sweep in some changes; they will hire a non-OBN superintendent who will promote non-GOB types. Years of "paying your dues" will go down the drain. When this happens, many of the GOB are bitter and angry or decide to retire. After all, they've been playing by the rules for so many years and now the rules have been changed. Life has been unfair to them.

Another occupational hazard encountered when attempting to "inherit" your job is having to learn how to be a bit player or even becoming "scenery" for long periods of time. In OBN systems, the boat-rockers get knocked off first, or just get disgusted and leave on their own (to the delight of the GOB). An "inheritance" approach means laying low. It means being careful, knowing when to speak up and when to shut up. When there's blood in the streets, it means "hunkering down." Longevity is what matters. Staying power is strength.

Many administrators we know simply inherited their jobs. Some didn't have to wait very long. One advantage to being a "squatter" is that you'll have an opportunity to make a lot of friends, providing you avoid the "pothole" jobs which are either positions that get everybody ticked off at you because of the nature of the duties (like Affirmative Action Officer) or dead-end positions from which one cannot get back to the line of promotion (Coordinator of Interstitial Space).

The other strategy is "going for it." It's risk-taking strategy. It's the Saul Alinsky style, the pole vaulter, organizational ju-jitsu at its best! It's the "damn the torpedoes and full speed ahead" style that will either get you there in one bold stroke or have you clinging to a life raft after the daring attempt.

To those who go for it, length of time served isn't nearly as important as the number of accomplishments completed within that time, for it will be their demonstrated competence which will serve as their calling cards for the next assignment and not the number of years notched on their seniority gun that matters.

This approach is for the creative and the impatient. It isn't necessarily the surefire road to popularity. Powerful enemies can be made along the way which can lead to an early departure from a school district. But life is, after all, a compromise, a trade-off. The free-wheeler, the risk taker, says "goodbye" to colleagues more often than he or she might wish, seldom stays in any one place long enough to build an empire, and may have to uproot and relocate the family several times before ultimately settling down.

Both methods work. We know hundreds of Administrators who fall in both camps. We know, however, *too few women* who made it *either way*. The dominant approach is the OBN and longevity. It is definitely the "chairs." That's a tragic loss to the profession when the best brains of half the population are sacrificed for the mediocre talents of the rest. Genius is always in short supply. To screen out half the population on the basis of sex discrimination deprives the nation's schools of the best leadership it's got for one of its most important functions: the rearing of its young.

Over and over again we have been struck with the obstacles we place in front of women to gain access to key administrative positions. There is even a piece of research by a female psychologist that documents that good looks for women are a definite liability for promotion in the work place. It seems the stereotype is that beauty and brains are accepted only for men, not women. The message is that beautiful women have more difficulty shedding the female role-stereotype than their uglier counterparts. What a pity! A double barrier.[1]

We still believe the words of Diane Ravitch of Teachers College Columbia University apply to both men and women, "The person who knows 'how' will always have a job. The person who knows 'why' will always be his boss."[2]

**THE RIGHT PEOPLE—WHO ARE THEY?**

By now, it should be clear that there are those people who can help you or hurt you (even if both of you *think* you are being helped). With examples from history, we can list those people who won't be able to help you.

| QUOTE | YEAR | PERSON |
|---|---|---|
| "Everything that can be invented has been invented." | 1899 | Charles H. Duell, Director of the U.S. Patent Office |
| "Sensible and responsible women do not want to vote." | 1905 | Grover Cleveland |
| "Heavier than air flying machines are impossible." | 1895 | Lord Kelvin, President, Royal Society |
| "There is no likelihood man can ever tap the power of the atom." | 1923 | Robert Millikan, Nobel Prize, Physics[3] |

These people all were non-risk takers. They had closed minds about the possibilities for the future. If they were in school administration, they would be saying things like "No woman can ever be a superintendent in this district" or "Computers in every classroom? Hogwash!"

The people the risk takers need are the big thinkers. In the words of Ole Sand, the NEA's former Director of the Center for the Study of Instruction,

> What all this means for us is that we should neither be optimists nor pessimists, but possiblists—if we are not to be in graves while we are still alive.[4]

Many of the people close to schools who are not educators can be true godfathers for the aspiring administrator to be. We think of some like the school board attorney. The ones who are excellent at what they do are well respected and known in many school systems by superintendents and board members alike. They know them on a personal basis. They get to know a lot of the "right" people. A word to any one of them about you can open a door not otherwise available in a short period of time.

Often the "right" people don't have fancy titles or even impressive ones. We know of one superintendent who had so much confidence in his secretary that potential adminstrators in the district were deliberately scheduled to sit in his outer office and chat with Mrs. Bonsoir as if it were waiting time. The superintendent would check with his secretary to record her impressions of the candidates. There was at least a seventy percent chance that this superintendent would "agree" with Mrs. Bonsoir's assessment. That's how much he valued her opinion. Although you won't find Mrs. Bonsoir's name anywhere on the organizational chart, you'd better believe she's alive and well and wielding a great deal of power in that district to this day.

There are ways around the OBN and its depressing influence on leadership in the schools of the day. Both sides seem to understand that in the ensuing battle for the posts of the future the balance can be tipped in favor of the non-OBN types by getting enough people in a critical mass in such positions to knock the other side out.

If you're female, black, Mexican, or a non-OBN male, this chapter is for you. When you finally get into the position to deal with the OBN and the good ole boys—kick ass and take names. The future of the business is in your hands.

### CAVEATS, CODICILS, AND CONUNDRUMS ABOUT CAREER PLANNING

- Nobody runs a business by the "chairs." Who perpetrates such garbage?
- The "chairs" are the property of the nationwide administrative fraternity, Omega Beta Nu (OBN) (the *Old Boy Network*).
- The *men* of Omega Beta Nu are the educational Mafia of the work place.
- The motto of Omega Beta Nu is "In Mediocrity We Trust."
- The more "hits" the Good Ole Boys get, the more they can weed out aliens and do-gooders (translated: women, blacks, Mexicans, Chinese, or anybody else they don't like).
- Organizational charts don't really chart the organization.
- There are two kinds of strategies for career advancement: advancement by taking risks and advancement by inheritance.
- School administration can't afford to lose the best brains of half the nation's population to be sacrificed to the mediocre talents of the other.

## CHAPTER 10

# Resumes, Headhunters, and Interviewing

A school administrator's resume is either his or her best foot forward or an epitaph on a professional grave. Bad resumes are legion in school administration. Most are filled with irrelevant information, placed backward in order of importance, and "stuffed" with garbage.

## THE RESUME AS DOUBLESPEAK

"Doublespeak" is the art of appearing to say something based on facts but which if examined closely is a mixture of *truth* and *tapioca*. Some resumes are mostly tapioca. We will take the case of William Latemoor. William was a sixth grade teacher desiring to be an elementary principal. The only thing Bill had to qualify as any kind of administrative experience was as summer playground director. This meant being on the grounds in the summer, organizing board games, checking balls in and out, and running a few bag races on Friday.

Bill's resume read like the *Who's Who of the East*. Here's what he said:

*PAST ADMINISTRATIVE EXPERIENCE*

Director of Summer Athletic and Educational Program, 1980–85

Responsible for the creation, implementation, and evaluation of a summer program at Halstead Elementary School which served 8 square miles including an adult population of 8,500 and a population of 1,500, K–12 multi-ethnic students. Responsible for budgeting, equipment inventories, and curriculum development which integrated student experiences with situations of everyday life. Halstead is located in the historic part of Rittenburg, home of the mayor and several prominent citizens in the region including Norbert Nutmeg, oatmeal millionaire; Rodney Rags, disposal magnate; and Harold Rugs, carpet tycoon.

This is an example of a lot of tapioca masking the reality of Latemoor's actual responsibilities. It is "super-puff" and most experienced resume readers can spot it a mile away. William has never gotten an interview. Instead of rewriting his resume he keeps puffing it up adding more to it. The only one who believes it is Bill. After the fifth rewrite of his resume he even asked for a raise as playground director! Somebody that good with as many duties as he had just wasn't making enough, he reasoned.

*Super puff* on degrees means that the resume exaggerates advanced degrees earned. Some say, *Ed.D. 1988.* That can mean anything from the person is planning on entering an Ed.D. program in 1988, to the person will finish an Ed.D. program in 1988, or it can be just wishful thinking.

*Super puff* on awards and honors will really stretch it out. Some examples are:

1957—Award for Outstanding Merit—Jones Junior High School (newspaper poll)

1959—Outstanding Musician, Trombone Section, "B" Band

1961—Selected Alternate Delegate to State Forensics Competition

1963—Runner-up Most Popular Dorm Counselor, State U.

*Super puff* on publication looks like the following:

- submitted numerous drafts and articles to *North American Gaelic Society Quarterly*
- authored two articles on building fykes for *Regional Fisherman* (in review)
- participated in the development of a report on the teaching of orthopterious, herbivorous insects in a unit of eighth grade science (with Herbert Hebert, colleague, under "Grasshoppers").

A good resume should be in the range of four to five pages and follow the principle of an *inverted pyramid*, the most information to the least. The three most important pieces of information which must be quickly ascertained are your *actual* experience on the job, your training and education, and your certification. Everything else is nice, but not necessary.

Leave out references to your age, sex, marital status, children, religious affiliations, high school attendance, or any awards at high school. Only major awards at college should be placed in a resume. All awards should relate to the job for which one is applying.

If you put the actual names of references in your resume, be sure you check beforehand with everyone that it is okay to use their name *and* be sure they will be positive about you.

Use reverse chronological order when listing events or jobs, i.e., start with your current employment record and move to the earliest such record. Don't use a photograph and avoid having your resume printed on special paper. The best resume is typed fresh on plain white paper and is tailored to the job one is seeking. A printed resume says to the reviewer that you've had hundreds printed and aren't choosy about whom you work for. It means you're "desperate" and actually have no real job choices. It's the portrait of a "loser."

This advice stands in stark contrast to what one may hear in business school. There, a fancy professionally printed resume on pink paper will "stand out" in the stack. Educators have different norms on these matters. Resumes say a lot of things about you. The last thing you want someone to think is that you're not choosy. This puts you behind the eight ball in negotiations should you get the job, but nine times out of ten you won't even get an interview.

In *Exhibit 1* we show you what a "lean and mean" resume looks like. At a glance a prospective employer knows Lawrence's training, his majors, and when he received his degrees. The employer knows Bob's standing with certification. Should Bob apply for a position in New York, a Board would know if New York had reciprocity with either Florida or South Carolina immediately. Also, Bob's actual responsibilities and duties are clear in each position he has held.

If a prospective employer is going through a stack of resumes of some 150 candidates, it must be immediately apparent if Bob is qualified in order to make the "paper cut." If an employer will not spend more than three to four minutes per resume on the "paper cut," information must stand out and be easily deciphered. One cannot spend a lot of time searching through a resume to know what a candidate actually did or if he or she is or can be properly certified. A "puffed up" resume works against a candidate in this regard. It prevents a prospective employer from making a clear decision at the paper screening level.

When administrative positions are keenly sought, ambiguity at the paper screening level will usually be negative. Lean and mean resumes are best to get one in the door. So save the "puff" for the interview. The first hurdle is to get through the stack and open the door to a face to face interview.

We are reminded of the story of a frugal New England widow who was shopping for a gravestone for her deceased husband. Stonecutters charged by the letter.

Her first lines to fit the headstone were:

> Beneath these stones
> Do rest the bones
> Together with the corpse
> Of one who ere Death cut him down
> Was Andrew Jackson Dorps.

After getting the price, the widow was staggered by the cost. She quickly recast her memory into these lines:

> Beneath this stone there lies the corpse
> Of Mr. Andrew Jackson Dorps.

However, the cost was still beyond what she considered reasonable. Therefore, she worked it over again.

> Here lies the corpse
> Of A. J. Dorps

Finally, she took her pen and eliminated all but the essentials. The grave marker read:

> Dorps'
> Corpse.[1]

---

## Exhibit # 1

SAMPLE RESUME FORM
Robert J. Lawrence

*EDUCATION AND TRAINING*

| | | |
|---|---|---|
| 1984 Ed.D. | University of South Carolina | Educational Administration |
| 1974 M.S. | University of Florida | Administration-Curriculum |
| 1972 B.S. | The Florida State University | Secondary Education |

*PROFESSIONAL CERTIFICATION*

| Year | Certificate | Expires |
|---|---|---|
| 1975 | Secondary Teaching/Florida | 1988 |
| 1982 | Secondary Administration/Florida | 1989 |
| 1984 | Superintendency Certificate/ South Carolina | 1989 |

*PROFESSIONAL EXPERIENCE*

1983 to present     *Senior High School Principal, Lombard High School, Columbia, South Carolina*

Executive leadership of a 2300 pupil high school, grades 9–12 which functions on a $7 million dollar

1981 to 1983  budget. Includes supervision of 155 professional
staff, 37 non-certified staff and coordinating functions to three feeder junior high schools.

1981 to 1983  *Assistant Principal, Rogers High School,*
*Columbia, South Carolina*

One of two assistant principals of a high school of
1935 students, 9-12. Responsible for supervision of
educational program in English, social studies,
foreign language, and mathematics. Developed
budgets for these areas with department chairpersons and supervised teachers and support personnel. Student discipline included for grades 9-10.

1977 to 1981  *Department Chairperson, Dumbarton Oaks High*
*School, Alachua County, Florida*

English Department Chairperson of a 2,500 pupil,
9-12 high school. Duties included curriculum
development and monitoring, supervision of 31 full
time teachers and four aides. Over 112 courses
offered in the English Department. Curriculum
included full scope from basic English to Advanced
Placement courses.

---

We suggest a similar strategy in putting together your resume.
Keep it to essentials—the resume is not for you; it is for a potential
employer to match against a job description or set of job specifications. The ability to quickly tell whether or not a person's background, interests, and experience match a job is what counts in the
paper chase. A "foggy" resume usually gets lost in the stack.

### ON BOGUS DEGREES: AVOIDING DIPSCAM

We are surprised at the number of educators who are tempted to
"buy" their diplomas rather than earn them the good old fashioned
way. There are no shortcuts to obtaining a bonafide advanced
degree. And such degrees are the necessary "union cards" to ad-
vance in school administration. Early in 1985 the FBI exposed a ring
of four men who churned out fake degrees in education, business,
engineering, medicine, and theology. These men had sold over 3,000
degrees for more than $2 million. Among those who purchased the
degrees (along with fake college class rings and alumni associations)
were a superintendent of schools, an elementary school principal,
and many other educators, administrators, and teachers.[2] The names
were turned over to the Internal Revenue Service. Some were made
public to discourage others from taking the same route.

We note that one candidate for the Public Utility Commission in

Pennsylvania had to withdraw when it was disclosed that he had bachelor's and master's degrees from fake universities.[3] Assume that your credentials will be checked at some point in the future. Fake degrees indicate not only a blatant disregard of the responsibilities of advanced administrative positions, but broadcast loudly and clearly that other things about one may also be fraudulent.

The list of bogus degree mills is shown below:

- American Western University of Tulsa, Oklahoma;
- Southwestern University of Tucson, Arizona;
- Southwestern University of Salt Lake City, Utah;
- Northwestern College of Allied Science in Tulsa, Oklahoma;
- Williams College of Boise, Idaho.[4]

A school administrator should be warned there are no shortcuts to an advanced degree. Programs which advertise non-campus work and no courses are only taking your money. In return you get something you can never use for fear of exposure.

Degrees are like money. When dealing with money one wants the soundest currency going from the most conservative country fiscally. Confidence is measured by the reputation of the country and in the case of a degree, by the institution. If one is going to invest the money, one should receive something that can be utilized. Fake degrees can't even be displayed on your office walls.

We know of a few administrators out there who took the short cuts. They are not only out the money, but they are afraid to even list the diploma mill doctorate on their resumes. A phony degree truly is useless to them.

## HEADHUNTERS, CANNIBALS, AND THE OBN

*Headhunters* is the name given to those consultants who help boards of education select administrators, normally superintendents, but sometimes principals. There are probably only about a dozen really powerful headhunters nationally. Not surprisingly they are all white males. On some superintendent searches, the *headhunters* will add a minority person or female to the screening team to ensure a balanced look.[5]

While some in the business would argue that the OBN (old boy network—see Chapter 9) is a thing of the past, we would *disagree*. Occassionally a female is selected as a superintendent, *but too few*. Some headhunters maintain "stables" of candidates whom they shuffle in and out of a variety of openings. A close tracking would reveal such candidates in the positions being screened.

In the business world, it is estimated that over 90 percent of the U.S. Fortune 500 companies have used headhunters (called "Executive Search Consultants"). There are approximately 1,500 such consultants/firms who employ 10,000 consultants who annually fill some 80,000 upper management positions in the U.S.[6]

Getting to know a *headhunter* who is strong regionally is the first order of business for the upwardly mobile school administrator. Many frequent national conventions and are on the prowl for new talent. After examining the position you want, see if a headhunter is being used. When you continually see the same name, you are onto the trail of a headhunter. Some headhunters conduct periodic workshops on resume preparation or interviewing. Attend them. Nothing succeeds like face to face meetings. Headhunters are human like everyone else. They also have an incredible underground network that is largely informal. This network tells them what jobs are coming open because those who think they want to move, *or will have to move*, call them for advice and counsel. Much of the informal backroom talk at national conventions is devoted to tracking professional movements around the nation. Most of the big jobs are "covered" long before they come open, in that the vacancy is known informally, and prospective "ducks" are lining up to see who the headhunter is that the board will select.

One of the first things that the aspiring administrator should know is if the headhunter is in reality a "cannibal." Most responsible headhunters won't play the cannibal game. Some are duped. Getting eaten by a cannibal means that a position for which you've declared yourself a candidate is "wired" behind the scenes, usually for an "internal" candidate. These are crooked searches. They are shams.

Playing the game means knowing if the job is "wired" and not going through the agony and anxiety of the interviews and paper forms only to "lose" the final to the chosen one. If one's name is on the front pages of the papers, it is impossible to keep your application a secret from your current employer and thus your candidacy endangers your current position. If all of that has been taken in a phony "search," *you've just been cannibalized,* wasted for nothing!

Most national headhunters will not take on a search if they know the job is wired. Understanding this, some boards will employ a national headhunter to convince the public the job really isn't wired, and then award the job to the internal candidate when the chips are down. In this case, the headhunter has been "had," as well as the finalists for the positions who had applied based on the reputation of the headhunter for an honest search. When this happens, a headhunter has a lot of explaining to do and knows that in the future many qualified and prominent administrators will not apply if he (there are no she's) is handling another search.

### INTERVIEWING YOUR INTERVIEWERS

Once one gets through the paper shuffle in an honest search, the next hurdle is the interview. Interviews can be one on one, or more usually, a group of people interviewing a single candidate. There are some important rules about interviews.

The first rule is that you should be interviewing your interviewers. It is the candidate that should control the interview and not those doing the interviewing. It's easy to do. Just answering the question is not enough. Your tone, your pace, the measure of your response are the keys to controlling an interview. That keeps you off the defensive and moving the interviewers to your pace and to your strengths and not your weaknesses.

Ninety-eight percent of the time the very first question is, "Tell us a little about yourself," and off you go! What you say, how you say it, and the speed of your response dictates the extent of your situational control. From the opening bell you must be in charge. The answer to the first question is crucial. Some interviewees have never recovered from it.

Now the questions should be coming based upon your first response which should have several "hookers" in it that will easily lead to a follow-up question. Once you're in charge, you must stay on top of the interview all the way through. A little humor, a question back to the interviewers, a call for definition of terms prior to answering a question are all ploys that can be used to "catch your breath" and take stock.

There are a couple of *sand traps* you should *avoid.* If you should get asked, "What are your weaknesses?" don't be like one chap who said, "After fast cars, fast women, and liquor, I don't have any." Always make your strengths your weaknesses such as, "I work too hard," or "I have high expectations for my work," or "I find I don't have enough time to do everything that needs to be done."

And be prepared for the old reliable inquiry, "What is your philosophy of education?" Most people, especially laypersons, don't really want to know your *philosophy;* they want to know your *ideology.* There are only four types of educational philosophies.[7] If you think they really want to know your philosophy, try an appropriate response such as, "I'm a classical realist" and quit.

Most people want to know if you "believe" in individualized instruction or schools without walls or open campus or homework or a dozen other things which have more to do with a closed system of beliefs, i.e., an *ideology*, not a philosophy at all.

Asking an educator to explain his or her philosophy would be like asking Edison to explain electricity. Where does one start? So have in mind some things to say that are not philosophical and therefore will not be metaphysical, epistemological, or axiological, but *nitty-gritty*. Remember, they don't really want to know your philosophy at all.

At the end of the interview have some questions to ask your inteviewers. Have some good ones going into the interview that you can alter if need be. Some of the ones we have found that really make your panel of inquisitors think are, "If I were to be selected for this position, what evidence would you use to determine if I were successful?" or "What is it that you want this (district, school) to become and how will you know if you accomplish it?" or "How do you know of all the things the (district, program, school) is doing that it is doing the *right* things?"

These questions are important ones to differentiate between means and ends, something which many districts have a hard time doing. The ones that do are way ahead of those that don't and represent a measure of sophistication which is an easy benchmark.[8]

### LEADS: DEAD ENDS, DEADBEATS, DETOURS, AND DIVIDENDS

A "dead end" is a job for which you have repeatedly applied and not been selected for an interview. That means you are getting screened out in the "paper cut." It usually means your resume is too confusing or you don't have the right qualifications or experiences required to meet the minimal entry criteria.

The best strategy is to shift targets. For example, if you are shooting for a superintendency but can't get to first base, try an assistant superintendency or perhaps a director level position. But don't keep sending out your resume and wasting postage, not to mention bent expectations. It is easy to acquire a defeatest attitude with too many rejections. So why do yourself in? Get smarter!

"Deadbeats" are those people who keep making you promises they can't deliver. They may be friends who keep saying they will write you a letter for your placement file or personnel assistants who keep urging you to submit your application after repeated denials and rejections. Deadbeats are any people who make you promises they can't deliver on. Forget them. Find new friends. Find people who can deliver. Find people who say what they mean and deliver when they promise. One of those is worth a hundred of the rest.

A "detour" is a route one takes to get to a job one really wants, but not directly. It usually means something or somebody is blocking the way. Suppose you want to be a principal of an elementary school but there are no openings. Waiting around forever will mean passing up opportunities to acquire non-building-level administrative experience that could be valuable for you. So aim for an administrative position to get the experience, but position yourself so you can get back to the main highway easily. This means avoiding detours that take you so far away and into such a specialized position that you discredit yourself for future promotions. Often these are hard to tell. "Line" positions in school systems are those concerned with operating the schools such as principalships and administrative officers to whom principals report, if not the superintendent. "Staff" positions are support roles such as guidance, pupil personnel, staff development, curriculum development, and the like. If you take a "staff" position and you really want to get a "line" position, don't get too far away from the line and don't stay too long in such a position.

"Dividends" means investing in your career. Go to conferences and choose the hard sessions. Take the challenging courses at a university and college. Challenge yourself to become competent. Learn skills that make a difference. Acquire theory that helps you explain or predict what may happen in school administration. These are the "dividends" that pay in interviews and in job performance. If you feel yourself becoming stale, that is a surefire sign that you require stimulation and it's time to invest in more dividends.

It's probably fairly true that if one is not growing, one is dying, at least professionally. People can become obsolete just like machines. People can become worn-out just like machines. People can be discarded just like machines. The unemployment lines are filled with them. The difference between people and machines is that people CAN REGENERATE THEMSELVES. It takes purpose and courage. It's a matter of will and energy. It's our business. We should know how.

### CAVEATS, CODICILS, AND CONUNDRUMS ABOUT RESUMES, HEADHUNTERS, AND INTERVIEWING

- "Super-puff" in resumes is mostly tapioca with a sprinkling of truth.
- A good resume follows the principle of an inverted pyramid.
- A professionally printed resume is the portrait of a "loser."
- A "foggy" resume gets lost in the stack.
- A phony degree isn't any use, even to a phony.

- A crooked search is run by a cannibal who may be a headhunter in disguise.
- Asking an educator to explain a philosophy of education would be like asking Edison to explain electricity.
- Getting nowhere on a job for which you have repeatedly applied is a "dead end."
- People who continually make promises they can't keep are "deadbeats."
- A "detour" is a route around the position you want but stays close to the main highway line.

## CHAPTER 11

# Academics and Abecedarians

Sooner or later those who wish to become school administrators bump into academics. *Academics* train prospective school administrators, or *abecedarians* (a student learning the rudiments of the alphabet), on how to run schools.

While universities have been around since 859 A.D. (The University of Kaurueein in Fez, Morocco[1]), the professoriate in educational administration is a little over eighty-five years old.[2] It is obvious that schools have been around for longer than professors of educational administration.

One of the ironies of school administration is that many of those training school administrators have never been school administrators. The situation would be like trying to train pilots to fly airplanes without ever having really flown one.

Professors are sensitive about this problem. Many feel that it isn't necessary to have been a superintendent to train them well. For example, Roald Campbell noted, "In seeking young men, we will need to cherish ideas more than experience. . . . For at least some of our professors, relationships with the university community are more important than those with the school community."[3]

Still others would hold the proposition that the "training" of school administrators is "beneath them." That is the role for vocational schools and they are more interested in developing theories than operating schools. Besides, professors are in search of "truth" in the nobler shades and hues than merely grubbing in the market place (except when they are in search of grants). Beware of a person who has spent his or her life in search of *truth* because he or she will be intolerant of the rest of us who settled for money and power. It's like a person on a Pritikin Diet watching a fat man eat ice cream dripping with Grand Marnier, a mixture of horror and envy.

One result of the distance between professors and practitioners is the plethora of research and articles in scholarly journals that have little or nothing to do with making schools more effective. That they

*131*

have nothing to do with schools in operational settings is *intentional*. First, few researchers are well acquainted with running schools firsthand. Notes Stanford Professor Elliot W. Eisner, "... the tack that has been taken in educational research by educational researchers has, in the main, distanced itself from practice."[4] If one doesn't know anything about running schools in reality, how can one practically improve them?

Secondly, research almost always *follows practice*. What is there to research if it didn't? One studies the real world and then tries to draw conclusions from the study that may relate to the development of a larger perspective and perhaps to improvement.

It is a quixotic malady in many schools of education that practitioners are held in very low regard, experience is devalued, and those without it cast in the mantle of experts who must study what the practitioners do in order for them to retain their expertise. Such scholars write paragraphs like the following:

> The relation of finite and infinite in man has the paradoxical property and boundless creative lures, outreachings for wider relations, and strivings for ideality, all of which transcendent tensions challenge the status quo of finite realizations, cause persons to negate transcendence in order to save themselves from the threatened dissolution of actual attainments.[5]

This passage was written in a book edited by the same critic of educational research who proclaimed that the text would be useful for "professional educators and lay people."[6] We know of few educators or lay persons who would even understand the paragraph let alone be able to use it.

Still other academics have studied what superintendents do, for example, and decided that superintendents *manage conflict* among other things. After interviews with twenty-five superintendents, a book is written describing the nature of the job. The book began after a discussion with an experienced superintendent during a teachers' strike in which the academic commented, "My professorial naivete concerning the situation must have startled him."[7]

The tension between academics and abecedarians is highlighted by the fact that the university culture denigrates experience and fosters the gap between what happens in the real world and what happens and is rewarded at the university. University culture demands publications and research as the benchmarks of a productive academic. We have no immediate quarrel with these benchmarks except that the people hired to conduct such studies in schools of education have often never worked in the settings they study nor handled, on a daily basis, the jobs they profess to know something about. The "objects" of study are akin to buffoons and rats in mazes and in the process of objectified study become one more variable to manipulate or control.

The downgrading of experience as a qualification for the professoriate is underscored by the fact that in many institutions of higher education, it is a secondary aspect in the hiring of a professor.

In 1964 Shaplin studied which four characteristics of potential professors of educational administration were given the most weight in the hiring process. They were:

- experience as a school administrator
- concrete evidence of research training
- study in depth in a social or behavorial science
- study in breadth in the social or behavior sciences

Shaplin discovered that the research training and breadth in the social or behavorial sciences were given more weight than experience. Of the schools of education that *devalued experience* were Stanford and the University of Chicago, two of the five schools responsible for training 44 percent of all recently appointed professors of educational administration.[8]

Twenty years later Eisner cautions about this emphasis on work in the social sciences as the major criterion of appointment:

> If the best work in education is indistinguishable from the work that is done in the social sciences, the best place to train educational researchers is not in schools of education but in the social science disciplines.[9]

Eisner also warns that the model of the past eighty years will probably result in about the same impact on schools in 2020 as in 1980, pretty near ineffectual.[10]

The de-emphasis of the practitioner continues to this day. To ascertain what value school administrative experience has in the eyes of those in the university we did an analysis of advertisements for professors in the trade publication, *The Chronicle of Higher Education,* during the time period March of 1983 through June of 1984. We examined thirty-one issues of *The Chronicle* covering some seventy-three advertisements from universities/colleges in twenty-eight states and the District of Columbia.

Our analysis appears in *Exhibit #1.* We broke the data into two main categories, those qualifications *required* and those merely *desired.*

## Exhibit #1

*Required and Desired Qualifications for Professors
of Educational Administration Advertised in*
The Chronicle of Higher Education, *March 1983–June 1984\**

N = 73

| QUALIFICATION STATED | | QUALIFICATION |
|---|---|---|
| *Required* | *Desired* | |
| 92% | 1% | 1. earned doctorate |
| 44% | 19% | 2. previous administrative experience in elementary/secondary education |
| 38% | 8% | 3. record of scholarly publications in the field |
| 26% | 12% | 4. record of research ability or background |
| 23% | 5% | 5. experience in higher education teaching |
| 19% | 5% | 6. experience as teacher in elementary/ secondary schools |
| 12% | 5% | 7. experience with computer/programs |
| 1% | 3% | 8. experience in higher education administration |
| 1% | 0 | 9. recognized as leader in educational administration |
| 1% | 0 | 10. experience or background with related educational agencies |

*Multiple answers were possible. "Professor" includes: assistant, associate, full professor.

Shaplin identified thirteen institutions that in his study in 1964 trained 68 percent of all professors of educational administration. They were Teachers College, Columbia, Chicago, Stanford, Wisconsin, Michigan State, Harvard, California-Berkley, Indiana, Iowa, Oklahoma, Pittsburgh, Ohio State, and Oregon.[11] Our analysis of *The Chronicle* for the time period March 1983 through June 1984 indicated that five of these institutions advertised for professors of educational administration. In no case was "previous public school" (elementary or secondary) administrative experience a "required" qualification. In one case it was stated as "desired." Under the area of required qualifications, after the doctorate, "record of scholarly publication in the field" and "record of research ability or background" were the most sought after experiences of potential professors.

The standard bearers in the field, Stanford, Harvard, the University of Chicago, and Columbia do not place a premium on actual administrative experience for their professors. Everyone else wants to be Stanford. The *prestige* goes to the researcher, not the practitioner!

So, the student of educational administration will soon discover that few of his or her professors have ever really done what they teach. Few have faced strikes, budget battles, board politics and backbiting, curriculum articulation problems between schools, right wing fanatics, student vandalism, faculty apathy, crisis management, or endless legal hassling in grievance and arbitration hearings. Few appear to know how to apply whatever research they may have completed.

And the prize for publications goes not to journals that practitioners read, but to one or two "refereed" journals dominated by academics who read prospective articles "blind." Such journals emphasize vast collations of research called "meta-research" or forays into theoretical topics. Rarely are such journals the places where radical new ideas that may impact practice are presented for the first time. Were that the case, these ideas would be subject to such an acid bath of scholarly criticism, they would die an early death by academic syringe in the editorial review process.

The reader is asked to cite what potent or really innovative new practice in school administration was first "discovered" in an academic refereed journal. We can think of none. But we haven't read them all either. As Eisner has so aptly stated, "If educational research is to inform educational practice, researchers will have to go back to schools for a fresh look at what is going on there."[12]

## THE PH.D. AND ED.D. OR INITIALS ARE EVERYTHING

One of the first decisions that will have to be made is whether to go for an Ed.D. or a Ph.D. The Ed.D. (Doctor of Education) is considered by some (usually those who have Ph.D.'s) to be *less rigorous* than a Doctor of Philosophy (Ph.D.). In theory the Ph.D. is a research degree and the Ed.D. a practitioner's degree. However, in practice, this distinction is often blurred. We know of many Ed.D.'s who can run rings around Ph.D.'s in research or in most anything else.

Research is a kind of *ritualized thinking*. It takes practice and the more schooled one is, the more steps one knows. It's sort of like learning how to dance. A beginner would learn how to do significance testing, measures of central tendency and variability such as the mean, median, and a standard deviation. The Ed.D. may end with learning the "t" test, parametric correlation, and the analysis of variance.

Precocious Ed.D.'s now get some non-parametric steps (which old-time Ed.D.'s used to get and now smart Ph.D.'s regularly get) such as the Mann-Whitney U-Test, Spearman Rank-Order correlation, and the Chi-Square test.

High-powered Ph.D.'s go on to do multivariate parametrics such as linear regression, canonical correlation, multivariate analysis of variance and multiple correlation and perhaps a little discriminant function analysis. A few Ed.D.'s may also get some of these steps as well.

If one were to obtain dancing instruction at Arthur Murray, it might take several years to learn the intricacies of the Latin American rhythms. It's the same in statistics. The Arthur Murray types who have been at it a long time are the Ph.D.'s. The beginners are the Ed.D.'s though everyone is a beginner at some point.

There was a time in the awarding of a Ph.D. that candidates had to select the largest computer and the most high-powered multivariate parametric measure available and get the computer to sing a high "C" until it laid a telephone book replete with hundreds of tables and data. A Ph.D. could write a series of telephone books.

An Ed.D. had to settle for a lot less "rigorous" statistics based on less sophisticated steps. Ed.D.'s would write case studies, archival studies, or ethnographies. Ph.D.'s were the scientists. Ed.D.'s were the peons. It wasn't important what they did anyway because the only research they would ever write would be their dissertation. So what the heck?

Then somebody decided, based on reviews of the literature, that such high-powered data didn't really indicate what was going on and that more "qualitative" data was necessary to really tease out what was actually going on in schools. In his controversial book *PO: Beyond Yes and No*, Edward deBono notes that:

> Since education is a closed and highly artificial world, it is never possible to check the validity of an idea to see how it relates to the real world. Instead the only criterion of validity is the logic by which the idea has been derived and with which it is defended. So logic is equated with truth, and this gives logic an unjustified arrogance which outlasts education.[13]

We are now in the midst of the return of the "softer" types of research. Not that we ever had a lot of problems, but those giving out the degrees did. We find the reception to the complexities of schooling refreshing and the emphasis on more open-ended methods of dealing with effective schools a lot more promising than burping a computer with input.

We advise prospective students to study carefully the actual requirements in their college catalogs and to note how much stat and other course work is required that separates an Ed.D. from a Ph.D. Despite the artificiality involved, our advice would be that if one believes he or she will eventually work at a college level or in industry, get a Ph.D.

## THE ALPHABET JUNGLE: READING THE LETTERHEAD

After getting your coveted degree from your university of choice, there is always the business of whether to put your new title on the stationary. We leave that question up to you. In the academy, most professors are always called "professor" no matter what their rank. Some journals make it a practice of never placing initials after the authors because it is assumed all authors already have their degrees.

We've found degrees necessary under a variety of circumstances. First, when making airline accommodations and restaurant reservations, a "doctor" is usually given some preference. In certain kinds of grant proposals, the initials will help. However, in most situations, even in the field, we recommend leaving the initials off the letterhead. If someone really wants to know if you are a "doctor" or "master," they can find out. Most folks will judge you on what you say and not on your degrees so it won't help you at all. When one is in a gunfight, it won't make any difference if your weapon was earned at Harvard—it's still how fast you can shoot that makes the difference. So let your competence be expressed in what you can do.

## PICKING THE RIGHT PLACE TO GET PLACED

One of the major benefits of picking the right college or university is that institution's record of placement. Some institutions have cut out this service as a result of financial stringencies. At least 50 percent of the value of your degree is the help the university and its professors will give to you to get a job after your work there. A Ph.D. without a placement service is like a man who knows how to have sex 153 different ways, but doesn't know any women.

So ask questions to find out what the university will do for you after you've paid your tuition and got the union card. Does their responsibility end? Is it all up to you? Strong universities with good programs have "outreach" into the extended professional community via networking. Private universities are perhaps more sensitive to this need than public ones since their lifeblood comes from successful placement. Get to know your professors. Who is involved in administrative screening and recruitment? Which professors are periodically called by prospective employers looking for administrative candidates? Whose advice weighs heavily in the field? These are the professors to know and to study with. Often doctoral candidates never ask the question until they are through with their program and end up perusing the classified section of the Sunday paper in search of work. Ask the placement question on the front end and do some serious questioning of your professors and how they are involved with field work.

## PROFESSORS AS PARTNERS

Some professors are live wires. They are involved in the issues of the day, sought after as speakers, involved in research, and are excellent teachers. These are the people to cultivate as partners and colleagues. They are not necessarily the "big names" on campus. "Big names" often decorate the course catalogs and bookstore with volumes of texts, but are never around to offer help to students in time of need or pick up the telephone to call someone on your behalf. They are on their way to Nairobi or Geneva for the latest symposia on this or that.

Good professors like students and cherish their time with them. They are never too busy and are approachable. They are at the university by choice, not by default, and are driven by inquiry and the embodiment of the human spirit. They are the ones who appreciate partnerships.

## LIFE IN COLLEGE CLASSROOMS

We believe in the words of Joseph Schwab, a mathematical geneticist and philosopher at the University of Chicago, when he wrote ". . . the professor of any profession is one well or best equipped (a) to conduct inquiries designed to better or to extend the scope of the profession's practice, and (b) to train able practitioners of the art."[14]

The sad fact is that too few professors are able to offer this to their students or to the practice of educational administration in the schools. So if your academic training has been dull and boring, if your professors are apparently not interested in your career in class, it's probably because he or she is too busy worrying about getting published in some issues of *Educational Esoterica* to worry about whether or not what they are teaching has any relevance to improving schools or your service in them. Promotions and raises in the academy are given for people who write in *Educational Esoterica,* a small but prestigious journal edited by selected Brahmins from prestigious universities, who decide which ideas are worthy and which ones are not. Most of the Brahmins have never been public school principals or superintendents, so they are not interested in what makes a difference to you or to field people. They are social scientists, not practitioners.

*Educational Esoterica* is not read by more than 3,000 people nationally. Most, if not all, are *other* Brahmins who have no linkage of any direct nature to public school classrooms or administrative offices. Your professor is writing for other professors, not for you. His or her time is spent developing acceptable ideas for other intellectuals. We've suffered through a few of these courses ourselves. We like the words of Mark Twain on the subject when he said, ''I never let my schooling interfere with my education.'' Hopefully this book will help with your education.

### CAVEATS, CODICILS, AND CONUNDRUMS ABOUT ACADEMICS AND ABECEDARIANS

- Beware of those who are only interested in the ''truth.'' They are not very tolerant of those of us who settled for power and money.
- Researchers have a hard time leading practice when they have to follow practice to engage in research.
- The university culture denigrates experience as a worthy base for recognition unless it can be made theoretical and testable.
- The most prestigious universities devalue field experience in the selection process of professors of educational administration. Everyone else tries to be like them.
- What potent or really innovative new practice in school administration was first ''discovered'' in an academic refereed journal?
- Research is a kind of ritualized thinking practiced by the schooled.
- Fifty percent of getting a job is picking a university that believes a job is important after you get their degree.
- Let your competence be told in what you can do and not where you got your degree.
- Don't let your schooling interfere with your education.

# Getting the Job Done Right

## CHAPTER 12

# The Job vs the Job Description

Superintendents, principals, supervisors, and teachers are never sure
under this system that it is safe to exercise responsibility for anything.
If they do so, the results may be unfortunate, so the surer way is
always to refer the matter to someone else. . . .

from Leonard P. Ayers
*Cleveland Education Survey*, 1916

*Passing the buck* has always been a problem with school administration. The report by Leonard Ayers of problems in the Cleveland
Public Schools in 1916 provides early details of what the consequences are for a school system: confusion, stagnation, poor morale,
and corruption.[1]

One solution is to carefully prescribe the duties of each person in
the organization and then see to it the responsibilities are completed.
Effective supervision rests on the premise that certain tasks grouped
into *jobs* are filled with people who know how to do them and on
making sure they get done.

Job descriptions as they are known today had their genesis in the
work of Frederick Taylor, a Harvard dropout who invented "scientific management" at the Midvale Steel Works from 1878 on.[2] Taylor
analyzed work. He did not simply accept it as it was done by the
people in the organization. In his historic work analysis of Bethlehem
Steel in the late 1890's he showed how, with his procedures on coal
shoveling, he could reduce the work force from 600 to 140 men,
reduce the costs involved, save $78,000 per year, and maintain the
same level of output.[3]

Later, Frank Gilbreth added the concept of work motion study in
the brick business. Using the motion picture camera he performed
micromotion studies of work which he analyzed using a process called
*chronocyclegraphy*. Via chronocyclegraphy Gilbreth was able to
raise productivity in the construction business from 120 bricks per
man per hour to 350 bricks per man per hour.[4] Gilbreth also invented
ways to code and classify work-subdivisions he believed were behind

*143*

all types of work. He called them "therbligs" which is the plural of Gilbreth spelled backwards.

Using "Therbligs" Gilbreth carefully constructed the proper way to mop floors. He meticulously derived his specifications from long hours of study and therblig analysis.

### For the Mop

- It should be made of good grade 4-ply, soft, roving, long-staple yarn.
- The length of the mop strands should be 38 to 42 inches taped in the middle with good cotton duck at least 5 inches wide.
- The mop is not to be sewed in the folded shape in order that both sides may be used to equalize wear.
- The average dry weight of the cotton should be 23½ to 24½ ounces for wet mopping and 31½ to 32½ ounces for dry mopping.
- The mop handle should be 60 inches long, 1¼ inches in diameter and have an aluminum knob at the end.

### For Mopping

- A "side to side" stroke is preferred over the "push or pull" stroke.
- The janitor should position himself in the middle of the stroke length with feet spread apart and at right angles to the direction of the stroke.
- The mop handle is grasped over the end with one hand down 15 inches from the other.
- The mop is placed flat on the floor and the arc should be slight.
- The mop should pass in front of the janitor and within three inches of his feet.
- At the end of the stroke the mop is slightly looped to reverse the direction (centrifugal force in describing the arc spreads the mop strands to increase the area covered in the stroke).
- As the boundary approaches, the janitor reverses his position 180 degrees at the end of the stroke and with proper timing there is no loss of time.
- The optimum length of stroke for a janitor of average height

is 12 feet, which with an effective width of 0.70 foot, will result in a coverage of 8.4 square feet per stroke.

Gilbreth also prescribed carefully how certain areas were to be mopped, whether lengthwise or crosswise strokes, the exact size of the water buckets to be used at the precise water temperature. In addition he finically noted that by belting shoes with a type of sandal, he could keep the janitor's feet dry, prevent slipping and increase output 5 percent. The bottom line was that the average janitor using proper therbligs could cover 2000 square feet compared to less than 1000 square feet before.[6]

The progenitor of the job description in schools never attained the precision in the factories we've described, to which we say "Amen." In fact we have not been able to find the idea of a "job description" in the literature of educational administration prior to 1952 with scattered references throughout the sixties.[7,8]

### WHAT MAKES UP A JOB?

As soon as you've landed your first administrative position you're going to want to know what is expected of you. You will be handed, or in some cases have to search out, what your duties will be. Most school systems have something called a *job description*, that is, a sort of general outline of what it is that comprises your job. It won't be designed using therbligs either. In some cases it may be a philosophical statement. In others it may be a simple kind of shopping list. *Whatever, it won't be very detailed.* Unless you work for a nit-picker, it won't matter either. *The job is whatever it takes to satisfy your immediate superior that you should be re-employed the following year.* That's it! No amount of therblig study will draw the precise boundaries for you. There will be no amount of detail that will satisfy an unsatisfied boss either. So your job is to find out what the boss really wants and construct your own job description with as much precision as necessary.

Doing this will take whatever documentation the district has and in whatever form it may exist. But don't stop there. Through your actions and questions and *interactions* with others (and most importantly your boss) you begin to define little by little the *exact* things that are required to be re-employed next year. We call this procedure *reciffo stniop* or (officer points). To be re-employed requires a minimum of 51 percent reciffo stniop level. The higher the RS level, obviously, the better. In fact we don't guarantee that a 51 percent will get you much either, beyond a bare passing grade.

## DATA, PEOPLE, AND THINGS

A job can be broken down into *three* distinct types of domains:

(1) people, pieties, and piffles,

(2) data duties,

(3) things, therbligs, and thistles.[9]

It should come as no surprise that the bulk of the building administrator's job is meeting with *people*. School administration is people administration. Principals meeting with teachers, assistant principals, students, clerks, the superintendent, counselors, other central office staff, aides, custodians, security personnel, and parents. People, people, people.[10] Over half of these contacts are initiated by the principal.[11] And the principal meets mostly in his or her office, but also in hallways, classrooms, lunchrooms, auditoriums, gyms, playgrounds, and the library.[12]

The school administrator comes to work only to be with people. People are his or her work. The administrator does three things that involve people:

(1) meet and talk with people,

(2) answer people over the telephone,

(3) answer people through the mail.

School administrators who don't understand that they don't come to work *to work, but to meet with people* are out of line *with their actual job.* No matter what the job description says, administrators exist to interact with people.

The administrator who sequesters himself or herself in his or her office and keeps people away is not doing his or her job. People don't get in the way of the job, *people are the job!* Anything other than talking with people directly, on the phone, or by mail should be done somewhere else other than schools. That is the only job that counts.

### CONTROL VS CONTROLS OVER THE JOB

Peter Drucker has maintained that there is a large difference between controls and control. "Controls is not the plural of control," notes Drucker.[13] The synonym for "controls" is data processing, i.e., information. It can come in a variety of forms: financial, attendance, scheduling, curriculum development, and time sheets. On the other hand, "control" means *direction*. It relates to the question of whether the school or the school district is a purposive institution that is going somewhere.

In the context of human interactions, the administration doesn't just "put out fires," "stroke people," "problem solve," or "mediate conflict" for the fun of it. Reports are not sent to whomever to fulfill bureaucratic obligations only. All of what the administrator does should be aimed at accomplishing a mission, reaching a goal, achieving some end. This gives the administrator's behavior a reason, a driving force.

Working with people means seeing them as both *means* and *ends.* People are simultaneously an end in themselves; they are their own best reason for being anything. However, in organizational life, *people make the organization.* The school or the school system is nothing more or less than the sum of its people and their collective willpower and energy.

The job of the school administrator is to wed that energy together into a force that accomplishes things for children. In this sense the school administrator should be modeling with adults what he or she expects adults to do with children. It should be a play within a play.

## RETROFITTING THE JOB DESCRIPTION TO THE JOB

In 1926 Professor William Cook wrote a text on school administration in which he described the principal's two responsibilities as involving both the mechanical and the artistic. Wrote Cook:

> Sadly enough, many a thorough office worker is a failure as principal, because he lacks the soul to draw and motivate people. Actual weight of personality counts enormously.[14]

Cook goes on to describe two large high schools. One principal runs the place like a business. The halls are always quiet. Students are orderly. "Here the machinist was in charge," says Cook. Then Cook contrasted this school with another where the halls were not so orderly. There was more friction in the classrooms. Students were more carefree and less restricted. The first principal got respect. The second got affection. "Statements of students betrayed the unmistakable distinction," avers Cook ". . . such was the work of an artist, a man who gripped people in the school and out in the world."[15]

We have seen such schools as Cook described. Many like them existed before our times. What Cook observed was some fifty years ahead of the "school effectiveness" research which has validated the central and pivotal role of the principal as the person who instills in a building "control," i.e., a sense of purpose and *direction.*

So "retrofit" your job description to the idea of "control." If the principal or superintendent doesn't know where a school or the district is going, nobody else does. And it is up to the administration to energize people to collectively move in a unified direction.

At the end of most every job description there is what is known as a "zipper clause." It usually says, "and all other duties as assigned." Strike this line from your job description and write PEOPLE over it. Move it to the front of your job description so that it reminds you of what you are about. Then, the second responsibility is to define "with people" the mission for the school or the school district. All other duties come after. They are the *therbligs* that don't really matter but may have to be done (after people).

People can never be *therbligs*. They aren't duties, things, or thistles. They are the reason administration is required. They are why *we need you.* If you are not comfortable with that fact, you are in the wrong position. Retrofitting the job description should *release* the people *in you.* It should mean making schools fit places for people *beginning with you.*

Just as *therblig* was the beginning of the micro-routinization of work, we should remember that it was only Gilbreth spelled backwards. Gilbreth was a person. When you take your job description and move people forward, you are ridding it of the therbligs and replacing it with people. Retrofitting is always moving forward— WITH PEOPLE!

Perhaps the best example of our philosophy of organization is provided by the Japanese billionaire Akio Morita, founder of SONY. It was SONY that produced the first magnetic tape recorder in Japan, the first Japanese transistor, the world's first pocket-sized transistor radio, the world's first transistorized TV set, the world's smallest TV set, the first home video recorder, and many more shattering technical breakthroughs.[16]

Yet Akio Morita does exactly the opposite in searching for such breakthroughs. Instead of beginning with work analysis, he begins with people. His approach to building SONY has been to find talent and then put it to work. He matches the work to the people. He practices retrofitting! Who else would have hired an opera singer with no business training or experience to be president?

Says one of Morita's colleagues in the United States:

> . . . Morita is one of the few top men who really moves through his company vertically, diagonally, and every way, seeking out the ideas and talents of everyone . . . he talks to warehousemen and bench technicians very naturally, without having to make any special effort to do so.[17]

Retrofitting reworks work by putting people first and the work second. In this way people are always means and ends together. We believe schools should model that idea more than any other human organization.

**CAVEATS, CODICILS, AND CONUNDRUMS ABOUT
THE JOB VS THE JOB DESCRIPTION**

- The job is whatever it takes to satisfy your immediate superior that you should be re-employed the following year.
- Any job can be broken into three parts: people, data, and things.
- The school administrator comes to work only to be with people.
- People don't get in the way of the work to be done in schools; people are the work!
- The administrator who spends time on control is never "in control" of anything.
- Your "zipper clause" should be "up with people."
- Retrofitting the job description should release the people in you to meet the people in your school or system.

CHAPTER 13

# Ploys to Avoid

## GIVERS, TAKERS, AND FLIMFLAM ARTISTS

Human relationships are made up of "givers" and "takers." A "giver" is a person who gets satisfaction from giving to others, thereby making them feel good about themselves. In turn, the giver feels good about himself or herself. A "taker" is a person who must receive in order to feel good about himself or herself. For a "taker" the good life is in the "getting" *not* in the "giving." Cris Evatt and Bruce Feld explore givers and takers in relationships in their excellent book.[1]

Whether the school administrator is a "giver" or a "taker" in his or her own personal life, those with whom he works who are less powerful will perceive him or her as a potential giver: of better teaching programs, better facilities, free periods, smaller classes, and a whole host of "freebies" and "fringes." On any given day over 90 percent of the people checking into the administrator's office *want something.*

The school administrator's office is the psychic blood-bank of the school. Parents, teachers, kids, other administrators, board members, secretaries, and custodians come in for daily transfusions in order to attend to their needs, to heal their bodies and minds, and to get their problems solved. And there's nothing *wrong* with that. It's a big part of the job.

But nevertheless, by the end of the school year, many administrators feel and look as though they have been hooked up to intravenous tubes connected to each of their arms, the back of both knees, and to their jugular veins for the purpose of donating their blood to others. How is it that some others look and feel as though they have just spent a year at the spa and are enhanced and energized?

Much of our disappointment, hurt, frustration, and resentment when dealing with people is a result of our giving to takers because

*151*

we were taught at a young age that, "It is better to give than to receive." This idea is fine as far as it goes, but it doesn't go far enough. Advice that would be more conducive to a feeling of satisfaction and fulfillment is: it is better to give to a giver and receive satisfaction than to give to a taker and get nothing in return because:

> If you give to Givers, it all comes back to you; but if you give to takers; you will get back about 10 percent.[2]

We believe that the administrators who look and feel as though they've been "bled dry" by the end of the year are those who have consistently given to takers all year. Giving to a taker is depleting. It's like throwing all your money into the Grand Canyon a dollar bill at a time. There's no payoff. There's only energy loss. *And no matter how much you give them, it's never enough.*

Who are the takers? How can you spot them? All of us are givers and takers to some degree at some time or another. The strongest givers also take once in a while and vice versa. By "taker" here we mean a person who constantly takes, asks, wants, and gives little (10 percent) or nothing in return.

So the most obvious tip-off in detecting a taker is the number of times the person is in the "request mode." The requests often come in the form of special privileges such as being excused from meetings or other obligations which the rest of the staff must fulfill.

Another clue to look for in order to detect bonafide takers is a distinct lack of words of appreciation or gratitude in their vocabularies. Hardcore takers rarely, if ever, say, "thank you," "I appreciate what you've done," etc. Almost never will you receive a token gift or card or note or kind word from a taker. The reason is simple. Takers take what they are given for granted. What is given them is coming to them. They don't even think about it as taking. The only way to give to such a person without feeling "ripped off" is with the knowledge that you will get no gratitude in return and that *this is not personal.*

The takers on your staff are basically selfish when it comes to parting with anything that they consider to be theirs. Therefore, their attitude toward "their" time will be another clue to whom you are dealing with. Often, takers will not want to give too much of their time away by coming in early or staying too long after they are allowed to go. Faculty meetings (while not a heavy favorite in many schools) are a special imposition on takers since many such meetings occur on "their" time (no matter what the contract says). Takers typically don't volunteer to do anything for nothing (at least not usually) since that is a giving gesture. Unless the stipend is cost-effective, as a rule, takers don't usually become class advisors, advisors to extra-curricular activities, or chaperone dances, trips, etc. In general, takers, no matter how much you have given them, do not give more of themselves than is absolutely necessary—*and that has nothing whatsoever to do with the administrators on a personal level.*

Givers, on the other hand, have no problem demonstrating affection, gratitude, appreciation, etc. They tell you by saying, "thank you," "I really appreciate that," etc. Sometimes they'll write their thanks in notes, cards, etc. Some even go so far as to give token gifts of genuine appreciation for kindness already shown (as opposed to bribes for favors someone wants). Often, the gift, note, or "thank you" even seems unwarranted or inappropriate. Often, you'll feel that you were just doing your job, what you had done for the giver you'd do for anyone, and you'll wonder why you elicited such feelings of gratitude.

Another dead giveaway of a giver is genuine personal concern which is difficult to fake. Givers generally give a damn about people, about you. They will notice if you look tired, sick, troubled, sad. And they'll ask you about it. And they'll mean it. And there'll be times when their concern about you as a person, as a human being, will touch you deeply.

Takers don't really care about anybody but themselves. They're too into themselves to be into anyone else—much less an administrator. They take what they can get from "administration" because, after all, administrators are overpaid, do nothing worthwhile anyway, and in the final analysis, "administrators may come and administrators may go, but teachers last forever."

*Faculty Givers, Takers, and Flimflam Artists*

Jane and Barbara provide an uncanny illustrative distinction between giver and taker types on a faculty. Both started their first teaching jobs in the Mathematics Department of the same high school at the age of twenty-three, having just completed their M.A. degrees. Neither of the girls knew one another when they began their jobs, but became close friends—even roommates within a year.

While both girls were pretty, Jane was cute in a vulnerable sort of way. She was a small-town girl (from Arkansas) in the big city (Chicago) on her own for the first time. The first of her family to go to college and become a professional, she was fresh and new and exciting, and Frank Marino, the principal liked her instantly. Her interview was a formality. He couldn't wait to get this eager young ball of fire on his staff. She'd be great for kids and perhaps her enthusiasm would be contagious for staff as well.

Frank's only concern was her naivete. Being from a small town in Arkansas would be a handicap in the "Windy City," where the sharks were sure to swarm. He was afraid that someone would try to take advantage of her, and, of course, he immediately assumed the role of her father–protector.

When her parents came to visit her shortly after the school year began, he met them and assured them personally that he would watch out for her. And that he did. When Judd Sloane, a married man with two children from one of the other schools seemed to be getting too chummy with her, Frank called her into his office for a long talk to let her know that Sloane had a reputation for hidden agendas.

But poor Jane didn't seem to know how to discourage Sloane, or so Marino thought. Even some of the teachers in Jane's department remarked that Jane was hanging around with the wrong crowd (Sloane's crowd).

Frank Marino wasn't going to let Judd get away with this one. This was his protégée. Before long, Sloane and Marino locked horns, while Jane claimed that she didn't want to "get in the middle." By the end of the year, Frank Marino wasn't sure who he was anymore. One of the genuine givers on his staff had walked into his office one day, closed the door, and said, "Look Frank, this is hard for me to say because I know that you are a family man and I know the rumor isn't true, but I think you ought to know that there's a rumor going around that you and Jane are an item."

Marino was dumbfounded by what he had heard but not nearly as dumbfounded as he was when he asked Jane if she had heard these rumors. To his surprise, she told him that she had known about the rumors for at least three weeks. Her only concern seemed to be who had told Frank about them! When Frank asked her how she addressed the rumors when asked, she replied, "Oh, I just told them they didn't know all the facts."

Five years have gone by since that memorable first year when she joined the staff. Frank Marino has grown up and learned a lot in the process. He sees Jane in a new light now. She's no hick, she's just slick. A genuine flimflam artist. Poor Judd Sloane was guilty of nothing more than being flattered and coquetted to death. The following year it was Tim Flannigan's turn, the swimming and tennis coach (also married), who got Jane's attention. Her real motive wasn't romance there either; it was free swimming and tennis lessons and an escort to an occasional sporting event plus his attention. In spite of this, she'd always make it *seem* to others—and especially to Frank—through a variety of ways that there was more going on.

And so it went. Jane played the flimflam game with Frank as long as it lasted, but her "MO" became clear after a while. She'd always come by Frank's office for favors, advice, etc. She wanted special treatment—and she got it (at least for a while), as Frank would listen to the soap opera of her life.

When she asked for a letter of reference "because her college wanted it" for her placement file, Frank wrote a two-page typed letter that was the most eloquent he had ever written in his career. She never said "thank you" or acknowledged it in any way.

But Frank's final realization arrived when Jane came into his office in tears halfway through her second year (she cried a lot in Frank's office). She was upset because she had heard that Frank was annoyed that she would not be able to chaperone the senior prom (it was tradition that all class advisors go to the prom and Jane had been advisor to the senior class). She said that her family was coming to visit her all the way from Arkansas, and she had planned on spending the evening with them.

Frank felt like a heel (as he usually did after one of her crying spells). He told her the truth. He had not been himself lately. He had undergone surgery recently to have a cancerous tumor removed and in fact was going to hear the lab report about the operation on the following day. Relieved, Jane thanked him and left.

She never even asked Frank about the results of the lab report. Not the next day. Not ever. As Frank looks back over the years with Jane, he realizes that, far from being naive, she has been quite a flim-flam artist. She loves being the center of attention and in the lime-light, even if the attention takes the form of gossip. She would take from anyone whatever she could get. Over the years from Frank, it has been recommendations, exemptions from faculty meetings, personal attention to problem students, permission to leave school early before the vacation breaks to beat the airport traffic (when flying back home), etc. But she had an uncanny knack of getting people in general to do things for her. She seemed to have an entourage of givers eager to help her move, paint her apartment, run errands, make repairs, and do in general what knights in shining armor do.

Throughout the years, Frank Marino could count on the fingers of his left hand the number of times he had ever heard her say "thank you" for his many kindnesses.

Barbara, also twenty-three when she began her first teaching job in the Math Department at Frank's school, seemed street wise, and even a bit hardened at first. She was a "tough cookie." Whether it was because of her life experiences, upbringing, or whatever, Frank knew he wouldn't have to worry about Barbara; she could take care of herself.

Being new to the school and to the profession, single, and the same age and in the same department, it was no wonder that the two girls became good friends. Soon they were referred to as "the Bobsie twins" by the rest of the staff. Eventually they even became roommates.

But the Bobsie twins were really opposites. Barbara hardly ever asked Frank or anyone else for anything, much less came to his office frequently. But the job she did with kids was fantastic. She turned around the most difficult class in the school within two months. By the end of the first semester Frank had written her a commendation for her personnel files. Her response was warm and genuine. She told Frank that she had been so moved by the commendation, she showed it to her father.

On one occasion she told Frank that she was going to be absent from school on the following day because her mother was to undergo a serious operation. When she returned to school, Frank immediately asked her about her mother. He had tried to telephone her the previous evening but was unable to do so because he was given the wrong telephone number. The following day, Barbara walked into Frank's office, laid a small gift-wrapped box down on his desk, and was about to walk out.

"What's this for?" asked Frank.

"It's for being such a great boss," she said. "I just can't believe how much you really care about people."

The gift was a pen and pencil set. Frank couldn't understand why Barbara felt compelled to give him a gift for just trying to call her to find out about her mother. If Jane had gotten him the pen and pencil set—if she had gotten him a hundred pen and pencil sets, he would have understood and felt *worthy* of them.

More recently, after word of Frank's cancer surgery had gotten around, Frank told a small group of people at a meeting (both Barbara and Jane being present) that he would miss the first couple of weeks of the new school year in September for reasons he didn't want to discuss (the meeting took place in June). Shortly after the meeting, Barbara walked into Frank's office. He noticed her lips begin to quiver and her eyes beginning to get teary.

"Hey, listen," she said, "You're not getting sick on us, are you?"

Frank gave her one of his famous Marino bear hugs. "No, kid," he said, "I've got a court case coming up the first week in September that can't be put off any longer. Don't worry about me, only the good die young."

Both Jane and Barbara are good teachers. They are good and decent *people* as well. Jane was self-absorbed, immature, and heavily into games. This didn't make her a bad person, but she was a taker, a "textbook example," that could have easily come right out of Evatt's and Feld's book.

Frank was a natural giver. But Frank learned over the years, "If you give to givers, it all comes back to you, but if you give to takers, you will get back about 10 percent"[3] *and it's not personal.*

And flimflam artists aren't all takers either. Some are givers too—to *their* departments, their programs, their schools, etc. Some are the smooth slippery, slick, and saccharine sages of the District who will sweet talk you to death in order to get what they want for their programs. Many are the "Music Man" types, showmen, actors, actresses, theatrical-types. They usually come fully equipped with melodious (often deep) professional announcer-type voices and the persuasive ability to talk a buzzard off a manure wagon.

Your job will be to look past their acts, beneath their flimflam to discover exactly what it is they are giving or taking to or from whom.

The bitchers and the complainers, the teachers who complain "nothing has changed" (in spite of a dozen significant improvements in the school within any given year), get Frank's polite attention. The teachers who cannot handle discipline in their own classrooms but who became leaders of "Discipline Committees," which then berate the "administration" for poor student discipline get Frank's polite attention. But he gives them nothing of his heart and soul the way he used to.

His heart and soul he saves for the Barbaras on his staff and in his life (his wife, kids, and special friends). He listens to all. He ignores the flimflam artists. He humors the takers, attempting to give to them only when necessary and never trying to satisfy them or attempting to make them happy. And he gives freely and openly to the givers. And at the end of the school year, he isn't as tired as he used to be.

## MEMO WARS AND TURF BATTLES

*The Written Word*

The written word
Should be clean as bone,
Clear as light,
Firm as stone.
Two words are not
As good as one.

Anonymous

There are some administrators whose motto is, "Never put anything in writing." Our hunch is that this statement is more of a rationalization for those who can't write well than it is a statement of wisdom. Those who know how to use the written word skillfully also know why "the pen is mightier than the sword."

Certainly, the memo is every bit as much the administrator's tool as are the nail and hammer the cobbler's. And while "talk is cheap," it is the written word that "nails it down." In fact, talk doesn't become official until it's in writing.

Perhaps that's why written contracts are so much more effective in modifying the behavior of acting-out youngsters than is the spoken word. Once kids "negotiate" a written "contract," which is then signed by the parties involved, they tend to live up to the written agreement, even though they have ignored verbal agreements that made the same promises dozens of times in the past.

Although *mightier* than the sword, the written word, like the sword, is "double-edged." While spoken words are eventually forgotten, the written word is immortal, often haunting its author many years after it is written. Therefore, we've got to be careful about what we put in writing.

So, if we can agree that war in general is dumb, then it should be easy to see that a memo war is even dumber. An actual war ends when one side surrenders, but a memo war just begins (to fester) with someone's surrender because the words are still there. And you can't usually win a memo war because of what you're up against.

Let's face it, real people who are reasonably well adjusted with a modicum of integrity tend to communicate face to face. Those who can't because they have problems with being able to look people in the eye when talking to them tend to hide behind paper and rhetoric. And because they're so skillful in the paper world, they're hell-bent on having the last word no matter what. So that's what you're up against for openers. But if memo warmongers retreat from the real world where they feel handicapped to a paper world where they feel safe and strong, why fight your battles on their turf?

The written memo used as a missile or bomb explodes upon impact and, therefore, loses its potency immediately. But used carefully as a stratagem, the memo is much more potent.

For example, what better way is there to nail a lunatic than by hoisting him by his own petard? Instead of being afraid to put anything in writing to a memo warmonger, on the contrary, a carefully worded stratagem will press his "Shakespeare button" and he'll retaliate in all his lunatic splendor, thereby handing you the rich documentation necessary to prove his insubordination, craziness, or incompetence, which you couldn't get on your own in the past.

An innocently worded constructive list of specific criteria and objectives written as part of a year-end evaluation to put the evaluatee on notice that he will be evaluated during the next school year based upon his successful attainment of these objectives can (and has) produced a Niagara of words in response that can all but hang the "linguamaniac." And, of course, it's all signed and part of the official record.

Just a few more well-placed similar provocations is all you need. Then gather them all together into a coherent package and share it with the superintendent (or the school board if you are the superintendent) IN WRITING, of course, and let him or her do the rest. No one can hang a fool better than a fool can hang himself—so don't try. Let the fool do it.

Memos are also vital in chess games with adversaries who are trying either to unseat you or who are, for reasons of their own, trying to "stick it to you." For example, if you feel that you are being "set up" to bear the blame for something not in your control, write a memo to your superior(s) informing them of your concern with whatever the problem is (demonstrating that you are a responsible administrator who is bringing the matter to their attention). End the memo stating that you will await further instructions, advice, etc. from your superior(s).

Whether your memo is answered or ignored, you will have an "I told you so" weapon in your hands should the situation explode later and should anyone try to make you the villain. As a matter of fact, not only do you have a documented "I told you so" but even more powerful, you have an official "I asked you for help and I didn't get it" zinger ready and waiting as a deterrent or a defense against an unjust evaluation charging you with the responsibility.

And, of course, a memo can be used as therapy. Blasting the hell out of the "bad guys" on paper can relieve an administrator of a great deal of anxiety, frustration, anger, etc. Transferring the venom onto paper and then locking it in your upper right-hand desk drawer overnight will allow you to leave that part of the job where it belongs—in your desk, as opposed to being home with you. Hopefully, things will seem a bit better after a night's sleep and the memo can be destroyed, having served its purpose. Now with the anger gone, you'll be ready to write a *stratagem* and play some "hardball."

Turf battles are dangerous because winning a piece of turf can cost you a war. Before getting involved in a turf battle you've got to ask yourself if the "turf" is worth the battle.

If someone is fighting you for the right to do some of your work, but your power remains intact, why fight? Let the dumb bastard do the work.

But even if the very source of your power is at stake, you must know who you are dealing with and what is at stake *over the long run* before getting into a battle that may very well cost you your job, albeit in a few years!

### FORCING DEMOCRACY ON DOPES

You would think that most teachers would give their dustless chalk for the chance to work with administrators who include them in true participatory democracy. Not true. Participatory democracy requires participation. It's so much easier for some teachers to let administrators make all the decisions and do all the work and then to bitch about the outcome and complain that they weren't consulted in the decision. Once they become part of the process, many of them begin to feel as though they are doing the administrator's work. Not only that, but being a part of the problem-solving process gives people a chance to experience for themselves how difficult it is to solve problems and to be fair. Since, as the saying goes, "Those who can, do, and those who can't, criticize," participatory democracy takes the wind out of the sails of the critics and the windbags—which is one of the reasons why administrators should use this method of problem solving whenever possible.

But criticism and opposition are occupational hazards an administrator can expect to encounter from "the troops" when attempting to give them a taste of true participatory democracy. Often, the critics will focus on the administrator being weak and indecisive—unable to make a decision without referring the problem to a committee (and, indeed, administrators who need committees for everything, to avoid making decisions, deserve this criticism).

Of course, in Japan, these "committees" are called "quality circles." But in many American schools, problem-solving committees are considered as smokescreens invented by administrators to hide their ineptitude. Americans, in general, have had little time to experiment with true democracy, and to many American educators, participatory democracy is still in the "cognitive concept" stage. Like the fermentation of fine wine, it can't be rushed.

*A Special Place for Special Teachers*

Grace Butler had just assumed the principalship of Robert Browing

Junior High School as her first administrative post. After being an excellent classroom teacher for ten years, she was determined that she was going to be the best principal who ever lived! As a teacher, she had watched administrators carefully for over a decade, and she felt that she knew just how they managed to irritate their staffs. But Grace was going to be different. She was going to be a new breed of administrator, and she was going to change things. . . .

Within her first year on the new job, she noticed that the Special Education Department was slowly emerging as a sizeable department (and getting larger almost every year). Yet, unlike the other departments of comparable size in the school, Special Education had no department office. Ms. Butler called the chief custodian to her office, and the two of them explored several possibilities, each of which impacted upon other people and/or on their turf since there were no empty rooms in the building.

Rather than make a unilateral and arbitrary decision which would surely alienate someone, Grace decided to go about the decision-making process democratically. First, she asked the Special Education teachers if they felt that they really needed a department office in the first place. The answer was a unanimous "yes."

She then appointed a committee comprised of each person who potentially could be impacted upon by the creation of the office, including several members of the Special Education Department. Once the committee was in place, Grace called for a meeting to agree upon the criteria or considerations to keep in mind when selecting the room to convert into the new Special Education office. After first writing their objective on the board as "the Problem," Grace and the group brainstormed and came up with four major considerations for committee members to keep in mind while they surveyed the building for possibilities. Grace then told the committee members to carefully consider various possibilities in light of the four considerations and to submit their ideas to her within thirty days, at which time they would reconvene to discuss each of the ideas submitted.

In thirty days, the committee met and Grace handed each member a sheet of paper listing the problem, the considerations, and the five suggestions submitted to her by committee members, along with a suggestion for a possible combination of the five ideas or perhaps even a new idea not already listed (see pages 162–163 for the complete document).

The committee explored each suggested site for the new office. One site was not suitable because the area was too noisy, another was not large enough, another was too large, another didn't have electrical outlets, and yet another had security problems. Finally, Ms. Smith, one of the two co-advisors of the National Junior Honor Society came up with an idea which wasn't even one of the five already discussed. Why not move the Honor Society office from Room 236 into one of the small rooms in the auditorium which was being used by the Music Department for storage? The Music Department already had access to three other places in the school and surely they could use one of them to store the robes which were in the room that could be used as a small office by the Honor Society.

Because no one from the Music Department was a member of this committee, Grace insisted that she first consult with them before she gave her blessing to this idea—which everyone seemed to endorse. Grace called for a meeting with the Music Department to explain the situation to them. They were most understanding and cooperative.

Within one week, the move was made. The custodians painted the floor and the walls of the new Special Education office. Desks and chairs were moved in, and even a telephone was installed! The Industrial Arts teacher made a beautiful sign for the outer door of the office which read, Special Education Department.

Grace asked each of the Special Education teachers to meet her in front of their new office when it was ready, immediately after school. When all were assembled, she handed each of them a shiny new key for their new office.

The Special Education teachers were obviously beaming, but Grace was even more excited than they were. She had succeeded in demonstrating that not all administrators were insensitive, dictatorial, and arbitrary like so many she had met over the years when she was a classroom teacher. And even more importantly, she had provided her entire faculty and staff with a role model and established participatory democracy as the official method of operation for her school.

---

## ROBERT BROWING JUNIOR HIGH SCHOOL

*PROBLEM:*  The Special Education Department, a growing department, has no department office for telephone calls, storage, etc.

*CONSIDERATIONS:*  1. Which solution would be easiest to undo if the configuration of the school district changes in a year or two and we would become overcrowded?

2. Should Special Education be confined to a specific location in the building or would this result in a "ghetto" or "segregated" area?

3. Which solution provides the maximum benefit to the greatest number of teachers and the least imposition?
4. Which solution is the best for the kids?

Many alternatives were considered over a period of months. The following alternatives seem to merit serious consideration.

*SOLUTION:*   1. Use Room 249 (present A.V. Room and Mr. Beach's office) as the new Special Education office. Make Room 216 the A.V. storage room (Frank's office).

2. Use Room 216 (used only for VCR now) as the new Special Education office and find another place for the VCR use.

3. Make Room 236 (currently used by Honor Society) new Special Education office and let the Honor Society use Room 216 (present VCR Room). The VCR remains in Room 216.

4. Use Room 216 as the Special Education Resource Room and use the present Resource Room (Room 136) for the VCR and for the Honor Society. Use Room 236 as the Special Education office.

5. Use Room 216 (VCR) as the Resource Room and use present Resource Room (136) as the conference room. Honor Society uses present conference room and Room 236 becomes the new Special Education office. Could VCR remain—Room 216?

6. Any other ideas? Combination of above or new ideas?

---

The only minor flaw was that the office needed one more desk, but there weren't any more available in the school except for the oak beauty which had been put into the new Honor Society office at Grace's request as a gesture expressive of her appreciation for their cooperation. A table in the Special Education office would have to make do for a while.

Approximately three months later, at the monthly meeting with the representatives of the teacher union's Building Committee (a group of teacher representatives who meet with the principal each month to discuss mutual concerns), the discussion turned to a problem concerning cafeteria management. Several solutions were explored when the other co-advisor of the National Junior Honor Society (the one who hadn't been on the committee to select a site for the new Special Education office along with his co-advisor, although he had been invited) shouted, "Are you going to make the decision unilaterally the way you kicked us (the Honor Society) out of our old office, or are you going to let the faculty have some input?"

Grace looked at the red-faced angry man and smiled. "Obviously, Mr. Kramer, you do not yet know the difference between a unilateral decision and a democratic one," she said calmly, "but you shall very soon."

After the meeting was over, Grace picked up the telephone and called her chief custodian. "Charlie," she commanded, "please remove the oak desk from the Honor Society office, put it in the new Special Education office, and take that table out of there and put it into the Honor Society office."

"What!?" was the chief custodian's incredulous reply. "Ms. Butler, what should I tell Mr. Kramer when he starts to yell and scream at me?"

"Simple, Charlie," she replied. "Just tell him that Ms. Butler has finally made a unilateral decision."

**YOUR TITLE AND YOU, WHEN TO TAKE IT SERIOUSLY**

The ancient Greeks knew well that "Power corrupts, and absolute power corrupts absolutely." Only, they weren't so wordy about it. One Greek word captures the essence of this idea and the ultimate ploy to avoid: HUBRIS—excessive pride often resulting in insolence or wanton violence.

It's hard not to think you're "hot stuff" in your own office with your name on the door—especially if there's a "Dr." in front of it and a title right after it. It's hard not to think you're "hot stuff" when people treat you differently—with respect (and some, even with awe).

But when you begin to believe that the respect, the awe, the invitations to social engagements, the flattery, the Christmas or Hanukkah cards, even the smiles, waves, and handshakes are SOLELY directed at you as a human being, you are on your way to becoming a Greek tragic hero.

The "beloved principal" in Chapter 14 learned the meaning of the above statement the hard way. It seemed as though everyone had been in his corner when he was being unjustly fired from his previous position. Yet, "after the speeches, the rousing parties, the demonstrations, the appeals, the press pandering, and hoopla," that letter from Albert Kraze, which was later framed and hung in his new office, was "the only tangible artifact that the beloved principal had received from anyone since leaving the school."

But you won't have to get fired to experience how the same people who previously treated you as Dr. William Rogers, Superintendent of Schools, will treat you as "Bill Rogers, Former Superintendent of Schools, and now just Person." Get a new job, and you'll find out. A superintendent of one of the largest public school systems in the country, whom we know well, puts it this way, "When you're out, you're out."

He claims that it doesn't matter if you leave a power post because you were fired or whether you leave to go elsewhere, the pain in the leaving is seeing how you are experienced differently by your "friends" and "admirers" while you're still in your position as a "lame duck." Even worse, he claims, is going back a year or so later to attend a retirement dinner or other such social function. You will see and feel how your former colleagues relate to you as a person, devoid of title. Perhaps Wolfe had this in mind when he wrote, "You can't go home again."

Of course, many of them will seem unchanged. But ask any administrator who has left a power post and most likely they'll tell you how they suddenly were ignored completely by some of the most avid backslappers in the district, how many former colleagues who were thought of as warm, personal friends had greeted them with formal politeness or with coldness or not at all.

According to our superintendent friend, a favorite past-time of his, while remaining in office as a lame duck before assuming a new post, is watching his former lieutenants jump ship ("kiss-up" to the new boss, or, even better, "kiss-up" to everyone because they aren't sure who the new boss will be).

Perhaps, going through this experience is the only way for anyone to understand—to really understand—what we're talking about here. And perhaps going through this experience makes one less prone to hubris. Certainly, Richard Nixon may have thought twice before condoning the Watergate break-in only to confuse national security with his own. Somewhere along the way he lost sight of where his personage left off and where his high office began. Luckily for our country, the Senate didn't, and a Federal court judge didn't, and two reporters didn't. The integrity of the Office of the President of the United States and of this Republic was preserved by a handful of people who could tell the difference between a man and his title.

We don't mean to imply that when you are in a position of power, all people will treat you like a god. They'll treat you in a manner consistent with how they feel about what your title represents to them. Many principals at all levels—elementary school through high school and all those in between—are treated by some members of their staffs as they were treated by their principals or the way they felt about their principals when they went to school—and many of these people aren't even aware of it. If your title represents "father," "mother," "authority," "priest," "king," "queen," "captain," or "janitor," to a person, that's the way he/she will relate to you.

Therefore, taking personally how your colleagues relate to you is usually a mistake because most of them, most of the time aren't relating to you as a *person*. And you'll never really know if and when any of them are, until after you slip out of your title and your position—and by then, it's usually too late to matter.

That's why it's a waste of emotional energy to get angry or hurt over takers. They took from your predecessor, and they'll take from your successor, and they'll take from a long list of others as well. Jane was and is a nice person and a good teacher. The fact that she was able to hook Frank Marino into a big daddy ego trip was really his problem, stemming from his failure to realize that she was relating to his title and not to him.

Even Harry Baylor, veteran high school principal, lost sight of this distinction for an instant. After "laying it on the line" with the Assistant Superintendent for Personnel on behalf of Rose Ann, the new English teacher, he had to fight a similar battle with the central office staff a year later. Harry had fought with the Assistant Superintendent for Personnel to hire her over another candidate in the first place, and then he had to fight to keep her from being excessed after her first year. He felt that she was that good as a teacher! Soon after his second near-mortal battle on her behalf was over, he had heard rumors that she was pregnant.

"Nah," he thought. "If Rose were pregnant, she'd tell me." The summer then came and went and Harry forgot about the rumor. In September, his chief custodian asked him on the way to the first faculty meeting of the new school year, "So, do you think it'll be a boy or a girl?"

When Harry looked puzzled, the custodian said, "Come on, don't you even know that Rose Ann is pregnant? Everyone else does." Indeed, Rose Ann walked into the meeting five months pregnant.

When she went on maternity leave the following semester, the letter requesting the leave went to the Assistant Superintendent—as it should. And when she decided she was coming back the following September, she once again sent the formal notification to the Assistant Superintendent—as was proper. Harry never even received copies.

Until May, Harry had heard rumors that Rose Ann wasn't coming back at all. Not until she stopped by his office to ask if there were any extracurricular advisorship positions available did Harry know for sure that she was really coming back, since the Assistant Superintendent hadn't remembered to tell him.

Ten years ago when Harry first began as a school administrator, he would have taken this as a personal insult. But he knows better now. On a personal level, Rose Ann probably thinks a great deal of him. But teacher contracts, leaves of absence policies, protocol, and formalities somehow get people to relate to titles, sometimes forgetting about the feeling, vulnerable human beings behind them.

But no matter how those with whom we work choose to relate to us, we must always remember that we *are* not what we *do*. There is no such thing in the real world as a janitor. There are men (and women) who sweep floors as a way of earning a living. The difference between how people relate to superintendents of schools and superintendents of apartment buildings usually has nothing whatsoever to do with the caliber of human beings behind the titles, and if the two switched jobs for a while, they would find this out quickly.

The most important thing to hold on to on your climb up and down the administrative ladder is a strong sense of *who you are.*

We hope that you are open, honest, caring, and yes, even idealistic. We hope that you love kids. We hope that you are strong enough to be vulnerable (because the alternative will make you less real). We hope that you will never forget your heritage. We hope that you will—through the power of your position—help others do the most important work on earth.

And if you persevere long enough and hard enough, chances are that you will see yourself as being an authentic human being—and that self-image will be strong enough to stand up to any title, no matter how impressive.

### CAVEATS, CODICILS, AND CONUNDRUMS ABOUT PLOYS TO AVOID

- "If you give to givers, it all comes back to you; but if you give to takers, you will get back about 10 percent."
- It is better to give to a giver and receive satisfaction, than to give to a taker and get nothing in return.
- The two words that summarize the purpose of most appointments to see the boss: I WANT.
- Administrators' blood is always the right type.
- Takers never get enough—ever.
- No one can hang a fool better than a fool can hang himself.
- Givers give a damn.
- Beware of takers bearing gifts.

- Don't waste your time trying to make takers happy; you don't have that long to live.
- Give your "consideration" to takers, but give yourself to givers.
- Caution: hicks may be slick.
- Participatory democracy requires participation.
- Japanese circles have quality.
- We are not what we do.
- Don't let hubris make a tragic hero out of you.
- A humanistic self-image should be strong enough to stand up to any title, no matter how impressive.

## CHAPTER 14

# Hiring, Shifting, and Firing

## WHERE LOYALTIES BEGIN AND END: HAVE GUN WILL TRAVEL

Professional school administrators come to understand that in the performance of their jobs, *popularity* cannot be traded for *competence*. Whatever loyalty is to be found lies in the knowledge that one's competence is ultimately one's sole calling card. It's the only permanent thing that counts.

Like Richard Boone in the old TV series "Have Gun Will Travel" the professional practitioner is a gunfighter who keeps his backside to the wall, particularly in faculty and board meetings and remembers the adage "There is no such thing as institutional loyalty."

We can recall more than once teachers, board members, and perhaps a PTA person or two who said, "Remember, ah, remember . . . er, what was his name?" Some administrators have literally fallen over dead at their desks, died with their boots on, and the flock of "faithful" couldn't remember that person's name long enough to put a tombstone on boot hill.

All institutions are amoral no matter what the motto says over the entrance to their hallowed halls. That's why some of the most venerable Ivy League colleges sell their liberal arts souls for defense contracts and investment portfolios in South African companies. Eastern bluebloods don't have any problem with loyalty and making a buck. And the same school district that begs someone to turn around one of its faltering secondary schools by becoming its principal will consider not giving that same person tenure three years later after that school has been turned around, if the board believes that such a move would be in the district's best interest because of possible secondary school closings somewhere in the uncertain future! So you don't owe anybody anything—least of all institutions!

Loyalty should not be a preeminent criterion for the selection of anybody, nor for that matter any institution. Loyalty should neither be a price a school administrator pays for employment or to anyone else. If you crave true loyalty, *buy a dog.*

**THE PROPER ATTITUDE**

On the wall of a high school principal's office in a place we know quite well, a framed handwritten letter catches the eye of some who enter. It is written in ink on the school stationary of another high school some miles away. It says:

Dear Friends:

We have missed you. And during the present round of parties and other holiday gatherings I've missed a lot of good laughs and pleasant moments because you weren't around. You're due for a good year ahead. I wish you and your loved ones a very happy holiday. Interested in Spring flounders?

PACEM
ALBERT KRAZE

Every once in a while, someone asks the principal why on earth this "ordinary" document is on the wall in such a prominent place. The principal responds, "I read that piece every day. It reminds me of where loyalties begin and end."

Our high school principal had been fired from his previous position. Everyone had appeared to "love" him. When his demise grew near, the adoration poured forth from the community, the students, and staff. But the boss (the superintendent) had decided that he had to go despite giving him a merit increase his first and second years and glowing evaluations.

After the speeches, the rousing parties, the demonstrations, the appeals, the press panderings, and hoopla, the principal was fired. After a year in real estate, his wife selling cosmetics from door to door, he was hired again as a principal.

The "ordinary" correspondence framed in the principal's office was the ONLY TANGIBLE ARTIFACT THAT THE BELOVED PRINCIPAL HAD RECEIVED FROM ANYONE SINCE LEAVING THE SCHOOL.

Loyalties generally begin and end correspondingly with the rise and fall to power and position. To bemoan this human frailty is to waste energy (and subsequently your own power).

Jesus fared no better in the loyalty department than the "popular" principal. While the Bible discusses at great length Christ's betrayal by Judas for thirty pieces of silver, let us not forget that Christ's favorite disciple, Peter (the rock upon which he had built his church) had also betrayed him—not just once, but three times—by denying that he even knew him "three times before the cock crowed." By these standards, that "ordinary" piece of framed correspondence was a precious artifact indeed.

An administrator must be his/her own best friend, confidant, and counselor (although a good marriage wouldn't hurt either). One suspects that the Superintendent of Schools of Cleveland, Frederick Holliday, who shot himself to death in one of his system's high school's, cursing board politics, corruption, fiscal dilemmas, and petty animosities as revealed in his suicide note, lost himself in the quagmire of system inertia. He stopped being his own best friend and paid the final dreaded price for personal self-alienation. What good did it do? Even his successor, Alfred Tutela, *was hired on a 4-3 vote!*

Not ever really being one of the "boys" is the price of leadership. Anyone who thinks that leadership can be embraced without paying that price is destined to dance with an imposter. The person in the mirror *is your only friend,* period.

For those administrators who have never experienced a trauma similar to the one experienced by our "popular" principal, we suggest a framed poster, perhaps written in handsome calligraphy, be hung in a spot where it can easily be read every day. The message:

The King is Dead. Long live the King.

And while we're on the subject, bear in mind that many administrators know that if you've never been fired, you can't be all that good. Perhaps this was best epitomized by a response made by an experienced superintendent being quizzed publicly about his past performance and job record by a prospective board of education. He was asked, "We see that you have had a few jobs where your service was, er . . . a bit short. Could you explain this?" To which the prospective superintendent said, "Yes, I've been fired twice, but I've never not had my contract renewed." (P.S. He got the job.)

The only thing an administrator has is his or her competence, the raw skills, the moxie, the guts, and integrity. As far as these qualities are concerned, they can't be sold because they shouldn't be for sale. It can't be compromised because it isn't absolute. It can get you hired and fired. Competence is a tough taskmaster. It makes one intemperate with mediocrity and corruption.

**THE SUBTLETIES OF STAFFING**

The only lasting mark any administrator makes on a school or a school system is the quality of staff he or she hires, promotes or demotes, shifts or fires. People are ultimately institutions. Institutions are no better than their collective brains, energy, and humanity guided by a mission or some other proxy that moves them to work.

While institutions have no souls, they do have staffs. They do make decisions. They do live and die. Sometimes they undergo transformations and are reborn. As our former World War II enemies, Germany and Japan, bombed into oblivion, proved, wealth is not measured in personal property or even capital. It is in the collective brains and skills of the population and their desire to succeed.

The school administrator does not compromise on competence. Competence is its own best reference and descriptor. Competent people come in all sizes, egos, races, sexes, looks, and body types. They are the administrator's greatest allies and source of strength. Competence can be a great deceiver, for although it may not dress in the fashion of the day, *it is always fashionable*. It is always in demand.

The school administrator who can look back and know that the people in a school are better than when he or she came has given that school the only lasting gift possible. But there are a thousand seductions, excuses, reasons, distortions, platitudes, and downright lies not to honor competence and replace it with mediocrity. Mediocrity is always pleasant. In the short run it can rarely get an administrator in serious trouble. Competence is a pain in the ass. It's not hard to find, but it's hard to hire, contain, and retain. Its uncompromising nature can get an administrator in trouble as easily as it can win one acclaim. This mercurial quality about competence in human beings is the professional school administrator's stock in trade.

Competence is the red blood cells of the corporate entity. It is the raw skill in teaching and in classrooms that can result in outstanding pupil learning. A good organizer can schedule better. A good business manager can save money. A smooth talker can make people feel better. But without competence as the essential element of all three, it makes little difference to kids and the quality of instruction they receive. Competent teachers are the *wellspring* of a school. With them it is hard to be bad. Without them, very little can be good, though things can run smoothly and be pleasant enough.

**HIRING GOOD PEOPLE OR HIRING PEOPLE WHO HIRE GOOD PEOPLE**

There has been great effort, time, and money expended on trying to figure out how to hire good teachers. A lot of money has been spent on instruments, questionnaires, descriptors, interview guides, national tests, and the like. We are reminded of the anecdote from World War II when the Royal Air Force sent out an interviewer to question the best RAF fighter pilot recruiter somewhere on the Scottish highlands.

When the researcher arrived at a modest Scottish home, he was greeted warmly by the recruiter who was puzzled by the visit. "You have selected the highest percentage of combat aces in the RAF," said the researcher. "I'm here to find out how you do it." To which the recruiter sat back, lit his pipe, and responded, "See that old sheep dog over there in the corner? If he likes 'em, I sign 'em up." So much for scientific procedures and statistical analyses.

The professional school administrator has learned that teachers who are outstanding defy the odds. Some are egocentric martinets. Others are lovable Mister Chips. Some are ugly. Some are misfits. Some are pretentious. All they seem to care about is what they do. There isn't a good teacher who wasn't demanding and there wasn't one who did not expect achievement and worked for it. Students are sweathogs. They are worked. They are expected to learn.

All the bunk that is taught in schools of education about lesson planning, delineating precise objectives, transitions, strategies, and culminating experiences can't make a good teacher. *While teachers can be trained, they can't be made.* It's the same with artists and athletes. Training and discipline can make them better, but it can't make them if they were not talented to begin with. Teachers have it or they don't. What is it? We will call it a God-given "presence" with pupils. A teacher is someone you feel first and think about second. That is what is meant by "presence."

We've found some questions to be useful in an interview to be the best ones in terms of separating the winners from the losers or the mediocre, for either student teachers, beginning teachers, or experienced teachers. But we don't know of any question or questions that are foolproof. It would be like Beethoven asking a prospective composer, "What makes a great musical composition?" The astuteness and brilliance of the interviewer is as much a part of the process as the answer itself. In fact, the answer per se may not indicate much of anything. It is *the process* that makes the difference. The interviewer and interviewee and what happens there are a kind of barometer of what will happen in a classroom.

When all is said and done, the administrator puts his or her reputation on the line and makes a decision. While we've studied effective schools, we have not studied effective recruiters of good teachers. Who knows what they do? We know it isn't grades in classes that make excellent teachers. We know it isn't how they answer national standardized tests. We know it has something to do with intelligence and verbal ability, but there is so much more.

There are those administrators who consistently pick winners and those who pick turkeys. Get the winners and keep them picking winners. If you can't figure out what administrators who select winners really do, at least keep them choosing teachers. *Hire people who know how to hire good people.*

Great teaching is an art form. Trying to select a prima ballerina on an interview alone would be unthinkable. The title and honor is earned little by little, performance after performance.

Teaching is different. The administrator makes a choice and for the teacher it's sink or swim. Somehow the good ones walk out and the bad ones don't make it. It's the old Inca throw-the-girl-in-the-well ritual and the virgins won't drown. At the present time we have no way to make incremental judgments based on expanding concepts of what constitutes master teaching.

Hiring is a guessing game, a complex pin-the-tail-on-the-donkey ritual in which the administrator is blindfolded by data which is meaningless, grades which stand for little actual skill in the classroom and often have nothing to do with sound training, with recommendations from professors who have not been in an elementary or secondary school classroom for years, if ever, passing judgments on candidates to teach, who often don't even know if they will like teaching until they end up surrounded by Indians and overwhelmed.

The administrator is alone in hiring. While lots of people may want in and demand to be "in" on hiring, however, see how many claim to be responsible when a "lemon" is hired. It's the principal who is left holding the bag. So when the teachers' union, the PTA, the board, and other administrators would like to be in on the picking, and they strike out, see who gets the blame?

So, as long as that's the way the game is played, make the mistakes on your own. Be hard-headed. From Missouri. Insist on interviewing the people themselves. Never take anybody else's word for anything. It's like taking a stranger's word for what makes a good restaurant. In order to trust a recommendation, one must know the culinary tastes of the critic and judge for one's self. Beware of personnel officers who are trying only to fill quotas with warm bodies. The best data to use in selecting teachers is to examine their past records and talk to people who have worked with them. This would even apply for brand new teachers. Talk with the teachers who worked with them.

## CON GAMES IN LETTERS OF REFERENCE

Examining a teacher's references is an art in itself. It is an exercise in decoding ciphers. If a teacher has a placement file, examine his/her past grades. These will indicate how strong candidates were in their chosen areas, though it may not be a good indicator that they can actually *teach* the material in those classes. Knowing and teaching are two different skills.

Discount any recommendation made by a professor who hasn't

observed the prospective teacher actually teach. Everything else is simply impressions. It would be like taking a recommendation on how well an automobile rides by listening to those who selected the color scheme or body style. Listen only to those who have ridden in it.

With experienced teachers, any time a referent writes, "If you have any questions about this person please call me," *make the call!* Those are "red flag" words that often mean *there was or is a problem.* This is particularly true today when personnel placement files may be inspected by the candidate himself/herself. Often that little phrase is the only cue that the person should make a firsthand check of the situation.

Teachers represent the general population. There are teachers who are sadists, child molesters, thieves, rapists, and murderers. Teachers suffer their share of alcoholism, drug problems, and psychiatric disorders. Talk to any personnel officer of a large school system. They will tell horror stories that will knock your socks off.

One of the co-authors was a personnel officer in a large school system. In the short time span of one year the following incidents were investigated:

- an instrumental band teacher who on trips slept with female students;
- a director of a drug project who sold drugs to students;
- a teacher who indicated he spoke with God and was told to exterminate God's enemies (this teacher was personally driven to the psychiatric ward and put in a straitjacket in front of the administrator);
- a teacher who was consuming a case of beer a day and who went through the DT's twice, refusing to admit he had a drinking problem even when the police and his minister admitted they had found him intoxicated.

To the author's knowledge, all of the above are still in the classroom today! Given legal due process requirements in court, the increasingly liberal attitude of the general population, strong unions, the reluctance of people to testify about such activities, and the view that a teacher's private life is his or her own no matter what, it is a matter of great concern to do one's homework in selecting teachers.

One personnel officer in a large metropolitan school district had an interesting way of stating it. If you are considering hiring a person and you know that the person has a past record, consider the *headline test* of the local newspaper, *"Principal Hires Known Child Molester."* If that doesn't stop and make you think how you would feel, not much else will. It's one thing to have one on your staff, but it's another to HIRE ONE.

These simple rules should be followed to reduce the chances of hiring the wrong person for a school:

(1) Check all references personally.

(2) Ask for references not listed by the candidate and check them.

(3) Make a site visit if there is the slightest hesitation on the part of anyone in speaking about a candidate.

(4) If there is any doubt, make a routine police check on the person.

(5) Ask for anecdotal records such as number of days absent (a pattern of Monday and Friday absences may reveal an alcohol or drug problem).

(6) Speak directly to other administrators and ask them pointedly, "Knowing what you know about this person, would you put your own child in this teacher's class?" If there is the slightest hesitation, investigate further until you are satisfied you have the truth.

Remember the best indicator of future performance is past performance. Forget what a candidate tells you such as, "I could have done better but I wasn't motivated. But I really am motivated now!" This is pure garbage. Past performance is the most tangible and reliable yardstick anybody ever has of what a person will do on the job. It is that record you want and which you must ferret out until it is clear in your own mind what this person did on the job.

In the beginning teacher, look for confidence, enthusiasm, the ability to relate to others, and the ineluctable "presence."

**SHIFTING PERSONNEL: KEEP YOUR EYES ON THE PEA!**

Seasoned school administrators within school districts play an interesting game of Russian roulette. At the end of each year it's "Pass the turkeys time." What this amounts to is that principals take inventory of their worst teachers and try to fob them off on other principals at other schools.

The game is usually played toward the end of the year in staffing discussions and enrollment projections. Principals come armed with hyped up evaluations, accolades and glowing reports, and excuses as to why this teacher just didn't work out at his or her building, but under the "right nurturing" could really blossom into the rarest of flowers.

Most principals understand rather well that a truly good teacher is never traded away, NEVER! It's more precise than the NFL "free agent" draft. In the NFL a football player can become a free agent if he refuses to come to financial terms with the owner. So *there are* good players who are free agents. Since school administrators can't manipulate salary and teachers can't become free agents, the only ones allowed to get loose are *the losers!* Sane principals know that even a great teacher who doesn't like them is better than a mediocre one who does because a great teacher keeps kids and parents happy and that means the principal won't have to deal with dissatisfied clients.

Bad teachers often don't know they are bad because school administrators have never told them flat out, "You are terrible." The reason is not too hard to discern. Administrators must have data. That data must be observable and verifiable. It must be made over a period of time. The teacher must have time to improve after having been told in writing.

This "due process" procedure takes time. It often takes more time than the administrator has. It means that with each observation, each summary, the teacher is challenging every little thing, grieving this or that, fighting and scraping all the way. At each turn there is confrontation and diatribes. Strong teachers' unions see to it that the rules are followed to the letter.

It often takes years to unseat an unsatisfactory tenured teacher and costs thousands of dollars and person hours. And then there are always appeals, charges of favoritism, discrimination, harassment that have to be endured. It's no wonder that so many administrators compromise and find ways to reduce the irritation rather than openly deal with the problem. But the most blatant cases of tenured incompetency *must* be addressed no matter how costly the process. Every child in an incompetent elementary school teacher's class loses one-twelfth of his or her entire public school education each year that person is allowed to remain on the staff. And every talented professional on the staff is similarly demeaned.

Some administrators will find closets to put bad teachers in. They will reduce class loads or staff classes with poor students who are apathetic because such students rarely complain about mediocrity. It is easier to do this in high school where staffs are larger. Such teachers are shunted off to the far corners of large departments. There are "closet cases" on every faculty. When unions propose collegial hiring and evaluation, it means that such people become part and parcel of the selection process and since likes select likes, a standard of mediocrity is firmly established. Few teachers in their right minds will hire more competent colleagues because it will expose them for what they are. The same goes for quasi-competent administrators. They will select people like them. An institution can become a victim of incompetency, a home for the mediocre, a haven for the jobless and alienated, a safe harbor for the unfit with tenure.

It is no small wonder that so many schools have sunk into a kind of mindless routine where excellence has no refuge since it is without honor and eschewed. The administrator who contributes to this norm should be tarred and feathered. He or she is worse than a "bad cop," since the influence of a bad school on children may last for generations, beyond even the immediate lives and fortunes of the current student body.

Shifting staff must follow the advice of the gambler in Kenny Rogers' ballad who confessed that every hand is a winner and every hand is a loser. It's knowing what to keep and what to throw away that makes the difference! Like poker, staffing should be done to strength rather than to weakness. Staff to the aces, look for three of a kind, draw to a flush. Patterns and possibilities are limitless.

## WHO MUST BE FIRED AND MAKING IT STICK

In the real world, "a new broom sweeps clean." Often, this is as it should be. Lee Iacocca could not have turned Chrysler around if he were unable or unwilling to dismiss anybody. But in the world of education, the administrator's powers in this domain are limited. Therefore, they must be used wisely.

## THEORY X AND THEORY Y

Of the prevailing notions about management and people, all three are at the end of the alphabet. Douglas McGregor, an industrial engineer at MIT, hypothesized that there were two concepts of dealing with people. One was the "X" model, predicated on the idea that people had to be kicked around to perform well. "Y" on the other hand, was a rosier view of humanity. In our times, the Ayatollah Khomeni would be a Theory X leader. Gandhi, a Theory Y. The Japanese use one called "Z."

The problem is that McGregor never dealt with elementary and secondary schools, unions, school boards, PTA's, and the deleterious impact of bad teachers and tenure. Some people are not motivated by "great expectations." Some people are motivated by fear. When dealing with the incompetent and bad cases of mediocrity, start on the problem as if it were going to the U.S. Supreme Court. Don't leave one stone unturned.

There is no fairy godmother. All of the theories can't make an incompetent teacher (note that throughout this section when we say "teacher" we mean administrator as well) into the handsome prince. The purpose of evaluation is not to deal with their growth, for the growth of such persons is infinitesimal if at all. They are not cut out to be teachers. They shouldn't be in the classroom at all. Your job is to get the bastards out, *period.*

So you enter the process giving the proper lip service to the prevailing ideology about growth and the good Theory "Y" stuff, but the bottom line is that you will get this person out of teaching and you set out to do it with the patience and diabolical attention to details that would even impress Agatha Christie!

Your homework in spinning your plot is to:

(1) Know the teachers' union contract by heart, line for line, passage for passage;

(2) Know the laws and legalities of the state, recent court rulings, litigation, line for line, passage for passage;

(3) Know the "hot buttons" of your personnel, what makes them tick, what they fear, how they react to various kinds of pressures, whom they turn to, and how they sustain themselves under fire;

(4) Maintain a good working relationship with your district's school board attorney.

Then, the cool administrator sets out to "put the screws" to the bad teacher in such a way that all of the rules are adhered to, all of the language in the contract is minded, and all of the laws are abided by—but the person leaves rather than taking any more.

We present four cases of such intrigue and intricacy in which the school administraor is pitted against the forces of evil in ridding schools of bad personnel. We use them to illustrate the weapons and strategies at the principal's command, the interplay among the players, and the final result.

The Case of Daisey Jones

Ms. Jackie Smith assumed her duties as Principal of Parker Peak Elementary School in July. Soon, she met Daisey Jones, the Special Education teacher. Ms. Jones immediately struck Jackie as high strung and inappropriately dressed. However, it was the summertime and Ms. Jones was upset over the scheduling of "her children" so she ignored it.

Not far into the school year it became apparent that Jackie's first impressions concerning Ms. Jones were more accurate than she had first realized. As it turned out, she was the object of much ridicule among members of the faculty, many referring to her as "crazy Daisey." She seemed to have an insatiable desire to be loved and accepted by everyone.

She referred to her students as "my little buttercups" and seemed to have a clinging relationship with them, which was particularly stifling. She would accuse any member of the staff who ever questioned her methods in any way of being hostile to her and to her "special" kids.

Unlike the students similarly classified in the other elementary schools in the district, Daisey's students were "hyper." They roamed the halls often with passes she gave them and they were everywhere but in her room. Their passes were calling cards for trouble.

Upon reviewing her personnel file, Jackie found that she had been given a good end of year evaluation by her predecessor the previous year, and because the year before that she had been employed by an intermediate agency, her employment records for that year were unavailable. Jackie's first year as principal was also to be Ms. Jones' tenure year.

A decision regarding her tenure had to be made in early spring. Her classroom observations weren't horrid because she wasn't a horrible teacher. She seemed unstable and her instability was having a spillover effect on her students.

The administrator had to make a judgment call. Was there time to save Daisey Jones? Jackie decided she wasn't running a Salvation Army stand. Parker Peak wasn't a soup kitchen for the homeless. Growth, to the extent that would enable Ms. Jones to be a first class teacher, was probably against her. Time was running out.

Daisey Jones had to go. Her instability, her inability to focus her class, her defensiveness, and her unapproachability presented a combination of elements impossible to untangle. She was not a candidate for tenure, *a contract for life.* Jackie could hear the staff saying, "If Daisey can get tenure, anyone can. *And,* if that's the case, why not me?"

The tender-hearted reader may be fretting. There wasn't much data. One year and it was good. The fact of the matter is that good administrators know how to make decisions on the right amount of data. For some decisions, there is never enough data. Any problem can be studied to death. Bureaucracies are rife with bad cases of "paralysis by analysis." And personnel decisions are the most painful and ambiguous ones in the book.

Working closely with the Director of Special Education, who concurred with Jackie's assessment, Jackie Smith conferred with the school board attorney. None of the reasons which were cited by Jackie could be used for the board. "So she's nuts and you think she drives her kids nuts, too," he said. "The board isn't going to want to hear that. How many times has she been absent and late?" Upon examination, Jackie found that Daisey had, in fact, been absent for nine days and had been late a total of eighteen times that year. "Fantastic," said the board attorney. "That will stick." The "telling" argument with the board was that if Daisey was late that many days during her tenure year, what could we expect from her after she obtains that "untouchable" status?

In executive session, the board voted unanimously not to grant Ms. Jones tenure. In her first year as principal, Jackie Smith had established that tenure was to be earned through performance and was not going to be bestowed by "squatter's rights." Were there others on Ms. Smith's staff who deserved to be dismissed? Certainly, but they would have to wait until next year. Since the administrator's time is so limited, and such cases absorb an enormous amount of such time, a good rule of thumb is "one at a time."

The Case of Ralph Plotnick

As serious and irritating as the Jones case was, Ralph Plotnick's was even more so. Ralph was a high school Social Studies Department Chairperson. He had tenure in his position for over twenty years. The females in his department were visibly afraid of him. This was one of the problems encountered by Joan Truegrit, the new principal.

None of the talents of the department were tapped. Each went his or her own way. The department was fractured. Ralph used the tactic of pitting one against the other for favorite classes or to attend conferences. His stock answer for why his department had not changed or tried innovations was, "There's no money for it."

An examination of his personnel file revealed a history of his not being able to get along with or take direction from all five of Joan Truegrit's predecessors. His file reflected repeated documentation of his poor leadership and his overt attempts to undermine the efforts of those five principals. Morale in his department was near zero. When asked, most of the department faculty responded that their best year in the school had been when Ralph was on sabbatical!

Ralph's personnel file looked like the Manhattan telephone directory because to each question, query, or criticism he attached lengthy rebuttals. Some of the statements were bizarre, revealing Ralph believed in plots against him. Students were enemies. Parents were in armed camps. He portrayed himself as Don Quixote jousting with the forces which would dilute quality education.

The portrait of Ralph Plotnick distilled from dozens of memos, anecdotes, letters, rejoinders, and inquiries was:

- An egomaniac who had wrapped himself in the mantle of the savior of public education;
- A picky, petty, vindictive person who was feared by his colleagues;
- A long time employee who knew the ropes and took advantage of the procedural weaknesses which existed, as well as the foibles of each of his administrators.

When Joan Truegrit met with the board's attorney about Ralph, she was told that the board could not afford the legal fees to remove him as a teacher and that as voluminous as the personnel file was, there was insufficient documentation as it pertained to his actual classroom teaching.

Joan constructed a detailed chronology from that file listing the dates and identified the specific documents from which specific excerpts were extracted. The documentary totaled twenty type-written pages. She then sent the entire document with a table of contents and appendices containing the original documents to the Superintendent and the Board of Education.

At the executive session of the board, board members took turns telling their own rocky horror "Plotnick" stories and the incomprehensible wrongs wreaked upon their own children. After they finished their catharsis and their questioning of Joan, they directed the school board attorney to take whatever steps were necessary to rid the school of Mr. Plotnick at *whatever the cost!*

The board's attorney suggested that they try to arrange with Mr. Plotnick a reasonable way out by resigning prior to engaging in all out war. The quid pro quo was that if Ralph was allowed to remain a teacher he would resign as chairperson.

While Joan believed Ralph was as unfit for classroom duty as he had been for chairperson, she was convinced that due to a lack of documentation, she would lose and so would the district. Two months later Ralph handed in his resignation as chairperson and became a full-time teacher. The only reaction from staff was, "What took them so long?"

The Case of Eleanor Trusty

Eleanor Trusty denied she had a problem with discipline in her elementary class. Before her principal, Sue Walters, she pointed out her exemplary student teaching record at a prestige-packed liberal arts college on the East coast. She came from a long line of educators. Her father had been a superintendent. She was destined to become a great teacher. It ran in the family.

Yet Sue Walters received daily complaints from parents by letter and by phone. Eleanor's grade level chairperson came to see her and indicated that she thought there was a problem. Other teachers were concerned about the noise from her room.

Finally, Sue determined that the problem had to be documented. She took a note pad and clipboard and went to sit in Eleanor's room. All she did was keep a frequency log of what happened without comment. It ran like this:

9:25 A.M.—Entered the room. Twenty-three children present. Eleanor said, "Now it is time for reading. Go to your reading groups."

9:28 A.M.—One boy left the room followed by another. No permission was asked. As Eleanor worked with one group, the others started to work.

9:30 A.M.—Both boys came back into the room and engaged in a mock Kung-fu fight. One swung his foot at the other, hitting him in the leg. The other said, "For that I'll take two shots." Eleanor glanced over at them and said nothing.

9:32 A.M.—One girl left the room. She was followed by four other girls. One reading group was in chaos. They were arguing over what they should do. One boy said, "We don't have to do nothing anyway."

9:40 A.M.—Eleanor said to the two Kung-fu fighters, "Will you two take your seats?" They ignored her and went on until one knocked over a table.

9:42 A.M.—Two boys left the room and one girl returned. Another girl grabbed the door and swung it back and forth laughing all the time.

9:48 A.M.—Eleanor looked over the reading groups and seeing one almost disbanded said, "Have you finished your work?" The children ignored her. The other reading group was opening and closing their books to make a kind of slapping noise, swat, swat, swat!

For one hour Sue Walters kept her log. Then she left Eleanor's classroom. She wrote up her observation point by point, minute by minute. Then she wrote at the end of the memo, "Please see me about my observation as soon as possible." When Eleanor came in some two days later, Sue said, "Is there a discipline problem in your class?" Eleanor looked at the floor. She cried. "Yes," she said. "Do you think you can get the class back with help?" Eleanor sat a long time. She looked out the window and said, "No." Sue Walters said, "I want your resignation on my desk tomorrow." She got it. Eleanor was gone on Monday.

The Case of Joe Falcone

Joe Falcone was the head custodian at Pete Jenkins' high school. Pete remembers Joe well. When Pete was made the principal, Falcone gave him a bear hug and a pat on the back to wish his new "boss" luck. He then put his arm around Jenkins and took him on a tour of his new school.

During Jenkins' first week on the job in July, Joe took him to lunch at his insistence so they could talk and so Jenkins could see where many of his high school teachers congregated. During lunch, Falcone "filled in" his new boss. He told him how unreasonably demanding the teachers were and not to let them pit the two of them against one another. He also told Jenkins how few—if any—staff members could be trusted, but that he (Falcone) would watch out for him.

Jenkins couldn't help but think that either Falcone was one of the nicest people in the world or that Joe was setting him up. Which was it? Within the next year, Jenkins found both to be true. Joe was a nice man, but he was also incompetent. He had no control over his crews, day or night. The crews did as they pleased while Joe covered for them in order to escape blame for not being able to supervise them properly.

Soon the teachers brought their frustration to Jenkins. The basis of their complaints was that, "nothing ever gets done around here." Joe was a consummate devil's advocate. He would think of dozens of reasons why something *couldn't* be done no matter what the request was or the occasion.

By the end of the first year it was clear that Jenkins was coming down hard on Joe, with the assistance of the Superintendent of Buildings and Grounds, Robert Stark. Falcone was beginning to feel the heat.

During an evening performance by the drama club, Falcone was unable to be found to fix a constant hum from the microphone, and the audience was left to grope their way out of the darkened auditorium when the performance was over because he was nowhere in the school to put on the house lights. Jenkins included this incident in a reprimand which went into Joe's file. A rapid list of reprimands for incompetencies followed. Falcone was no longer able to maintain a front which hid his own inadequacies.

Within months, encouraged by Jenkins and Stark, Joe handed in his letter of resignation and selected retirement as an alternative to continued documentation of his problems. Jenkins had cleaned up the custodial crews and the school, literally, and in the process, sent out a message that incompetence would not be tolerated anywhere on the staff.

### TAKING YOUR LUMPS, THE DIRTY WORK IS PART OF THE JOB

There is no doubt that the principals involved spent the better part of their time doing unpleasant house cleaning, bird-dogging, and close supervision. Nobody, except perhaps a sadist, likes to hurt people. Joe Falcone was a warm, personable man, old enough to be the principal's father. Daisey Jones, despite her peculiarities and problems, really did "love" her children. Ralph Plotnick did try to "fly right" when he figured out what was going on. Eleanor Trusty was bright and well educated. She was even witty in the faculty room. But these people were not fit for the jobs they had. They had to go.

And each of the administrators paid a price for the decisions. On the one hand, the replacements for the persons cited were much better. Things happened that never happened before. But these were soon forgotten. Each administrator endured the caustic petards of bitter people. When the decisions were made, as staff stayed on, they chose to "bad mouth" the administrators, create insinuations of "hidden motives," and other reasons for the actions taken. Daisey Jones even undertook a personal letter campaign against the principal, with letters mailed to board members and the superintendent.

Joe Falcone walked around the school grounds for six months looking like a wounded animal. Anonymous hate mail was sent to the superintendent about Joan Truegrit. Was it from Plotnick? It could not be proven.

Few people will say "thank you" to administrators who make the decisions about people. While people may be relieved and they may secretly admire you, no one will publicly admit, "You're right, the bastard did have to go." The dirty work is there. It will have to be confronted. It won't go away. It can be put into different piles but it won't go away.

The administrators did their homework. They knew how to gather data, to prepare the data, whom to talk to, and how to make the decisions stick. They didn't expect any cheers and they didn't get any. Instead, each has a new enemy. The unsigned "fan mail" continues. Will the administrators obtain tenure? Most don't know. Most don't care. The quality of life in their schools is better. Each likes what they are doing. If necessary, they can pack their guns and ride out of town, *proudly.*

## THE ONLY THING THAT LASTS

The only criterion for the school administrator is competence. Competence in every classroom, competent custodians and secretaries will create a vibrant and lively environment. But medals are not won for the dirty work it takes to ensure competence in the schools.

There isn't a bad teacher who wasn't loved by some kid or some parent somewhere. You won't get any public accolades, libraries named in your honor, scholarships given in your memory, editorials praising your vigilance. Unions will despise you. Some teachers will fear you (but they will probably be performing). Some other administrators will consider you a fool because you make them look too comfortable, like the fat cats they are. In short, you won't be loved. Respected, *absolutely!* But expect to be vilified, not appreciated. If you're the kind of person who needs lots of positive strokes, the job is not for you. And be prepared to pay the price.

## RETROSPECTIVE

School administrators won't qualify for sainthood. We know hundreds who would fit the description of the Agatha Christie mastermind. They do their jobs but they don't believe they are loved or popular. They know what it takes to create a competent and disciplined staff. They know how to "kick ass" if they have to, *and they have to!*

Every now and then one takes a dive and succumbs to the crowd. It's hard not to want what the crowd offers. It's hard not to want to be somebody's friend. But the nature of the job is different. *Dedication to first rate teaching.* To deliver a first rate education takes energy, struggle, singlemindedness that borders on being a zealot. Far from being the uncompromising procrustean leader, the most competent administrator is infinitely flexible about all things *except* a commitment to competence.

Who cares? You do. We do. Integrity means doing what you have to do, knowing what you have to do, and doing it. Without fanfare and pomp. Without expecting anything but grousing and bitching from everybody. The best administration is invisible. It happens because it is supposed to happen.

*Selling out* means accepting less than what you know you could have gotten if you had hung on. It means accepting less from faculty, students, and the community than they could give. And it means *you know it.* Yes, it is hard on you, but it is harder to know you settled for less. That's the job. Some administrators still have the job even though they turned their badges in years ago. If you still want the job, get the badge back. Start now. The only winners are the kids. Since all human accomplishment is incremental, there won't be much spectacular about it. But the big difference *is inside you.* It makes a difference. Everything else depends on it. And—you can take that to the bank!

## CAVEATS, CODICILS, AND CONUNDRUMS ABOUT HIRING, SHIFTING, AND FIRING

- Hire people for their competence not their loyalty.
- Fear incompetence. It will hurt you and the kids.
- A teacher is someone you feel first and think about second.
- Popularity may make you feel good, but it isn't a substitute for good feelings about yourself.
- The only friend you need and can count on looks back at you in the mirror . . . if you think you can fool this person, you are a fool.
- People are ultimately institutions, yet institutions have no souls and are amoral.
- Mediocrity is always pleasant, competence is a pain in the ass.
- Teachers can be trained, but they can't be made.
- If you think you can hire someone with a past, *try the headline test!*
- The best predictor of future performance is past performance.
- A good teacher is never traded, never.
- Competence is its own best tenure.
- Integrity means doing what you have to do, knowing what you have to do, and doing it—without fanfare.
- The purpose of evaluation is to keep good teachers in and get bad teachers out, not to have incompetent teachers grow.
- Staffing should be done to strength and not to weaknesses.
- Check all personnel references personally.

- Keep administrative winners picking winners, even if you can't figure out how they do it.
- Not ever being one of the "boys" is the price of leadership; anyone who thinks that leadership can be embraced without paying that price is destined to dance with an imposter.
- If you crave true loyalty, *buy a dog!*

## CHAPTER 15

# The Emmetropia of Evaluation

*Emmetropia* refers to the normal ability of the human eye to accurately focus light rays on the retina resulting in a correct reflection of reality. Evaluation in the schools bears little resemblance to the reality going on in them. Emmetropia does not exist as it pertains to evaluative practices.

The standard phrase for the evaluation of people in the schools found in most contracts, policies, or platitudinous philosophies is that the practice is supposed to "stimulate professional growth." Any administrator who believes that deserves the fate awaiting him or her when the teacher's union lawyer carves him or her up like a Thanksgiving turkey on the witness stand before an arbitrator or judge in a court of law.

The purpose of evaluation is not to "promote growth" but to (1) ensure that quantitative and qualitative standards set for all personnel are maintained in their day to day performance of their work, and (2) provide a solid base of data to support fundamental personnel decisions in the schools, namely hiring, transfer, or firing (as cited in Chapter 14).

## GROWTH VS PERFORMANCE

The whole emphasis on evaluation as "growth" distorts the personnel function in schools. It takes our eyes off the object of why schools exist (to educate children) and makes teachers and administrators the objects for schools, and not their performance in them, but "their growth."

The evaluation of physicians is not to promote their growth, but to ensure the highest level of medical practice possible. In this sense doctors come to hospitals already fully "grown." One would think that with all the talk about "growth" for teachers they were a pack of professional pygmies instead of fully trained professionals.

There is historical data to support the "growth" function of teachers as the central reason for teacher evaluation. When anyone with an eighth grade education and a year or two of normal school training could be a teacher, *all teachers* required more intensive training.[1] Teaching was only half a profession then. They got the other half with OJT (on the job training). So evaluation couldn't be aimed at discerning the truly competent, since the training process was so universally abysmal, and a lot of partially trained recruits and other "irregulars" were the bulk of the teaching force.

Much of that has changed. Despite repeated criticisms of the quality of teacher training that echo through schools of education today, modern teachers graduating from four-year programs, with a fifth or sixth year of specialization beginning to be required, are a far cry from their predecessors in one-room schoolhouses of the past.

With this change in the work force, the function of evaluation is to hire competent and fully trained teachers, be sure their work is of a consistently high caliber, and get rid of the deadbeats, the unfit, the apathetic, the incompetent, and the destructive types that damage kids with their ego trips, sarcasm, and cynicism in the nation's classrooms.

### THE SEARCH FOR THE ONE "PERFECT" SYSTEM

Evaluation is a problem in schools because of logistics and because of the mythology surrounding its purpose. *Any* system used to evaluate teachers is imperfect. Teaching is a complex act. Much of great teaching is improvisation along with mastery of a set of skills and content, just like a soloist in a jazz band.

Administrators trying to evaluate what teachers do are faced with enormous problems. They take one of two approaches. The first is that they try to "capture" the teaching act observed "holistically" in the same way a person would tape-record a great musician. Think about trying to do that with paper and pencil. Imagine writing the music on paper as a musician played a jazz riff. Even if it could be done, the "essence" of the musician's excellence is lost in translation, i.e., it is screened out. Such evaluations are more like inkblot tests, i.e., they are more a measure of the evaluator than the evaluatee.

The second approach is to go to a teaching episode with a checklist and note when certain elements are utilized, such as anticipatory set, guided practice, feedback, and correction and supervision of independent practice. It is assumed that since good teaching includes these elements then, if also utilized by our observed teacher, use of them all would result in an "excellent" lesson. That this may not be so is abundantly clear to any novice administrator.

Both assumptions may be based on the false premise that

whatever is being observed is "typical" of what the teacher does when the observer is not in the classroom. Some new evidence suggests that a teacher's effective delivery of a curriculum changes with the nature of the discipline.[2] This means that the fundamentals of a good lesson in mathematics may not be the same for social studies.

The logistics of evaluation often make a mockery of the practice in schools as well. Assume that a classroom teacher must be observed at least three times (normal) during a 180-day school year. If the teacher instructs a five-period day for 180 days, that would be a total of 900 class periods. If the teacher were observed three of them, that would be .003 percent. We can immediately see that some very serious consequences for the teacher will be rooted in a very thin data base which fails to include a sample of time in a classroom equal to at least 1 percent (which would be nine observations) of total class time. Add to this the lack of assurance that those three observations are "typical," and the value of direct observation of a teacher in the classroom is nil.

For this reason and some others, the bulk of administrative judgments about teachers rests on non-observational or *indirect* data, e.g., parental complaints, student requests for transfer, grades given, etc. In essence, evaluation of teachers in most school settings is indirect rather than direct, and it is monitoring by exception, not the norm. This means that the administrator will not spend time with teachers for whom there are no complaints or problems. Rather, the administrator will spend his or her time on the "exceptions." This is the only way the problem becomes manageable. It is no wonder that good teachers complain that they never see their principals. They don't.

And we give to most principals an unmanageable job with supervision. The typical principal has direct supervisory responsibilities for twenty to thirty teachers or more. If all the teachers had to be observed three times for a full period, that would mean a maximum of 270 fifty-minute observations or 13,500 minutes or 225 hours of classroom observation.

Given the jam-packed days most school principals face, devoting 225 hours to instruction is impossible. With a span of control of twenty to thirty teachers, the job would be unthinkable in the business world.[3] But the public and most boards of education continue to misunderstand the demands made of administrators and the nature of school administration today. So the result is that the typical school principal concentrates on the turkeys. These are the most intractable problems for people in the business (see Chapter 6 for a few examples of "turkeys").

For these awful teachers the principal must spend not only classroom observational time, but hours conferring with the teacher, other administrators, lawyers, parents, students, other teachers, and union reps to ensure due process. To seriously get involved in ridding a school of a turkey teacher, a principal is faced with 200–300 hours of time demands on just one teacher, knowing full well that the teacher will be given every benefit of the doubt and every legal protection there is in the law books. In any such procedure, experienced principals know they are the ones on trial, not the teacher.

It is no surprise that faced with such decisions, many principals try to "rope off" the turkeys and minimize the damage they do to colleagues and kids. This compromise is often the only practical one available if the superintendent is a "chicken" about getting into a real donnybrook with the union in front of the community without a guarantee that the administration will win. Teacher unions bank on it. They know that superintendents run the risk of a serious loss of face when they lose badly in front of the community on a teacher dismissal.

And beware of big-talking board members who sound tough about backing you in your efforts to run the turkeys out. Most of them turn to piles of jello in a sustained legal firefight. Most board members don't have the foggiest idea of how complex and demanding the legal procedures are to jettison a bad teacher and how vulnerable the administrator really is in laying his or her neck on the line in "going for the professional jugular vein."

It is axiomatic that some kid will like the worst turkey on your staff. So the safest assumption to make when you are going to decide to "get a turkey" is to know *you will be alone*. Expect no support and you won't be disappointed, and know if you decide to run the rascal out you must be a cold-hearted son of a bitch, or it will be your body in the streets and not the rotten teacher's. In short, to be successful, you must be a Mafia hit man. You must take the attitude expressed in *The Godfather:* "No hard feelings. It's just business." And then do it cleanly, accurately, and as quickly as possible.

A lot of administrators come to realize this and find the irony of the situation too much. We are supposed to be in a nurturing and helping profession. How can we tolerate behavior which is so contrary and which goes against our professional "calling." The fact is that our culture is a perfect one for the ne'er-do-wells and nincompoops of the world to use our "calling" against us. They will nest and breed in the mantle of the nobler virtues of our profession and ruin it with cynicism and incompetence. In the end, schools reap what they reward. If we desire instructional excellence, we must be prepared to fight for it, demand it, and rid the ranks of those incapable or unwilling to be excellent. To fail in this is to sell out. You're a wimp! If you find yourself weaseling on the matter, look yourself in the mirror and ask, "Would I put my own children in this teacher's class?" If you hesitate at all, you have no right to put anyone else's kid in that teacher's class. So get busy.

## HARD VS SOFT DATA

It's almost impossible to "prove" anything about classroom teaching in the conventional manner courts and boards of education understand. One must remember that classroom teaching is not merely a mechanical set of operations, it is at its best *a performance* that is *instructional* (reaches specific objectives) and is *inspirational* (fills a student with the desire to learn). As such it is neither discrete with a definite beginning and end but rather a continuing series of encounters. In brief, it is not a novel, but a bunch of serials with a lot of "mini" beginnings and "mini" endings. These are classes.

Few people who have not been teachers or administrators understand the frailties of deriving data of any kind from a series of performances done over an extended time period. As such there are no "control" groups in schools from which to establish a pre-treatment *zero* and then measure pupil progress from that point. All students are being subjected to a "treatment," i.e., teaching, all the time. So children are always on the move. This means that there can only be estimates, not measurements. For this reason, when comparing teachers, the administrator can say with some certainty, "This teacher is better than that one." However, no administrator can say, "This teacher is *twice* as good as that one." To be able to *prove* one teacher was indeed exactly twice (no more and no less) as good as another teacher would be impossible. It would be like trying to say one actor was twice as good as another. Meaning it and proving it are two different problems.

Even in activities where there are more measurements than teaching, such as sports, we can say one baseball pitcher is better than another. One may have won twice as many games as the other. However, the number of games cannot be equated to a judgment about the pitcher. To be able to infer that the number of games won is an indicator of the quality of a pitcher, one must be prepared to offer evidence of the caliber of the opposing hitters, days of rest in a pitching rotation, and playing conditions. Even when those conditions are comparable, the answer regarding "twice as good" is speculative because there is no solid standard and no definitive absolute base upon which to determine a pitcher's total performance at any one time.

When examining teaching, it doesn't mean we can't evaluate it nor apply standards about what teachers do. It means we have to settle for less than the precision of industrial standards and contexts, where there is an absolute zero. When the first product (widgets to autos) rolls off the assembly line, there is a definite #1.

In teaching, there is no such starting place. Students are always changing. They are never static. There never was a time they didn't exist. They were not at the same starting point when instruction began and the better the instruction, the wider the diversity which will exist in what they continue to learn. The more effective the school, the less uniformity exists as instruction continues. This is in sharp contrast to industrial settings where quality control is aimed at reducing discrepancies between the product and standards, with a finite capacity to measure changes against the standards as a product is produced, and where the product can be "frozen" in time in an unfinished state and remain fixed until a decision is made to proceed and "unfreeze" it. Judging human performance is difficult even in these controlled circumstances, but infinitely easier when compared to evaluating the contribution of an individual teacher to the life of a child under noncontrolled conditions.

This is why we say that the data to evaluate teaching is "soft." Take any checklist for teacher evaluation we've seen and fill it out. The mere sum of the categories cannot be used to identify a superb teacher or a dud. Any great teacher will defy any set of categories we've ever seen or had to use in classrooms in schools where we worked. The administrator must always fill in between the lines and the categories and checks with judgments about the quality of that performance without getting bogged down in subjective quicksand.

To help the administrator in this process we must define a few terms pertinent to evaluation:

A *fact*: evidence that can be verified by observation or physical replication that is the same each time it is presented

*Example*: On March 23, 1986, Mrs. Jones' roster showed she had twenty-six students in her class for fifth period.

By showing Mrs. Jones' fifth period class roster for March 23, 1986, we can affirm or deny to anyone whether or not there were twenty-six names listed as pupils.

A *judgment*: an interpretation of a fact or an event. Judgments are made to explain the meaning of a fact by leading to a conclusion which in turn forms the basis for an administrative action.

There are two types of judgments, i.e., those that can be *sustained* and those that can't. In preparing a teacher evaluation, the school administrator is not forbidden to make judgments. On the contrary, that is the reason for having an administrator in the school in the first place. But those judgments must be capable of being *sustained!* Let us see how a fact can be changed:

> On March 26, 1986, Mrs. Jones' fifth period class roster showed she had a combination of twenty-six hoods, rowdies, and dirtbags that would intimidate most hardened street gangs!

This is an example of an *unsupported judgment*.[4] Just what information in the roster would lead to this conclusion? If the roster showed the number of absences or tardies or even referrals to the assistant principal, would it sustain the inference made that these students were hoods, rowdies, or dirtbags?

If, on the other hand, the roster showed how many times Mrs. Jones removed knives, zip guns, razor blades, or brass knuckles, would that be indicative of the reasonableness of the judgment? If it did, then we would need to have some standards by which it could definitely be known *at what point* a student with a knife became a hood. Is the possession of a knife proof a student or any person is a hood? How many times do such possessions occur before a student is a dirtbag? This is an example of an *unreferenced judgment*.[5] Unreferenced judgments cannot be sustained. If we concluded that possession by itself constituted the basis for being a hood, we would be using an *implied judgment*[6] that also could not be sustained.

When an administrator decides to go after a teacher turkey, each and every judgment must be capable of being sustained to make the "hit" stick. Going for the throat means making judgments within an evaluation that can be sustained before an arbitrator or a judge and *following the rules to the letter!* It means no shortcuts. If the contract calls for three visitations of not less than twenty minutes apiece and not more often than once a week and never on Mondays, it must be adhered to strictly! To do otherwise is to risk the entire evaluation being thrown out, not on its content, nor even on the quality of the judgments, but on the basis of failing to follow procedures. Being *ruthless* within this context means playing by rules—exactly! It is a game for the strong-willed and strong-minded. It is a posturing of willpower. It is a war of attrition. A successful school administrator is one who is a combination of Michael Corleone, Perry Mason, and Bulldog Drummond.

The administrator who is impatient, careless, or who can't stand the pressure when the bleeding hearts feel sorry for the teacher in the squeeze *is a goner.* His bullets are blanks and the strategy to be rid of the turkey will have been blown. This is not a game for the weak-kneed. One is talking about real people and real emotions. It is never pleasant. The administrative hit man is selective.

We separate the "hit man" from the "hatchet man." The latter refers to an administrator for hire brought in by a board to conduct a pogrom of the administrative or teaching staffs. Hatchet men are indiscriminate hacks who can't stay in any one place very long because of the vicious political retribution that comes from too much blood from normally trumped up evaluations.

All data about human performance in schools is basically subjective. Those that argue for an "objective" base either are naive or up to no good. The creation of criteria and the application of them is essentially selective, arbitrary, but not necessarily capricious.

For any evaluation system to "work" there has to be some trust between the people involved. We've seen terrible instruments used to make crunchy personnel decisions and be accepted when there was trust among the people using them. Likewise we've seen great paper evaluation systems and instruments founded on zero trust situations. Paper and forms cannot create trust, only people can. Both the context and content of evaluation are subjective and always will be in the final analysis. What makes any of them work is trust, not intricacy or length.

The evaluation of teachers is a subjective exercise. It involves judgment about one human being's performance from another human being. In this sense, it will always be "soft."

**FLATTERY WILL LOSE YOU A GRIEVANCE**

Once in a while a casual remark made in good faith will get one into trouble. Consider the plight of Wilber Hawkey, elementary principal of Falmouth Crest School. Wilber made a practice of trying to put something "positive" in every teacher's evaluation and observation, no matter how bad they really were. He believed "love" conquered all, eventually.

However, Hawkey finally had to go to the wall over the pitiful performance of Ivan Tinker, known as Ivan the Terrible. Wilber prepared carefully. His case looked pretty good. However, in arbitration, the union attorney simply put together Wilber's *paeans* to Ivan over many observations as follows:

> How can you say this teacher is as bad as Mr. Hawkey alleges when he himself wrote the following remarks over two years of actual observations of Mr. Tinker:
>
> "Today the children were smiling, filled with satisfaction with your science lesson. Your classroom was filled with the smell of fresh

flowers, a touching reminder of the tragedy of Hiroshima. You seem to take great satisfaction in coaching the reluctant learner. Your interest in spelling correctly is obvious, the children respond positively. Your lecture on commas was innovative."

I ask, Mr. Arbitrator, can this teacher be so terrible? Is this the teacher Mr. Hawkey calls "unprepared, cynical, even sadistic"? Either Mr. Hawkey is not describing the same Mr. Tinker or he is mistaken in his view of him. Which is it?

Hawkey was foiled on his own flattery; it was the result of the "growth" mentality regarding teacher evaluation. An evaluation is not a tool to spur growth; it is a tool to assess performance, period. Extraneous comments will lose you a grievance.

## FACTS ONLY COUNT FOR SO MUCH

Facts will only take one to the heart of an evaluation, which is judgment. From judgments, conclusions are drawn and decisions made about re-employment, raises, or promotion. The essence of a judgment is the nature of the factual data used to sustain it.

Often administrative evaluation is the worst of them all. Part of the reason is that most administrative behavior is hard to observe because it is not confined to any one place such as a classroom is for a teacher. Administrative behavior occurs all over the school, the central office, the telephone, the halls, and the community. To fully observe it would require a "shadow" and would interfere with the administrator's effectiveness in truly sensitive and delicate personnel matters.

So administrative behavior is judged by results based on mostly non-observed and indirect sources. For this reason, the judgments developed may not be capable of being sustained at all.

We offer the following administrative evaluation as an example of how a school administrator was "evaluated" by his superintendent.

---

*The Evaluation of Gale Peabody*
*Junior High School Principal*

| THE SUPERINTENDENT'S COMMENTS | OUR COMMENTS |
| --- | --- |
| (1) This constitutes my final year-end evaluation of Mr. Gale Peabody. | (1) A fact. |
| (2) Mr. Peabody reinstated the drama club and established the "run for hunger" to help starvation in Africa. | (2) A fact. |

*(continued)*

| THE SUPERINTENDENT'S COMMENTS | OUR COMMENTS |
|---|---|
| (3) However, Mr. Peabody must realize staff talents must be channeled and evaluated. | (3) Unsupported judgment. What evidence is there to sustain Mr. Peabody's use of staff talents or his evaluation of them? |
| (4) Mr. Peabody publishes a monthly newsletter to keep the community informed of his school goals. | (4) A fact. |
| (5) Mr. Peabody must be more involved in how delegates perform the work assigned to them. | (5) Unreferenced judgment. Mr. Peabody is now "involved" but, how much is "more"? At what point would Mr. Peabody or the evaluator *know* when he was meeting an implied, unstated standard for involvement? |
| (6) Mr. Peabody rarely makes suggestions for implementation of programs or procedures and tends to follow rather than assume leadership. | (6) Unsupported judgment based on unreferenced standards with an implied judgment as a conclusion. Does the "rare" frequency of suggestion (to which there is no quantitative standard stated nor frequency of Mr. Peabody's contribution to validate the judgment "rare" being utilized) mean he is a follower? It could also mean Mr. Peabody agreed with, supported, and implemented all programs and procedures as presented and was therefore a leader. |
| (7) He served on the Red Cross Board and has been at all meetings as evidenced by his monthly reports to me. | (7) A fact. |
| (8) Mr. Peabody leaves considerable room for improvement in the management functions of the principalship. | (8) Unsupported judgment. What management functions? |
| (9) Finally, Mr. Peabody must give more attention to the "nuts and bolts" and less to public relations. We would like to see more involvement of the principal in the effective day to day running of the school. | (9) Unreferenced, unsupported, and implied judgments used. What is "more" and what are "nuts and bolts"? What is "more involvement" that will lead to "effective" running of the school? Is the school now effective? If not, in what ways is it not effective? |

This is an example of an unsustainable set of judgments being used in an administrator's evaluation. There is a total lack of any factual data base that will support, reference, or provide evidence that the judgments are valid. Mr. Peabody is left guessing as to what was desired to change his administrative actions in the future.

In reality, the purpose of the comments were to "salt" Peabody's evaluation. "Salting" refers to a personnel practice of sprinkling negative comments throughout an evaluation to set the evaluatee up to be demoted or fired by accumulation. "Salting" a mine is to put fake "ore" in it to make it appear that a vein has been struck. The strategy to use in dealing with a "salted" evaluation is to attach a memo to it and identify it. Point out the faulty judgments, the contradictions, and the unanswered questions. That is what Peabody did. He attacked the evaluation and exposed its "phony" evidence for the forgery that it was. Not to do that is to accept by default all of the comments as possibly valid data when it is laid before a third party later.

In many school districts, evaluation is not used to promote anything. It is used to assassinate enemies of those in power, the non-conformists, the creative, or the non-groupies. Most evaluative systems are corrupted with misinformation, bias, unsubstantiated opinions, false conclusions, phony evidence, and unsupported judgments. Part of the furor raised by proposing a merit pay plan which uses such systems as a data base is the almost universal absurdity of most of the evaluative instruments and techniques utilized in school systems we know. The fuss is only partially quelled with the utilization of peer review panels, objective tests, and the development of personal portfolios to counteract the rotten evaluation system in place. With this in mind it is no wonder that even a mediocre union lawyer can have a field day when the administrative evaluator is on the stand. Facts only count so much because there are so few of them in most evaluations.

Our words about being alone when the chips are down are highlighted by a case in point. On August 22, 1985, in a closed-door eight-hour meeting ending somewhere around 4:30 in the morning, Superintendent D. Louis Christensen was stripped of all of his duties on a four to two vote of the Board of Education in Elk Grove, Illinois. The charges against the superintendent were:

Insensitivity to staff members, inconsistently spending money without board approval, publicly supporting programs prior to board approval and leaving a convention one day early without board approval.[7]

In his last several years, Christensen had shed about one-third of his administrative staff and tried to close the high school of one of the most politically powerful communities in his school district, the largest high school system in Illinois. Christensen's comment: "Only people who play it safe stay in one place for long in this business."[8]

### CAVEATS, CODICILS, AND CONUNDRUMS ABOUT EVALUATION

- Since teachers are not a pack of professional pygmies the purpose of evaluation is not to promote their growth.
- Great teaching is improvisation along with mastery of a set of basic skills.
- Most teachers are never observed more than 1 percent of the total time they teach in any one school year by a school administrator.
- The typical school principal has time to concentrate only on the turkeys.
- "Would I put my own children in this teacher's class?"
- In teaching there is no starting place; students are moving all the time.
- The mere sum of the categories on any checklist doesn't mean anything.
- A successful school administrator goes after a turkey like Michael Corleone, Perry Mason, and Bulldog Drummond.
- There is a difference between a "hit man" and a "hatchet man."
- One deals with a "salted" evaluation by adding an addendum as a little "pepper."

## CHAPTER 16

# Budget Skullduggery

## BUDGET CONTROL AND HIEROGLYPHICS

Most citizens and uninitiated administrators find school budgeting to be a kind of archival search for meaning in an ancient crossword puzzle in an unknown language. Most boards struggle vainly to educate children and control costs simultaneously. They may be doing neither well, but chances are their budgetary control is purely perfunctory.

By *control* we mean the capability to:

- direct money to priority needs;
- track dollars to programs;
- relate dollars to costs, specifically priority costs;
- provide an accurate framework with which to monitor financial transactions;
- utilize the budget to provide a record of financial accountability to the public.

The typical school budget does not do any of these things, so there is little *control* of school finance at the local level except to question an occasional fund transfer or a bid for ice cream or gym towels.

The school administrator who wants to learn how to control the budgeting process even *if it is out of control* must be educated in some simple *budget basics,* some ideas not found in the traditional books in administrative courses on school finance.

## WHAT IS A BUDGET?

A budget is not *reality.* It actually is a fluid process frozen for a short time period, usually a year. A budget is an *estimate,* an educated guess, about revenue (income streams) and expenditures (disbursements of cash resources). That's all it is.

Once these estimates are accepted by the powers that be, then the flesh is put on the bones of the budget and it is shaped up and massaged appropriately. *Budgets don't control anything!* People control costs by using a budget to understand costs and where the money is going and, more importantly, where it came from.

Budgets are fleshed out in four basic forms. They are:

*line-item budgeting* in which the objects of control are expenditure categories like administration, instruction, fixed costs, transportation, food services, etc.

*program budgeting* in which the objects of control are programs like elementary science, junior high school mathematics, or high school industrial arts.

*performance budgeting* in which the objects of control are fixed on the work to be accomplished. Work units or cost centers are developed by which to relate budgeted dollars. These may be such items as elementary science curriculum guide construction and printing or repairs of the track and field.

*zero base budgeting* in which the objects of control are on "decision packages" which relate specific budgeted funds to goals and activities within the schools including a statement of the consequences of not funding the package.[1]

Most school budgets are line-item budgets in which costs are not related to programs, services, results, or decisions. Rather they are related to expenditure categories. The school board cannot, therefore, control or direct dollars to program priorities. Costs cannot be contained rationally. Ineffective programs cannot be curtailed because they cannot be identified. Only the most arbitrary and self-destructive actions can keep a lid on costs in most school budgets. It is sort of like pulling the pin on a grenade and letting it blow one's hand off.

The lack of sufficient budgetary connections to educational programs in most school budgets denies to the board any effective means of supporting good programs and weeding out bad ones. Everything is lumped together in one glob. Most boards are not able to do much except to be budget *patsies* or budget *hackers*.

### ALL BUDGETS ARE PADDED

Finding the padding in a budget used to be simple. Most of the unspecified amounts (the pad) were lumped into a category called "miscellaneous." In many states such categories are now forbidden by law.

Thus, skillful school administrators have learned how to pad their budgets so that most of the time the money is never found, *but it's there!* Therefore, actually looking at most school budgets for spare bucks is futile. By the time the budget book is printed, it's too late. The figures have all been finagled. They all add up. Everything is neat!

We know of one board member who intuitively "knew" in a $40 million budget that it had a $1 million lining. He spent long nights with the budget searching every category and cranny for the million. It was there, but he couldn't find it. The school administration knew it was there but publicly denied it. They kept referring to the budget. He looked at the budgets for the last five years and couldn't find it. The problem was that he was using the wrong document. If you're looking for budget padding, the budget isn't the place to find it. *It's in the budget parameters that the "pad" is placed.* The budget simply irons out the wrinkles.

The document the board member had before the budget was the critical one. That was the one that estimated revenues and expenditures. For at least five years, the administration had overestimated expenditures and underestimated revenues. That meant that the "pad" was on both ends, i.e., somewhere between the actual revenue and the projected revenue which had been underestimated. This meant that *more money* was really going to come in than was stated. In the case of the expenditures, *less money* was going out than projected.

For example, if the administration expected fuel to increase by 6 percent, it estimated 7 percent, a 1 percent overestimate. If it had so overestimated consistently over the past five years, the overestimate could not be traced easily through past budgets. If the administration were questioned about the estimate compared to falling OPEC prices, it replied "we think it is prudent to be conservative at this point." The estimate can be lowered *as long as it contains the padded overestimate on top.*

## HOW NOT TO BE CAUGHT WITH YOUR PADDING DOWN

A simple procedure to "catch" such padding may occur when the board and the public receive some sort of financial statement or report, normally quarterly in most school districts. This shows actual expenditures compared to budgeted expenditures. The difference on the *plus side* (more left in the category than spent, compared to a *projected amount to be spent*) would reveal the padding.

All the administrator does is to *transfer* the pad prior to the quarterly report going into the computer. The pad can be split up into dozens of smaller amounts, and if done over a period of time it is impossible to trace without a computer since there are thousands of such transfers within budgets each and every year. This process systematically reduces the amount spent to the amount budgeted *to be spent*. The "pad" is gone. The account balances.

The "pad" is never placed in one lump sum anywhere in the budget. Rather, it is placed here and there and within budget categories in which there is a historical problem of fluctuations that may be large. Such categories may be salaries and fringe benefits, insurance, or fuel. Big money can be placed in these categories easily. Arguments about how much should be placed in such accounts must fall on *the conservative side*, i.e., it is better to overestimate than underestimate since one would not want to be caught short. This is particularly true if there can be no contingency account in the budget.

Budgets are usually cut in non-salaried or fringe benefit categories. Cuts in non-salary and fringe benefit codes are *peanuts*. Salaries and fringe benefits may run between 70 percent and 80 percent of the total school budget. Add to this fixed costs, plant maintenance, capital outlay, and transportation, which normally don't vary much, and one can easily see that what's left is less than 10 percent of the budget. Quite literally they are searching for nickels and dimes. What's cut? Paper and pencils. Classroom chalk. A few record players or overhead projectors and maybe a few books here and there. If these areas are cut, they can easily be replenished from the "padding" in the big cost categories via budget transfers at a later date in the school year.

**THE TELLTALE EVIDENCE: THE SAWDUST ON THE FLOOR**

The only actual evidence of this practice will occur at the end of the year when the accumulated overestimated expenditures, when added up, can be considerable. So it must and usually is spent prior to this time. What remains is the "pad," i.e., the actual revenues which were underestimated in the budget. Most of the time these can be blamed on the agencies which collected them for the district.

For example, underestimated state aid can be laid at the usual bureaucratic doorstep of the state department of education. Since the states normally screw up anyway about 50 percent of the time, it is a plausible excuse. Local tax collectors also have a generally unreliable record, so overages can be laid to a "good year" for collections.

What is left accrues to the carry forward balance and hence usually results in a lower local tax rate required in the ensuing year. There is nothing illegal about any of the procedures described. Taxpayer watchdog groups are usually watching budget categories like everyone else. They find nickels and dimes rather than the thousands or millions of dollars which are "moving around" inside the budget and which, while there in front of their eyes, are really not even stationary in any category very long. Thousands and millions are spent while taxpayers are fixated on pocket change.

Once we knew of a situation where the administration bought an unbudgeted $70,000 school bus out of the teachers' salary budget code (i.e., "instruction"). The teacher's union president jumped to his feet to question such a transfer, fearing a loss of funds for teachers. Of course, the administration *knew* the salary code was padded and there was no danger, but the union president didn't know it. He was simply pulled aside and told that the actual funds for increments on the salary schedule were overprojected because not as many teachers had obtained advanced degrees as thought. That was plausible.

When explaining the school budget, one doesn't have to be right, just *reasonable*. No one has any data to the contrary, so you can't be challenged with evidence, only suspicions which result in nothing but further questions. With time they stop.

The real telltale evidence is the tax rate at the local level. In the district using the practices described, the tax rate never was as high as projected. The reason was that the carry forward balance was always higher than projected, resulting in the need for less of a hit to the local taxpayer than projected. The larger carry forward balance was the result of underestimated revenue and overestimated expenditures. The news was always treated as "good luck," the smile of dame fortune, rather than ascribed to the practices that consistently produced an actual tax rate which was lower than required. Besides, few taxpayers will really argue with that kind of news. They consider themselves fortunate and let the evidence go, something like getting too much change at the grocery store and smiling all the way to the parking lot. Our own greed disposes of the evidence.

## CONTROLLING COSTS

To really control school costs would require a much different kind of budgeting and accounting procedure than exists in the majority of school systems today. Few boards of education or taxpayer groups would really pay to install the kind of budgetary *jaws* necessary to put an end to the practices we describe. It would mean acquiring computers and more staff. And it would mean thinking about budget decisions in a much more sophisticated way than most are willing to learn. Besides, almost everyone believes that they can control costs under the old budgeting system. Change appears as a luxury. The reality is that boards are not sophisticated enough to ask the right questions, and taxpayers are too cheap to insist on the additional funds necessary to effectively monitor such funds. Nobody believes they have a problem so why change it? Even when we have tried and indicated the savings would pay for themselves, we haven't had much success.

Even a new budgeting and accounting system won't control the really big costs in a school budget. If 70 to 80 percent of such costs are in people, their salaries, and fringe benefits, then costs are controlled in contract negotiations and not in budgetary procedures. Budgets simply *reflect* what was negotiated. Since many unions often elect board members who are committed to wage hikes, controlling costs is impossible. It would be something like a home owner putting in air conditioning for the summer, but turning off the light in the basement to trim costs.

Since most boards spend so much time on nickel and dime categories, a little padding will usually get one by just fine. Remember that all boards must appear conservative, *so they will cut the budget regardless.* In order to give them room, the school administrator must add some padding or else boards can cut into the muscle and sometimes the bone of the educational program. Remember that the budget used in most districts is non-discriminating about good or bad programs. So board members determined to cut budgets are *hackers* every time. Hackers can be dangerous unless they have plenty of padding to beat on. It is also important that to keep hackers happy, it is necessary to spill a little blood for the crowd.

Just as professional wrestlers will conceal razor blades between their fingers to cut an opponent over the eye (where a little cut produces the most blood) and give the crowd some real blood when they want it, so must the administrator be prepared to do a little public bloodletting. Everyone likes to watch somebody powerful get knocked around. So make it another round of *Rocky* for the fans. In the end, you'll make friends for defending your budget, the program will be safe, and the hackers will be happy that they've made their point about school costs. All the agendas have been fulfilled.

If you have to come up with big cuts from the budget, it is simply a matter of readjusting the *parameters of the budget.* Move the overestimated expenditures back a little, and the underestimated revenues forward a little. A lot of money can be generated very quickly, but *don't do it too fast!* Everyone must believe you got it by squeezing the *categories* instead of the *parameters.* That will mean that you reduced the budget, but not at the expense of riffing a teacher, losing a school bus replacement or a blade of grass on the football field. *Nothing has been cut!* However, you must call them "cuts" and remind everyone that you've reduced the budget by an overall percentage or two and "saved" the taxpayer "x" dollars on the tax rate through "prudent management." That keeps their eyes on the categories where you want them.

A school administrator who plays this budget game any other way is risking having real things cut. That means teachers won't get the proper materials. Class size may go up, and children will be deprived of real educational opportunities. If one doesn't care about what kind of education kids get, don't pad the budget. But remember, there are no awards for being a budget bastard. Not in education anyway. You're *not* in the business to make or save money. You're in the business to educate children. Your first priority must be to ensure that each and every child has the best future you can squeeze out of the taxpayers. They're not thinking about the future. You can be sure if you're not, *they're not.*

And remember that public schools compete with all other public services: police, fire, sewers, parks, transportation, garbage collection, roads, libraries, welfare, medicine, hospitals, and defense. The cost of one B-1 bomber would run any one of the majority of the school districts in the U.S. well into the twenty-first century.

Yet education is one of the few things that are still subject to the local taxpayers' wrath and whimsy for having to pay for a $25 million dollar F-15 fighter plane that's grounded 60 percent of the time, $9,609 for a wrench, $400 for a hammer, $2.5 billion for a defense gun that is incapable of doing its job, or $12.7 billion on an air-to-air missile that may never be fired.[2]

For the schools not to be scapegoats for the profligacy of the federal government and state bureaucracies, the school administrator is well advised to learn the ropes of budget skullduggery. If we're going to saddle future generations of taxpayers now in the schools with the costs of tanks and submarines, we should at least educate them to be able to pay for them when the bills come due.

## CAVEATS, CODICILS, AND CONUNDRUMS ABOUT BUDGET SKULLDUGGERY

- A budget is never reality; it is always an estimate of two parameters, revenue and expenditures. *That's all it is.*
- Budgets never control costs; they reflect costs. People control costs.

- Board members are either budget patsies or budget hackers.
- All budgets are padded.
- It's in the budget parameters that the "pad" is placed. The budget simply irons out the wrinkles.
- Don't be caught with your padding down—transfer it!
- Big money is hidden in the categories with the largest fluctuations and the largest amounts.
- Most boards spend over 90 percent of their time on less than 10 percent of the budget.
- When explaining a budget it isn't necessary to be right, *just reasonable.*
- The real telltale evidence of budget skullduggery is the tax rate at the local level.
- Our own greed helps dispose of the evidence of budget skullduggery.
- All boards will cut the budget, *regardless.*
- Budget hackers can be dangerous unless they have plenty of padding to beat on.
- The administrator must be prepared to lose a little blood in the budget process to keep the fans happy.
- If you need money fast, squeeze the parameters, not the categories, of the budget.
- You're not in the business to make or save money.
- If we're going to saddle future generations with the costs of tanks and submarines, we should at least educate them so they can pay the bills when they come due.

## CHAPTER 17

# Textbook Tyranny, Curriculum Chicanery, and Testing Insanity

If there is one area of public service in which shoddy performance pushes families to change their address it is the kind of education their children are getting in public schools.

So wrote David Savageau and Richard Boyer in the *Places Rated Almanac* that examined the educational systems of hundreds of school districts around the United States. There can be no doubt about their conclusion as it pertains to public education. The question is how to make them better if they have slipped.

## THE EDUCATIONAL MUGWUMPS

The Algonquin Indians referred with disdain to a "great man" by calling him a mugwump. At least a person with the airs of a great man might be called a mugwump. We've got a number of them hobnobbing around the U.S. with their bag of nostrums for curing the ills of public schools. Very few, if any, have ever served or taught in the public schools as a teacher or administrator.

That would include Ted Sizer, Mortimer Adler, John Goodlad, and Ernest Boyer. Not one of them ever had to face a howling mob at budget time and justify funds for staff development or defend cuts in programs or athletics or propose an attendance or discipline policy. Not one, to our knowledge, ever had to make the hard decisions between reducing class size at the elementary level, maintaining art or music there as well, and revamping the chemistry lab at the high school, or increasing teacher salaries and fighting it through a divided board, union pressures, and special interest groups. Not one was ever shot at on the editorial pages or in the letters to the editor columns for working through changes in curriculum, deleting electives, or trying to close a neighborhood school.

We will never forget some of the fights we've had in communities where we served as administrators. In one, after a narrow budget defeat, the mob cornered us on the second floor of the volunteer fire department and there for over two hours subjected one of the co-authors to the most brutal grilling on the ins and outs of the schools one could experience. There was no hiding behind academic degrees or titles; it was just one against the mob who wanted an answer to every question they asked including "Why was the home economics teacher seen at 10:30 A.M. at the grocery store?"

In this respect, we feel a little like Sam Rayburn, considered as one of the great Speakers of the House, when he observed all the brain trusters arriving from Harvard to join the J.F.K. administration. Said Sam, "I'd feel a lot better if some of them had run for local sheriff."

We find it hard to give credibility to those advocating a single track curriculum for all students, like Adler, who have never faced the loaded political issues of what that means for dropouts at the local level and the enormous and real political weapons wielded on policy makers as a result.[1]

We find it hard to get too excited about Sizer's observations about rigid scheduling practices and his recommendation that students should be allowed to spend as much time as they need on one subject and stay in high school until they master certain skills.[2] Where was he when those of us in the field tried to implement some of J. Lloyd Trump's ideas and got hit with union grievances,[3] lawsuits,[4] and charges of allowing "kids everywhere but in the classroom—in the bathrooms smoking, loitering in the parking lot, and in the woods making love."[5]

And John Goodlad, who has never been a superintendent, downplays the importance of central administration in improving good schools, when any novice administrator understands the phenomenon of "sub-optimization" where one part of a school system can be successful, while the whole system fails its central mission. A school system is quite different from a system of schools. And a school is more than a confederation of classrooms. Being a dean of a college, a philosopher, or even commissioner of education is different from being a high school principal or a superintendent. One has to be in the trenches, face the day to day grind, the pressures, the unions, the kooks and nuts, the taxpayers, and the kids to fully understand what is possible and what isn't. And it's *more* than interviewing teachers, walking the halls as a guest, or taking a turn in a classroom or two as a visiting dignitary.[6]

The pressures of public schools are unlike private schools or colleges and universities. The mass movement of a captive clientele, many of them not wanting to be there, with a captive teaching force, many of them also not wanting to be there, in a building that creaks with age, with supplies and materials that are meager or non-existent, and a community that is apathetic about the public schools create an ethos that is very different from anywhere else. And we've been college professors and worked in college classrooms and even in the private sector. So when those who haven't been there take the rostrum and tell us what's wrong and what to do about it, we listen to the ring of authenticity about the context of the remarks, and whether or not they will work in the environment we know all too well on a daily basis. And frankly, we haven't heard much that is new or hasn't been tried before, or what we hear are the recommendations of someone who has never faced the crossfire on the battlefields we've known.

## PUTTING IT TOGETHER IN THE SCHOOLS

Putting it together in the schools requires some understanding of the relationship between what teachers do, what prescriptions they are given by their school systems, and measuring or evaluating what has happened as a result. The available data indicates that the single, most powerful tool for determining what teachers do is the textbook. Our own anonymous surveys of teachers on this matter likewise confirms what we already know. The fact is that the textbook *is* the curriculum in most schools. It does indeed dictate what happens in most classrooms. We have noticed that when teachers begin to write curriculum, they will often simply copy the major ideas and content from the textbook they are using at the time. So the curriculum doesn't dictate the textbook; it's really the other way around in most places.

Those in the business understand that textbook publishing is a for-profit business. As such, the adoption process is critically important for the industry. The two most important adoptions are in the states of Texas and California.[7] What happens in these states determines what happens in many others. We know people who work in textbook companies. They tell us about the campaign strategies. They tell us about who and what influences the shape of textbooks.[8] When these two states change their guidelines, they are changing the national curriculum!

Textbook companies have been notorious for influencing purchases of their wares through a variety of means. According to historical accounts, "textbook salesmen were not above using alluring women as accomplices to blackmail school officials into favoring their wares."[9] Early muckrakers Upton Sinclair and Lincoln Steffens reported cases of bribery and collusion between textbook publishers and administrators and board members.[10] That textbook publishers backed board candidates in political elections was cited by Ayers in his review of the Cleveland Public Schools in the early 1900's.[11]

At many national educational conventions and a host of smaller state conventions, the textbook salespeople host free cocktail parties and dinners for supervisors and administrators. It is through these contacts that books, maps, globes, equipment, and a variety of other wares are commonly sold later. So much for competitive bidding!

Textbooks are geared for the lowest level of educational attainment in the largest markets where adoptions are critical. As such, we have it on good information that the educational conservatives have a large sway over what is placed in textbooks, particularly history books. One contact of ours who works in one of the largest textbook companies has said that even in a subject like mathematics, the viewpoint of the Southern Baptists holds. There are no examples on presenting probability that utilize cards or dice in this company's math series because they want the Texas adoption.

It's no wonder, with the influence of special groups and opinions, that there is no "coherent design" in the curriculum.[12] The curriculum is the textbook, and the various states and local school districts have wide latitude in their adoption. Then the teacher controls the actual utilization of the book with children.

If a school district wants to be sure that the curriculum *body* is not wagged by the textbook *tail*, the development of local curricular objectives must *precede* the adoption of textbooks. In this way, the book with the largest congruence (overlap) to local objectives is adopted. The textbook then exemplifies the curriculum rather than establishes it.

Even when the development of curriculum does precede the adoption of textbooks, because of its lack of details, it often is not specific enough to be able to select a book. What we look for is a precise objective keyed to a textbook page with the example in the book matching the one in the curriculum and the one being tested. That assures both a content and methodological match.

The "real" curriculum isn't the one in the curriculum guide. Most curriculum guides are too big and bulky to be effective for classroom use. So teachers give lip service to using them and they gather dust in countless closets in thousands of classrooms around the country.

Most curriculum guides are also cluttered with too much garbage about methods and very little concrete specifics about what should be taught, how much time should be spent teaching it, or the sequence of what should be taught. In most guides there is little or no information regarding the tested curriculum. Teachers simply aren't told what is going to be tested, when, or how it will be tested.[13] So most teachers work in the dark following the mushroom theory of school administration, "I must be a mushroom because they keep me in the dark and feed me manure." Probably the best words we've ever heard about curriculum came from a silver haired school principal in Fort Worth, Texas who remarked, "I've been in this school district forty years and no one ever stole a curriculum guide."

Once we saw a curriculum guide in an elementary school principal's office in Columbus, Ohio. Since it had a lot of dust on it, we asked if he had ever "shared" it with his faculty. "Yes," he said slowly, "once. It was awful." "What happened?" we asked. "Well," he said, "it came from the central office one day with a note that made it mandatory that the principal take the faculty through it. So I called a meeting of the teachers and got them around the table. (Note: the guide was in a red three-ringed binder over 400 pages.) Then I said to the staff, 'Now the purpose of today's meeting is to review the curriculum guide.' Well, they looked at the guide and they looked at the clock and cracked up. What a mess. After that I just dismissed them. That guide," he said, "has been there ever since. In fact, I'd say that guide was an insomniac's dream."

The way most teachers write curriculum guides is to do it in four meetings. The first happens when they meet and decide which districts they will write to get a copy of their curriculum guides. The second happens when they get a few back and get out a large pair of scissors and a big pot of glue and cut and paste and turn it into the typist. The third happens when they look it over, make a few corrections, put their names on the cover, and submit it to the superintendent. The fourth happens when they show up at the board meeting to present the "curriculum." What does the board know? Some can't even spell it! So they bless it and send it out to the rest of the teachers. They use it for a lot of things—paperweights, doorjambs, etc. Or one teacher we met in Hartford, Connecticut told us he had no dust on his curriculum guide because he had kept it in a hermetically sealed file for over ten years. It was in "mint" condition, untouched by human hands!

Over the years we've had to read too many curriculum guides. We've read them, rated them, and ranked them.[14] We've been impressed by their bulk, their vapidity, and their stupefactive impact on teachers. We prefer a lean and mean curriculum guide, one that fits in one's pocket or goes in one's purse. Our motto is that the more important a document is the smaller it gets, not larger.

Furthermore, we would never put curriculum in a three-ringed binder because it gives teachers all the wrong messages. The reason curriculum directors put curriculum in three-ringed binders is that because the curriculum is "always becoming," it is "never done." Can you imagine walking into a busy teacher's class and telling him or her to work this tome to humankind into their lesson plans but remember, "it isn't done yet"? That's one reason teachers don't take all this curriculum guide stuff very seriously. They know if they wait long enough, it *will* go away! That's why the powers that be put it in a three-ringed binder. Who takes seriously something that will change quickly, particularly if it is huge? So, few take time to go through the curriculum guide. It's a waste of time.

Curriculum chicanery is the insidious practice of spending lots of bucks on writing documents no one will read or use. It's spending hours on philosophical harangues and word games that won't make one iota of difference to one child in one classroom, and . . . it's pretending it all will make a difference! That's trickery, subterfuge, a joke! We force teachers to "pretend" that these documents are important and will make a difference. All of the evidence we have seen, the documents we've reviewed, and the teachers we've interviewed plainly show otherwise. Teachers use two things to make decisions about what they teach: their own ideas and the textbook. That's it.

So curriculum people have to come face to face with the facts. Local control of the curriculum in the same sense that there is local control of the budget is non-existent. By "control" we mean a selection of content in classrooms that is in harmony with board policy and with locally developed curriculum guides in terms of which texts and tests have been selected. Normally, textbooks and tests *establish the curriculum*. They lead rather than follow.

## TESTING INSANITY

Statewide testing has become rampant. State after state has moved to expand student testing, particularly in the basic skills. The states are not using new powers. They are using old powers in new ways. State testing is a kind of quality assurance effort to make sure certain curriculum content has been taught at the local level. The state is moving toward conformity via the back door, since to go through the front door would be political suicide.

By the front door, we mean that the state would propose a curriculum to which all districts would agree and teach. That would raise the hackles of all the local educators, politicians, and citizens. So the state bypasses that quagmire and gets the same results via statewide testing. While few locals are against testing, almost all are opposed to a statewide curriculum. But a statewide curriculum is the result. And it is monitored by the state in the cheapest form possible. They don't have to hire umpty-umph supervisors to monitor the state's curriculum; the test does it for every student. The New York Regents Exam has monitored the New York curriculum for over 100 years. Now some thirty additional states have adopted a form of the Regents Exam.

When the test scores of hundreds of school districts are printed on the front pages of the newspapers all around the state, all of the qualitative data is lost, and all of the local contextual variables that impact on the scores in addition to what is going on within the classrooms of the school districts are gone. And then we have the absurdity of superintendents' saying that their districts are providing a Cadillac program to students on a Ford budget if the scores are high.[15] Such statements are fatuous when such tests measure a narrow slice of the curriculum, usually mathematics, language arts (not all areas), and reading. What about the other areas of the curriculum? What about what students bring or do not bring to school in the way of previous skills?

There is the belief that tests in and of themselves will in some magic way bring new rigor to an old curriculum. On standardized tests such an argument or belief is insanity. Such tests do not measure much of any specific local curriculum, so what do they mean? Let's take district "A" and district "B." In district "A" the "Gombah Test" fits only 25 percent of the system's curriculum. In district "B" the match is fully 74 percent. That means that in district "B" 49 percent more of the test is taught than in district "A." By shear exposure alone students in district "B" should do better on the Gombah Test.

If the curriculum content has been taught systematically for mastery in district "B" and at the same methodological level as it is tested, students should do even better (other factors being equal). Testing will never raise curriculum standards unless the testing content is matched with the curriculum content, in which case students are being examined rather than tested.[16] The historic difference between an examination and a test was that the exam was "loaded" to the curriculum that was supposed to be taught and the test was not. That is why we have been warned "not to teach to the test."

As far as we can tell, the only people who ever really got upset with teaching *to the* TEST were the test makers. Why? Because it blows the bell-shaped curve every time! As educators we want a skewed curve to the right. We want all the children learning. Why would we test children on things we had not taught them?

One of the reasons teachers have made little use of standardized tests is that they were never connected to the curriculum. In this case there was very little to do with them instructionally. They could be used to label children. But what do the labels really mean? A norm-referenced test can be valuable to the extent that it measures one's objectives and a school system's curriculum. To the extent that this is true, norm-referenced data tells a school system something meaningful about how well students are learning what they have been taught. From that data we can use the information as feedback and make adjustments in the instructional program. But it really plays havoc with a bell-shaped curve.

Take the typical norm-referenced test which is not directly related to the curriculum (or if it is we're not really sure how or where). We know that Johnny got 91 percent on math and Suzie 85 percent. What does it mean if none of the math was taught in school? What is the school to do with it? Most school districts do only one thing with norm referenced data. They graph it! Then it's given to the board and they comment, "Look at that sucker go down!"

The insanity of testing is that test results, no matter how bad, will not improve learning unless they assess what it is children have been taught. Raising test scores may lead to a concomitant change in the curriculum that is being delivered in the schools. And the madness that comes with test driven curriculum is that the whole curriculum becomes only what is tested. Indeed many schools who historically score at the bottom quartiles of any kind of testing program have little that they can change but the time *within the school day* devoted to what is tested. That, in turn, forces a lot of other things out of the curriculum and leads to a lopsided educational experience for many children whose only experience in any formal sense with the arts and humanities will be in the schools.

The dominant utilitarian value structure of the person in the street is that the schools should teach the basics and with that we don't disagree. However, *when that's all schooling becomes,* we have lost sight of the mission of the schools to develop an educated person. That goal will have been sacrificed in the name of the teeny tiny bits of textbook tedium to which millions of children are tested and re-tested ad nauseam. On the altar of efficiency we will have sacrificed the culture itself.

We are reminded of the memory of school of movie director Steven Spielberg, creator of *E.T.* the all time money maker among films, and *Jaws, Raiders of the Lost Ark, Indiana Jones and the Temple of Doom, Close Encounters of the Third Kind,* and *Gremlins:*

> During class I'd draw a little image on the margin of each page of the history or lit. book and flip the pages to make animated cartoons.[17]

It is within this framework that teachers try to work and not kill the creative spirits of the children in the process. But our mass educational system grinds on and grinds up our youth in the plethora of paperwork in the name of a monolithic curriculum developed for Texas and California and driven by Regents exams from New York as the national model. It is an industrial model gone mad.

## CAVEATS, CODICILS, AND CONUNDRUMS ABOUT TEXTBOOK TYRANNY, CURRICULUM CHICANERY, AND TESTING INSANITY

- A mugwump is an expert who has never done what he or she preaches.
- The textbook is the curriculum in most places; we just pretend it isn't.
- In order for the textbook not to dominate your curriculum, you must develop your curriculum first and adopt your book second.
- Most teachers are subjected to the mushroom theory of administration: "Keep them in the dark and feed them manure."
- No one takes seriously a voluminous document that isn't done yet, particularly someone who is busy.
- Local control of the curriculum is non-existent in most places; it's been traded away with textbook adoptions and test purchasing.
- Testing will not raise curriculum standards unless the testing content is the curriculum content.
- The only thing to do with norm-referenced test data is to graph it.
- When testing becomes all that school is about or can be, we will have sacrificed our children on the altar of efficiency and the culture itself.
- Our mass educational system grinds on and grinds up our youth in the plethora of paperwork in the name of a monolithic curriculum developed for Texas and California and driven by Regents exams from New York as the national model. It is an industrial model gone mad.

# Adversaries and Friends

## CHAPTER 18

# Secretaries and Custodians

## THE "SHADOW" ADMINISTRATORS: SECRETARIES BEHIND THE THRONE

Secretaries in school and school districts are the "shadow" administrators of them. No one else works more closely with the boss, and no one else's daily working relationship is more intimate or unique. No one else sees the number and kind of confidential memos, and is privy to more inside information than a secretary. Secretaries are the equivalent of military cryptographers in school systems. They know the secrets of the inner sanctum. They are often its gatekeepers. You must know the password to get by them. And you must know how to work *with them.*

Unlike the business world, secretaries in schools may often be tenured since most are part of the Civil Service System. Administrators "inherit" secretaries. In most places it is not the secretary adjusting to the boss that is the key; it is the boss being able to understand the importance of the secretary and to work with her (most are female) to run the place that spells success or failure *of the boss* (not the secretary).

When the boss is away, the secretary "stands in" for the boss. She interprets his or her messages. She communicates *intent.* She is your alter ego. Your staff looks to *her* to understand *you.* They *know* her importance. Do you?

A productive relationship with a secretary results in mutual loyalty "above and beyond" merely looking out for one another. Did Rosemary Woods really erase twenty minutes of the famous Watergate tapes by accident? Perhaps we'll never know for sure. We do know that she never denied it or made excuses in an attempt to make herself look good, such as "Mr. Nixon never showed me how to work the tape recorder properly."

A secretary who works for someone who cares about her and whom she *cares about* will stick her neck out when necessary. We know of one incident in one community where the secretary to the boss found out via her "sources" that an influential member of the community who disliked the boss planned to embarrass him at a public board meeting. Carefully covering her "sources' " tracks, she politely told the boss what was going to happen. He did not press too hard because he knew that if her "sources" were revealed, her effectiveness was also diminished. He prepared for the attack. The attacker was defused at the board meeting very skillfully. The "shadow" administrator had struck again!

We don't want to imply that good secretaries are "stool pigeons." We don't advocate that they ever be used that way. What we do advise is that administrators foster a rapport with secretaries in which a productive relationship develops that enhances the organization by making the boss more aware, more sensitive, *and more effective*. To do that requires learning something about the place, importance, and role of secretaries.

### SECRETARIES AS MEDIATORS AND POWER BROKERS

Secretaries are the first line of defense for a school administrator. The angry parent, the irate teacher, the insolent student, or the petulant administrative colleague usually run across the secretary *first* in an effort *to get to you*. How the secretary handles each situation will make what you have to do more or less effective. If she adds fuel to the fire, you have got a more irate teacher. If she further provokes a petulant administrative colleague, you may have an explosion.

Secretaries have got to be skilled. For sure, they must be able to type and do secretarial things well. But more importantly, and critically, they must be able to handle "people" problems with ease, tact, firmness, and fairness. Secretaries are therefore mediators in the "sticky" problems that arrive at your doorstep.

If your secretary doesn't act as if she knows that your image and reputation and, to a large degree, the image and reputation of your school, department, or district is conveyed directly through her, then you'll need to tell her so in a way that she will not only believe it intellectually, but will dress, act, speak, conduct her office, and conduct herself as if she believes it.

If your office seems mismanaged, the message to everyone is that you are a poor manager. Telephones which ring unanswered (usually by the third ring), reports done incorrectly or sloppily, low office morale, an office appearing slovenly and in general disarray reflect badly on the rest of the organization and specifically on the person who is supposed to be in charge.

Physical appearance, "climate control," image, office management, and public relations should be the basic priorities of a good
secretary. Over many years as school and central office administrators we've constructed the matrix below to show off a good
secretary. By her actions, secretaries enhance the boss or detract
from the boss.

---

### SITUATIONS IN WHICH SECRETARIES CAN BE A PLUS OR A MINUS TO THE SCHOOL ADMINISTRATOR

| SITUATION | DETRACTOR | ENHANCER |
|---|---|---|
| 1. The telephone rings | • Sometimes leaves phones uncovered<br>• Lets phones ring too long | • Always sees to it that phones are covered. Always answers by the third ring. |
| 2. Answers the phone | • "Yes" or "Hello" | • "Good morning, Dr. Bingley's Office" |
| 3. Caller "demands" to speak to the boss instantly | • Puts call through | • Politely "screens" the call, discovers nature of business, refers caller to other persons if appropriate, follows the "chain of command." |
| 4. Caller leaves message | • Misses important info such as content of call or phone number or gets it incorrectly. Fails to note time. | • Gets the entire message and all necessary information correctly. Places in a conspicuous place so the boss can find it quickly. |
| 5. Administrator not in office | • "I don't know where he/she is right now, they were just here."<br>• "No, he's (she's) not in yet." | • "Dr. Bingley stepped away from his desk right now, may I help you?"<br>• "Dr. Bingley is in the building. I expect him back shortly. May I take a message?" |

*(continued)*

| SITUATION | DETRACTOR | ENHANCER |
|---|---|---|
| 6. The assistant principal reports to the office and shouts, "What the devil does Bingley want me for now?" | • "Who knows? (rolls her eyes) Be ready for anything. Bingley's in rare form today." | • "Dr. Bingley just wanted to make sure you had enough chaperones for the dance."<br>• With a smile, "Nobody's died yet in the office. I'm sure it's important. Let me see if you can come in?" |
| 7. Staff member who wants to "burn up" the boss's time with idle chit chat—an habitual offender | • "You can run in when the door opens. I expect him out soon." | • "He's tied up. If you can tell me what it's about, maybe I can help." |
| 8. Mail comes | • Opens mail, forgets to stamp important correspondence, or sort neatly into piles. | • Opens mail, sorts it by importance, stamps all mail. Routes some pieces to the proper subordinates. Makes notations where appropriate, such as "Taken care of." |
| 9. Angry parent or staff member wants to blow off steam personally or on the phone | • Refers the problem intact, or exacerbates it. "Mr. Jones is here to see you." | • Interacts with person. Sympathizes. Gets person to see a conference would be more productive after a good night's sleep. |
| 10. Member of the public walks in | • Ignores the person or doesn't notice. Finishes work before paying attention. | • Immediately acknowledges the person's presence with a smile (no matter how pressed) "May I help you?" |

If you want to make a check on how your secretary sounds to others on the phone, call her sometime when she is at her desk. Some administrators have done this and been shocked! While a secretary may be pleasant enough to the boss, when she is interacting with John Q. Public, she may sound differently. Take the telephone test and find out!

Good secretaries are not only cryptographers, unofficially licensed people mediators, they are *power brokers* in the strongest sense of the word.

A "power broker" is someone who channels the authority to make decisons in an organization. Power brokers are people who *make things happen.* They do so by arranging meetings, scheduling events or conferences. In short they bring people together to meet, solve problems, or confront one another. That is a large part of every school administrator's secretary's formal or informal job description. Secretaries are emissaries par excellence. They are diplomats without portfolios. They work the "infrastructure." That is their territory.

The infrastructure is the networking beneath the surface, the informal alliances, the grapevine, the "klatches" at the coffee pot or water cooler. Secretaries know the infrastructure. They talk to one another. As a matter of fact, your boss has already gotten the word about you long before you probably met the boss via the secretarial infrastructure. And your boss is probably getting information about you right now because the reputation and the success of an administrator is carried by your secretary.

That a secretarial infrastructure exists is no secret, but what is uncanny is the accuracy of its perceptions. Perhaps one reason for this accuracy is that secretaries see both sides of most issues. They type the memos their bosses dictate, but they often read the boss's incoming mail (memos in response typed by other members of the infrastructure's bosses). What a memo really meant can be detected in the infrastructure. Infrastructure "memo wars" usually only surface in the infrastructure.

## SECRETARIAL SIGN LANGUAGE EVERYBODY KNOWS

Your secretary communicates with people not only by what she says but with her body language. The rolling of her eyes, shrugging of the shoulders, winking of the eyes, frowning, smiling, and raising of the eyebrows are only a small fraction of the repertoire of messages she sends to people. When these gestures are added to words, they can say something else than the words convey. Often a secretary "cues" the visitor as to how the boss is feeling. If the boss is grumpy because he or she had a flat tire on the way to work or was jumped by an angry parent in the hallway of one of the schools, the first person coming into the office may be in for some static. Watching the secretary's facial cues when you walk in may be a warning that you could be in for trouble.

If the secretary says, "He is just waiting to see you," and grimaces visibly, one knows one is about to be either attacked or shot. One enters the inner sanctum wary. If one is a good friend of the secretary, she has done you a favor. You are forewarned. However, if not a friend, a visitor is given the same cue. Body language and voice intonations are an important part of a secretary's arsenal. Used properly, they are invaluable signals to keep the system running smoothly. Used improperly, they can be arsenic in its table of command.

There are also misuses of a secretary too good-hearted to let you know. For example, having your secretary write "thank you" notes, arranging for trips for one's spouse, and getting a baby-sitter for your night out are unprofessional uses of one's secretary. And these days, most women resent being asked to buy gifts for someone else's spouse or being expected to make coffee. A secretary is not a waitress. Ask your secretary how she feels about these issues before asking her to do them.

Secretaries also cue the boss to important personal things happening to people in the school district. If the wife of a fellow administrator has cancer or a child was hurt or a teacher is going through a divorce with a lot of personal stress, these are important human messages that sometimes get lost in bureaucratic structures. Secretaries carry such information. Such infrastructure data can increase your sensitivity to the human dynamics of the school system.

Secretaries who "keep to themselves" and "mind their own business" are not assets to the school administrator. Many able-bodied high school graduates can type and take dictation. With a little training they can answer the phone properly. The real value of a secretary is her prestige and stature in the infrastructure. Her human relations skills must be superb, adult to adult.

A school administrator who only sees a secretary as a typist, stenographer, file clerk, receptionist, or telephone operator is not only narrow-minded, but may wonder, when he or she is ambushed somewhere in the organization, why they weren't warned first. Chances are your secretary knew about it beforehand. She just didn't know you well enough to tell you. *So who is the loser?*

### THE REAL BASICS ARE ALWAYS CUSTODIAL

Next to secretaries, custodians are about the most valuable support people in the school. Most often they are men, but not exclusively. Sometimes called "janitors" they can be observed sweeping, cleaning, polishing, digging, fixing, spraying, carrying, moving all kinds of objects, dusting, dumping trash cans, brushing, scrubbing, painting, replacing broken this and that, and interacting with staff and kids.

Custodians are not lowly people. *They are people.* The best ones run their schools as if the entryway to your office was their own living room. A bit of graffiti in the bathroom is a personal insult. A ground crayola on a waxed floor was done in their kitchen. In short, a custodian who treats your school as their own is one who takes pride in the cleanliness of odor-free hallways, restrooms, classrooms, faculty rooms, labs, locker rooms, showers, art rooms, and stock rooms.

Custodians we know who make a difference know the kids and the teachers. They go out of their way to help teachers build and maintain safe environments for kids. They fix things. Classrooms are always spotless. Spilled paint, ink, grease, paste, chemicals are gone overnight.

Those kinds of custodians are always busy. You will never find them in the boiler room playing cribbage with the boys. The day is never long enough. They never have enough time, enough paint, enough supplies, enough equipment. They want more so they can do more.

Organizations filled with people six or more hours each day, hundreds of people eating and moving about and doing all the things people do become messy. And there is always mischief with kids. When the girls' restroom has wads of toilet paper stuck to the ceiling, when some student has gotten sick in the hallway all over five lockers, when another student cut himself and bled to the nurse's office, when a student with a magic marker engraved obscenities all over the cafeteria tables, who do we call? *The grime busters!*

We know custodians that have cleaned up after dances, fights, parties, food fights, flu outbreaks, and we even watched one with tears in his eyes pour sawdust on a pool of blood and scrub it down after a student was killed by a car just twenty minutes before in front of the school.

The key person who works with custodians is the chief custodian. Chief custodians can make things happen that no one else can. They can be human magicians in a school. They can also block things from happening. They can be whiners and moaners who are never around when you need them. They find a thousand reasons why the room was not set up for the Curriculum Council, why the gum was left on the hardwood floor, why burned out light bulbs are not replaced, why there is no toilet paper in the bathroom stalls, and why the place looks filthy and unkempt.

Unless your chief custodian is a fireball himself or at least someone who can get his crew to attend to the custodial needs of the building or the district adequately, you won't be able to make much else happen. A trashed out school is an advertisement for an ineffective one. It doesn't matter if anything else is happening, the stain of the mess leaves a bad impression on anyone entering it.

Take early and careful stock of your chief custodian. If he is incompetent and can't change or won't change, he's got to go. If he is a blocker, a person who always finds a reason why it can't be done, and he can't change or won't change, he's got to go!

There are countless ways to make your chief's job unbearable so that retirement, transfer, or even resignation looks more attractive. We blame their former administrators who tolerated messy schools and who didn't care enough to keep schools clean. Ineffective custodians work for administrative wimps. If you can't keep the school clean, chances are you are not able to improve the learning in it either. So who needs you?

We emphasize the chief custodian must be your chief because there is a difference between the chief custodian being *your chief* or being *the chief*. The chief custodian is *your* chief if he enhances *your leadership* of the school. If he is *the* chief, he doesn't work for you or even with you. His allegiances, and probably his time, lie elsewhere. He is collecting his paycheck.

The chief custodian must first know you *care* about the way the school looks and you hold him responsible for it. We know of one rare high school principal who had worked as a custodian when he was in college at night. In his first principalship, he spent two nights working with his new custodial crews on all of the tasks they did. Then he redesigned their routines based on first-hand knowledge. No one can tell him the job can't be done—because he did it. His school is spotless. He won't tolerate anything less. The men know he notices what they do and don't do. No excuses.

Bureaucratically, secretaries and custodians don't appear on most organizational charts. But the school administrator who doesn't know that they are important is not going very far in the business. These are the "little" "big people" who make schools effective or ineffective. You won't learn anything about them in courses in school administration in schools of education. Nobody has written a book about school secretaries or school custodians for potential administrators. Seasoned school leaders know only too well their importance.

## CAVEATS, CODICILS, AND CONUNDRUMS ABOUT SECRETARIES AND CUSTODIANS

- Secretaries are the cryptographers of school systems.
- The secretary is a "stand-in" for the boss.

- Secretaries are the first line of defense for a school administrator.
- If your office is mismanaged, the message to everyone is that you are a poor manager.
- Secretaries are emissaries par excellence. They are diplomats without portfolios.
- Everybody who reads your secretary's body language know's what mood you're in today.
- Secretaries do professional work; domestics do chores.
- Did Rosemary Woods really draw a blank—or did she take a fall?
- When the power behind the boss is the boss's secretary—that's power!
- An administrator's first order of business is to gain the confidence of his/her secretary.
- The "front office" is not a front; it's *the* organization as most people know it.
- Nobody can make you or break you like your secretary—nobody.
- Have you smiled at your secretary today?
- The real basics are always custodial.
- The best custodians run your school like it was their own home.
- When a student gets sick in the hall, slops ink on the walls, whom do we call? *The grime busters!*
- The chief custodian is *your chief* or there are too many chiefs in your school.
- Ineffective custodians work for administrative wimps.
- If you can't keep the school clean, chances are you are not able to improve learning in it either; so who needs you?

## CHAPTER 19

# Unions

We once asked an experienced labor negotiator for management, the senior partner in one of the nation's leading law firms, what the difference was between the AFT and the NEA. He paused, then snorted sardonically, "That's sort of like having to choose between syphillis and gonorrhea."

We know a lot of superintendents who feel the same way. Nobody likes unions in administration, but like warts, obesity, freckles, and hangnails, they are part of the real world of the school administrator. They won't go away and they can't be controlled by administrators. About the only thing one can do with unions is to learn to live with them. You don't have to ever *like them*, but you will have to learn to work *with them*.

## THE AVON LADY IS CALLING: COSMETIC VS CUSTODIAL ROLES

There *is* only one union which has always been and acted like one. That's the American Federation of Teachers (AFT). Founded by two women in March of 1897, the Chicago Teachers Federation (CTF) was the product of the apron strings of Catherine Goggin and Margaret Haley.[1] Unlike the Avon Lady, Goggin and Haley not only rang door bells, they knocked doors down! Within three years of aggressive work, half of Chicago's teachers were unionized.

The CTF was instrumental in killing certain laws in the Illinois legislature that would have changed the schools of Chicago. The CTF was forward-looking. For example, it supported such issues as:

- women's suffrage,
- direct primaries,
- the popular election of U.S. Senators,
- municipal ownership of public utilities.

The CTF was also active in passing the Illinois Child Labor Law of 1903. Meanwhile the NEA (National Education Association) was firmly in the hands of professors, college presidents, and school superintendents. At that time there was no division for classroom teachers in the NEA[2] let alone one for a woman as a voting member. So the NEA was the "good ole boy" network of its day. It never became militant until forced to do so by the AFT's blitz of the cities beginning with New York.

We've negotiated with both the NEA and AFT. We've found laggards in both groups and occasionally officials or negotiators of great skill, insight, and idealism. While the AFT is tougher on bread and butter issues, our experience is that the *union* understands the role of management and doesn't really want to manage. The AFT's bottom line is always salaries and working conditions.[3]

On the other hand, many of the NEA types want the salaries, but they also want to run your job. The NEA would be *both* management and labor if it could. This makes bargaining with the NEA an exercise in dealing with a person who has a severe identity problem. This brings them into more conflict with administrators over non-salary issues. Both groups will strike. Both know how to play dirty pool and both groups are so involved in politics at the state and national levels that it's hard to tell them apart at times.

For example, in Kentucky, after a "reform" piece of legislation was finally passed in the Senate, Senator Joe Travis noted, "All we ever do is grease those squeaking wheels. I sometimes wonder how President Lincoln ever got elected without the KEA" (Kentucky Education Association, an affiliate of the NEA).[4]

A dispute in Massachusetts reveals the influence of the Massachusetts Teachers Association in electing Governor Michael S. Dukakis. Carol Doherty, once president of the MTA, was promoted to head a state-supported center to study strategies for improving public schools following Governor Dukakis' election. However, she was fired shortly after that along with her deputy. She wrote a letter to the MTA which stated, "It is apparent that the governor has not fulfilled his pledge to teachers."[5]

So today, the Avon Lady is a seasoned politician and savvy infighter in Congressional halls and in state capitals and powwows. As the legislative lobbyist for the AFT once explained to us, "I tell the legislators who don't support us, we don't get mad, we get even."

Alice Harden, the leader of Mississippi's wildcat strike, in which the Mississippi lawmakers suffered the wrath of the 14,000 member teachers association after giving themselves a raise and denying one to teachers, suffered fines and two suspended jail sentences. The former junior high school teacher of science said, "I'm a product of schools in Mississippi. When I tell you what's wrong with the public schools, I know what I'm talking about. This may not be the last strike of teachers that you see.''[6]

## UNION TACTICS AND VICTIMS

Unions have never led the way for education innovation or serious reform. They are conservative by nature and in order to wield influence they must come to terms with where the power lies in any community. If those in power are corrupted, so eventually are the unions who depend upon that power to deliver what is promised in negotiations.

Unions are therefore not champions of justice and truth in a vacuum, though they may start out that way. If the only card game in town is crooked and one has to play, that's what will be done. In this sense, unions are normally quite realistic. While they may back an opposing candidate for the city council or school board, once in power they will try to work with the elected person. Most unions don't have a long memory because there is always the next contract to be negotiated with whomever is in power. So the school administrator can never trust or count on the union because loyalty is always *issue specific*. The administrator is balancing the best interests of the school or school district with many other interests. The union has no such obligation or mission. A union is loyal only to its membership and their aggregate needs and usually the lowest common denominator of their fears and biases.

The school administrator should never be afraid of working with the union "pros." The "pros" we've met and fought with understand fully what your problems are with boards and politics, and if you think you know some of your teachers are real SOB's, the union knows them, too. Nine times out of ten, a teacher "thorn in your side" has already been one in the union's side. Professional union organizers know the foibles and frailties of their own ranks better than most administrators because they have to. Whereas administrators, especially the superintendent, must know the eccentricities of the board before those of the teachers, the union people we've watched screw up the process were the rank amateurs because they didn't understand the eccentricities of their own rank and file. Especially irritating are those teachers who come to the bargaining table and want to use it as a platform to solve all the social ills of the world, instead of as a place to hammer out salaries and working conditions.

Or the teacher who negotiates for a five-cent increase in hourly extra duty pay, who is "insulted" when the board will only pay four cents because they (the board) don't appreciate what a "professional" will do. It never occurs to these amateurs that if teachers were professional, they wouldn't even be talking about five cents and the only reason the board offered four cents was because they insisted on talking about it.

There can be little doubt that teacher unions have met legitimate needs in improving salaries and working conditions in the schools. Tangible gains were achieved that would not have been given by shortsighted boards or penurious superintendents. But sometimes a kind of creeping union mentality sets into a school system, and this has been the cause of more than one program's decline.

We can think of numerous examples where systems trying to engage in staff development were hindered by contractual constipation. A guest speaker who exceeds the forty-five minute stipulated contractual length for a meeting sees half the teacher audience leave because he exceeded the time allotted. Some contracts allow the meeting to be extended only by majority vote of the faculty. We were amused to note in one case where, after being informed of a bomb threat, one faculty debated for over thirty minutes, and voted seventeen to fifteen to adjourn with nine abstentions!

The union mentality of "I won't do one extra thing around here unless I'm paid to" has ruined many excellent schools and extracurricular activities programs for children. A true professional looks at the total job and puts in the hours necessary to get it done. A union person is concerned only with the hours and doesn't care if the job gets done. This approach is antithetical to "we want to be treated like professionals" (but paid like an employee on an eight-hour day and for overtime, too).

Teachers can't have it both ways. Unions in education have stood as barriers to the full professionalization of the teaching profession by blocking the emergence of a senior cadre of professionals.[7]

### LIVING, LOVING, AND LAUGHING WITH UNIONS

The smart administrator knows that the teachers' union is another administrative arm of the school system. After both sides have signed off on the contract, the union must enforce the contract along with the administration. Instead of just the principal and other administrators, the schools now have building representatives (shop stewards) who also enforce the contract. The reason is not hard to discern. As grievances come to be filed, the *past practice* of the parties defines the meaning of their words in the contract. If one party allows the other to act in a way inconsistent with what they think that section meant, they agree with the action by default.

For example, if the union watches the administration implement a certain contractual clause it believes to be wrong, it is forfeiting its chance to assert its meaning if it fails to grieve such actions. Any arbitrator will look for past practice as the guide for what the parties meant when they signed the contract.[8] Therefore, the union watches and reminds teachers of what is proper in a contract. The trick is getting good language into the contract that both parties must enforce.

## GRIEVANCES AND ARBITRATION

The teachers' union has two weapons in balancing administrative power. The first is the strike to compel agreement to a contract. The second is the grievance procedure cemented with binding third party arbitration. What this means is that an outsider, an arbitrator, will decide with FINALITY what the parties meant when they signed a contract.

Normally the union grieves an action of the administration as not being consistent with the provisions of the contract. The union files a grievance and it is processed through a series of levels ending before an arbitrator.

To be prepared for an arbitration means going to court. It means there will be evidence, witnesses, cross-examination, and summation. Legal briefs may be filed. Then the arbitrator rules. Arbitrators are not seeking for truth. They are searching for what the parties meant when they signed a contract. An arbitrator is searching for a solution that will satisfy both parties. Sometimes it is impossible.

### Some Tips About Arbitrations

When a school system has a lot of arbitration, both the union's and the district's lawyers will track arbitrators, i.e., note how many times an arbitrator has found for the union or for a board. Picking one is sort of like following race horses. Arbitrators who have done poorly by either side are scratched from the acceptable list at a later date.

The basic rule of the proceedings is that if the arbitrator likes the grievant, the odds are greatly enhanced that the arbitrator will find for the union. If not, he or she will find for the board. So the trick is to establish the administration as "very reasonable" and the grieving teacher as a curmudgeon.

This can be done in direct testimony and cross-examination. While the teacher is generally given every benefit of doubt, if the teacher is perceived as *frivolitigiously* inclined, an arbitrator can be turned off from the beginning.

The second point about arbitrators is that if the district has protected the due process rights of the teacher, the arbitrator will be reluctant to substitute his or her judgment for the administration, even if the union can prove another, alternative course of action was indeed better. Most arbitrators know any administrative action can be second-guessed forever, always with hindsight. So don't worry, you don't have to be "right" to win. You do have to provide the teacher with every opportunity to be heard and not be shanghaied.

*Two Basic Approaches to Arbitration*

There are two different approaches to arbitration. The first we call "stonewalling." This means that as the grievant proceeds up the levels of the grievance procedure ladder towards arbitration, at each rung the administration merely says "grievance denied." No reasons or rationale is ever given so no card in the administration's hand is ever revealed. Some educational lawyers like this approach because it means during arbitration they can use any argument or line of attack at the union as a weapon of surprise without inhibition.

However, there are distinct disadvantages to this approach. The first is that *everything* winds up in arbitration. Legal costs what they are, a completed arbitration may cost between $3000 and $5000 per case. In addition, the administration may have to pay any backpay or other fine if they "lose." Since the grievance has not really been processed up the ladder, the arbitrations take longer and become costlier.

The other approach to looking at grievance is the "full hearing at each rung" tack. This means a full, fair hearing is held at each level. The issues, facts, and evidence are weighed fresh at each level. As such, the administration shucks its losers early in the game when it is clear it goofed or cannot sustain its position on past practice or some other basis.

This prevents many grievances from reaching arbitration and those that do are processed more quickly because the issues have been well-defined at lower levels. Similarly, the board's attorney is constrained to arguments on the evidence as heard at the lower levels, and his case will rest on that evidence. Some attorneys don't like the constraints.

The advantage to this second approach is that it keeps the administration honest. A full hearing puts everyone on notice that an egregious administrative faux pas will not be stoutly defended against all odds. Such actions force the administration to examine its actions thoroughly at every level. Furthermore, we believe that is what a grievance procedure is all about. Used properly the grievance procedure is a wonderful safety valve to keep potential sparks from becoming general conflagrations, and while the grievance machinery can be clogged with the staff kooks and crazies flailing at ghosts and goblins of persecution, at least it ensures they remain harmless. The grievance procedure prevents the kooks from pumping the grapevine full of rumors, lies, innuendos, and distortions, and riling everyone up. Even though the faculty kooks burn up hundreds of hours of union and administrative time, the grievance procedure minimizes the deleterious impact to the rest of the school system. In this respect, it's kind of like *damage control.*

### THE GODFATHER: UNDERSTANDING UNION LEADERS

Some superintendents look on union leaders as little more than paid pimps for the union cause. In turn, union leaders look on superintendents as plantation owners and principals and other administrators as cronies and stooges. Often valuable conversation and communication is lost because of these two stereotypes.

Administrators should know some things about union leaders. Smart unions have smart leaders and union leadership is generally more demanding than administrative leadership simply because most teacher union leaders rest on a power base less stable than that of superintendents. Many union leaders have only their brains, cunning, and charisma as political tools. They have no contracts and no guarantees. They learn to live close to their constituencies and particularly the emotional issues which move the masses to action.

Union leadership understands gut issues. They know how to say things to their teacher colleagues to get them hopping mad or cool them out. They have to, to survive. So, look at your union leader as a savvy, tough infighter who understands the fine art of politics and generally you won't underestimate them.

From this perspective, union leaders are generally more realistic about politics than most educational administrators. They will settle for incremental steps towards goals they feel are important rather than the "all or nothing" attitude. Smart union leaders don't pick fights they can't win because, like the administrator, they can't afford to lose too many. This doesn't mean they won't toss a few barbs at you from time to time to show their own troops they're "vigilent and virulent." As long as you know the difference and don't take it personally, you will avoid unnecessary skirmishing. The administrator should not rise to every occasion when poked by a union leader. Otherwise, you will be baited all the time. And no matter how big and strong their union is, they will always pretend they are David peering at Goliath. They will always label any action they don't like as "union busting."

Union leaders depend upon the spoils system in-house. Those who backed them and are "in" get the spoils, such as choice committee assignments with travel privileges or paid posts on negotiating teams. Patronage works in unions as it does anywhere else. Union leaders are like Godfathers (or Godmothers as it were). They will do teachers some favors in return for their votes or support at union election time.

The school administrator should understand that unions play favorites in the same way he or she does. Sometimes the same teachers get rewarded by both, but more often than not, the union taps a different level of teacher leadership. Sure they have toadies and groupies and gripers. They also have some of the real teacher leadership of the school system who don't admire administrators or want to be one. And what's critical for you to understand is that your faculty will listen to them and trust them more than they will listen to or trust you.

Most of your teachers can discern the union hacks from the true leadership. If the true informal teacher leadership cadre are also solid union card carriers, the administration faces a formidable obstacle on most every count. And if the teacher union leader is the true teacher leader, that person is a force to be reckoned with.

If all is quiet and the administration has not riled teachers up, union leadership will limp along without a cause until you give them one. The worst enemy of school administrators is not teacher unions by themselves. When teachers revolt, it's because of miscalculations by the administration that set off a chain reaction of union countermeasures which are predictable.[9] Unions thrive on adversity; they hate too much harmony.

When union leadership is not strong, the administration may be tempted to make them look bad in a dogfight. Do so at your own risk. If you discredit the union leadership too much too often, they will be replaced. Then you will be facing a stronger, not a weaker, adversary. So, if you've got a pliable and positive union, it's to your benefit to make them look good by letting them win a round or two now and then so they can keep face with their own rank and file. Knock out the leadership and the next group may be real guerillas (or gorillas, depending upon how you spell it).

"Winning" is not being all powerful and getting your way all the time. And remember to separate *teachers* from *teachers' unions*. The administrator who fails to grasp this fundamental fact will make every teacher a foe. There are more of them than us. We like the words of the late Paul Salmon, Executive Director of AASA, on this point when he said, "Teachers are never the enemies, but teacher unions make worthy adversaries." Unions are here to stay. Stop worrying about them and work with them. It will never be a love affair. Only a marriage of convenience.

### CAVEATS, CODICILS, AND CONUNDRUMS ABOUT UNIONS

• Like warts, obesity, freckles, and hangnails, unions are part of the real world for the school administrator.
• The AFT's bottom line is salaries and working conditions.
• Bargaining with the NEA is an exercise in schizophrenia—they would be both labor and management if they could.
• Most unions don't have a long memory; they will deal with whomever is in power.
• Union loyalty is always issue specific and has nothing to do with you.
• Most teacher unions want to be treated like a white collar professional, but paid like a blue collar employee with overtime, too.
• In terms of contract enforcement, the union is another arm of the administration.
• If the arbitrator likes the teacher grievant, you have probably lost the case.
• You don't have to be right to "win" at arbitration; you do have to provide every opportunity for the teacher to be heard.
• The administration should shuck its losers early, way down on the grievance procedure ladder.
• Most of your teachers know the difference between a union hack and your true faculty leadership.
• Remember to separate the difference between teachers and teachers' unions. Make every teacher an enemy at your own risk.

## CHAPTER 20

# The Lunatic Fringe

Every school system has within its boundaries an assortment of wackos and flakes that consume an enormous amount of administrative time, sometimes drive teachers up the walls, and make a tatters of the best planned board meetings. We can think of the following real events that have happened to us in our careers:

- a mother who objected to having her son exposed to sex education in the fifth grade, but had no problems with the fact she was painted in the nude in a portrait that hung over the mantle in their home;
- a man who had sued everyone around, the police department, his own minister, and who was bringing a suit against a teacher for not grading homework given to his child;
- a woman who scanned all of the school libraries and objected to all books about witchcraft;
- a mother who continually requested to see all records kept about her son and who believed there were always "secret" records kept somewhere;
- a citizen who read everything published by the district so he could find spelling errors and write derogatory letters to the editor and point these mistakes out along with the high salaries paid to school administrators who couldn't spell.

## PRUDES, CENSORS, WACKOS, AND BIRCHERS

Prudes and censors are out to keep the ugly part of life and living from their or other people's children. Something in a textbook or a library book is found offensive, so they petition to have it removed, protest at a board meeting, write letters to the editor, badger school administrators, or publish their own newsletter blasting the books.

Gone are the days when all an administrator heard about was J. D. Salinger's *Catcher in the Rye*. During the 1984–85 academic year, objections to books and content in curricula were lodged in forty-six states.[1] It has gotten to the point where some parents object not to the content of the material per se, but to the author who may have written some other material that was offensive.[2] This moves the objection from the material to the author per se.

In Palm Beach County, Florida, one parent objected to a school book *Let's Talk About Health* because it contained passages dealing with abortion, homosexuality, and selecting a life style. This parent was instrumental in getting out 350 people who stormed a board meeting carrying signs quoting from the Bible.[3]

In Radnor, Pennsylvania, a mother objected to Richard Wright's *Black Boy* because it was "the pits." She complained bitterly on the front page of the *Philadelphia Inquirer* about a disease in the schools called "secular humanism."[4]

Phyllis Schlafly's *Eagle Forum* developed a long list of "objectionable practices" in the schools following the passage of the Hatch Act. The list was in the form of a letter to any school board president. It specifically states that no materials, curricula, textbooks, AV materials, or supplementary assignments of any kind be given without prior approval of the parent.

Specifically the Schlafly letter objects to values clarification of any kind, discussion of religious or moral standards, discussions of suicide, death or dying, alcohol and drugs, nuclear war or nuclear policy, discussions of witchcraft or Eastern mysticism, autobiographical assignments, log books, diaries, or personal journals.[5]

The Schlafly intrusion into the curriculum is a full-scale assault on the capability of teachers to deal with anything in the way of attitudes and their development in children. Attitude development is the heart of teaching. It is the essence of making teaching the dynamic, human enterprise that it is. In September of 1985, *USA Today* ran a special feature of "10 Great Teachers." These teachers were highlighted and given space to explain their unusual ability to deal with children and help them find success.

The overwhelming message from these teachers was that they cared and they changed attitudes about learning, school, life, and work. P. J. Jackson, a teacher in Morgan Park High School, says, "It may sound corny, but I incorporate love." Richard Myers teaches politics at Clearlake Elementary School in Brevard County through a political convention of the Bull Moose Party. Diane Moore in Tulsa, Oklahoma, started a "We Are the World" hunger studies curriculum now being used in 400 school districts around the nation.[6]

Every one of these teachers is dealing with attitudes and would be violative of the Schlafly "guidelines." Good teachers, let alone great teachers, could not survive the censors in the schools. The National School Boards Association has written members of Congress and warned them that the Schlafly "guidelines" would have a "chilling effect on the teacher/student relationship."[7] As many experienced school administrators and teachers will testify, sometimes the children who are in most need of love and understanding are the very ones whose parents are most afraid of exposing them to it in school. These parents fear a loss of their children. They are afraid of being questioned by their own children about values they hold and don't want questioned because they aren't sure they can defend them.

So down deep the prude, the wacko, the censor, and the Birchers are full of fear and doubt. They are dangerous because their fears are not rational, which may explain their aversion to psychological and psychiatric examinations of any kind. And as many school administrators who have dealt with them will testify, they are ruthless in the social and political arenas.

Our advice for the school administrator is that you stand as the first line of defense against the lunatic fringe from mucking around in your curriculum and your school. Successful administrators do several things to protect their schools against the wackos and nuts of the world.

## (1) Install Thorough Procedures for Handling Complaints

A good paper system of forms and committees constitutes a sound defense that will impersonalize the venom of the censor. People who object to a book, a passage, a practice, or the study of something must state their objections in writing. They must actually read the material and extrapolate what they find objectionable. It must be within the context of what is going on in the school and not whatever they "imagine" it to be in their own minds.

Then the written objection must be processed through a committee. We would suggest that the committee be composed of teachers, parents, and at the secondary level, some students as well. This committee examines the complaint, reviews the nature of the curriculum and the context of the teaching, and gives a recommendation to the principal. Then the principal reviews it and it is sent on to a district committee and then perhaps to the superintendent.

## (2) Brief the Staff on the Presence of the Objectors

As the administrator, one must make the staff aware of the presence of objections and those who are objecting. This should be done calmly and without forcing anyone to change anything. Assure the staff that you will be solidly behind them. Be sure what your school is doing is within state law, board policy, and district guidelines. If it is, no teacher can be singled out for breaking anything. The fight will be fought at higher levels over the policy, the guidelines, or the law.

(3) Expose the Wackos

The more zany and eccentric the wackos, the more you want to expose them to the populace. They are their own worst enemy. Invite them to come and speak to your PTA (with the consent of the PTA) or come to a board meeting. This exposes them to the media and to the citizens of the community. The last thing one wants is to fight a zealot alone. The more irrational they are, the more exposure you must give them. If necessary, the administrator must invent forums for them to be heard. It may be a long process and certainly one to try one's patience. But remember, the process of exposure is keeping them away from the teachers and the curriculum, the real targets of their wrath.

(4) Remain Vigilant

The book burners, the flakes, the censors are always out there. We have met a lot of them over the years. Some of them sort of self-destruct over time or run afoul of the law. We can think of one self-proclaimed patriot in Arizona who saw a Commie under every book cover in the schools. After surviving numerous attacks, our modern day Minuteman was arrested by the I.R.S. for failure to pay his taxes because he was opposed to Social Security. It was the only time we ever cheered the I.R.S.!

### THE LAST CRUSADE: THE RELIGIOUS FANATICS

Public school people are confronted with a cresting tide of religious fanaticism that seeks to remove anything that exists in their schools that would lead a student to learn how to think. Students are not supposed to think. They are not to question. They are to be *told!* Just as Socrates was accused of corrupting the values of Greek youth for daring them to question the established order, so public school teachers and administrators stand accused by the religious fanatics.

The Jerry Falwell types of the country pander to the need of some of the populace for certainty, not relative certainty, but *absolute certainty!* And as our world becomes more unstable with the possibility of nuclear holocaust, scientific data on shifting geological land forms and ice ages, which have caused huge upheavals in the past, demonstrate that the earth is anything but a block of granite.

To promise the insecure absolute certainty in return for absolute faith is the medium of exchange for the fanatic. It's a cheap promise. Nobody can ever prove anybody else is a liar when it's made.

But the one thing a fanatic cannot tolerate is doubt. To doubt, which is the genesis of the thinking process, particularly in science, is itself *a sin*. So we must not doubt, *ever!* No matter what facts cascade upon us, the doubters are the ones who are wrong.

Those who require the security of certainty are themselves the most serious doubters and have the greatest personal need for the antidote. So a religious fanatic begins with the assumption of the gospel of inerrancy, which means anything described in the Bible happened as stated, no more and no less. There are no symbols, no allegories or allusions, or actors. Everything said and done is fact.

Naturally, one of the first clashes over inerrancy occurred over the theory of evolution in science. Such an idea strikes at the heart of Biblical history. First with the famous Scopes "monkey trial" in 1925 and later with "creationism" there has been repeated and numerous attempts to displace evolution with creationism in schools. Despite the fact that the courts have repeatedly ruled that creationism is not science and not a theory,[8] evolution has been downplayed in the textbooks to the point where a California text-book panel urged rejection of all science books because they treated evolution inadequately.[9]

The quest for certainty means that no school subject or teacher can or should motivate a child to consider an alternative to his/her parents' values or phobias. Teachers should reinforce the parents' values, not cause skepticism about them. So the fanatics have prob-lems with any curriculum that comes a cropper of the kernels of doubt that the values espoused by them are not real, are not true, and are not absolute. Anything short of unquestioning acceptance is amoral. Relativity of any kind is, therefore, amoral by definition because it admits to the possibility of error. If there are no errors in one's beliefs, any other idea is heresy.

And so it has been through the ages. Science was once the pawn of the magicians, soothsayers, and astrologers. Yet science belongs to no one, for it is human inquiry and because of the myriad of forms it takes. But the soil of science is *doubt*.

Hard science is rarely the subject of vilification by the fanatics. It is in the realm of the social sciences that the greatest controversies abound. Few fanatics will want to ban the chemistry textbook. A lot will have trouble with psychology, sociology, or anthropology text-books. These are the sciences that attempt to apply science directly to human behavior and probe behind human beliefs and actions. Sowing the seeds of doubt about human behavior is hardly a popular cause, especially to those who believe doubt is a sin. When the tenets of science deal with the value base of opinions held near and dear and inviolate by the devout, they are condemned. Today such practices are labeled as "secular humanism."[10] This is a code word that means there is something in the school or the curriculum that threatens the infallibility of the value held by the fanatic.

The public schools' value to a pluralistic society is that they belong to no group exclusively, just like America. It is neither "value-free," which would be an absurdity in contradiction, nor does it embrace as true any specific value except inquiry. The fact that the public schools did not always do this prompted the Catholics to leave them in great numbers and ultimately form their own system of schools. Is it any wonder, when the textbooks of that day taught that "Catholics are necessarily, morally, intellectually, infallibly a stupid race?"[11]

The public schools are vulnerable to attacks by fanatics since they cannot counterattack generally and do not have a unitary value base to use as a defensive strategy because of the pluralistic composition of their clientele. A student body of broad protestantism, Catholics, Jews, Buddhists, Muslims, and agnostics cannot use the faith of any exclusively. Such a student body can only be defended under one common roof.

The very nature of a pluralistic student body prevents the public school from forming a tight defensive line against the fanatics. The public school is secular because it is the only way it can be functional with the clientele it must by law serve. By protecting the full range of student values by not offending them, it places the institution in the position of belonging to no one's God. That conversely offends the fanatics for not reinforcing their perceived divine destiny in the world and, of course, corrupting their children with exposure to alternatives.

School administrators have not, in general, been well prepared for these attacks. Fighting a religious war is a "lose–lose" proposition on any front. Most public school administrators would walk a country mile to avoid this kind of fight. We think that posture is a mistake, especially given the concerted attack on the public schools by such groups as the Moral Majority of Jerry Falwell and others.

We recommend a strategy based on demonstrating the diversity of the responsibility of the public schools to educate children of all faiths, including the faithless. Any school administrator who has ever had to deal with the intensity of religious sensitivities will agree that the first line of defense is to protect the rights of all of the children to believe in their chosen way in an atmosphere of mutual respect.

We've had to adjudicate sessions where children of Jehovah's Witnesses wept in our offices as their classmates cut out Christmas trees, where Hindus were offended at the sight of eating a turkey at Thanksgiving, where some Jews found the three wise men offensive. We have been dumbfounded that some people want the right to celebrate at the expense of the distress and discomfort of others. It is so easy for the joy of one group's celebration to be the chains of persecution of another. Too easy.

The fanatics would destroy the public schools as we know them. The overarching value that the public schools should at least be neutral in matters of the observance of holidays and celebration would become lost in the slavish adoption of a majority, moral or not. As long as one child's religious beliefs are transgressed by the others' for any reason, the public schools have failed that child.

The full-scale onslaught on the public schools amounts to a crusade against a fragile compromise of administering a system of schools designed to serve all, but which belong to no one ideology or belief except one—to protect *all* against the persecutions of the others *in any form.*

Those who advocate prayer in the schools fail to understand the extreme sensitivity of the religious experience, the privacy of religious passion, the intimacy of one's relationship to the Almighty. As a polyglot nation of religious peoples from around the world, most of whom have known persecution, the schools' ''secular humanism'' is the umbrella under which all can be free to pursue the sacred. When the schools are assaulted as being amoral and godless, they are neither. They are morally sensitive and respectful of each person's right to believe and worship as his or her conscience may dictate. As such, the teachers, the curriculum, the procedures, the methodology must remain above censorship by the views of any of the particular groups served by the schools.

The Schlafly people would substitute *their* values and fears for those precise values that protect every citizen's child against religious persecution. Schools are not value-free places. Before we displace one set of values with another, we must examine the proposed alternative carefully.

### THE ASSASSINS—WHEN THE BULLETS ARE REAL

No one doubts that reality is at hand when a fanatical Muslim's car bombs the U.S. Embassy and kills 250 U.S. Marines. School administrators face the equivalent fanatics every day, whose bullets are rumors, innuendos, distortions, and outright character assassination.

In Red Lion, Pennsylvania, a school teacher has sued 113 people, including the Red Lion Citizens for Decency, three ministers, and the Pennsylvania Roundtable, a conservative organization, for defamation, invasion of privacy, interference with a contractual relationship, and intentional infliction of emotional distress. These people had contended that the teacher had "promoted" homosexuality and premarital sex in the teaching of health.[12]

In Connecticut, a student suicide focused the wrath of the local minister on the policy of the board of education to permit the playing of the game Dungeons and Dragons at the high school. A petition of some 450 signatures demanded that the board withdraw the right of students to play Dungeons and Dragons. Said a spokesperson for the Christian Information Council, "Playing these games can desensitize players to murder, suicide, rape, torture, robbery, the occult, or any other immoral or illegal act."[13] The Board was unimpressed. The evidence indicated the student had been involved with drugs and that that was the factor, not the board game. Students at Putnam High School can still play Dungeons and Dragons today.

We know school administrators who have been tracked by wacko groups. We know of one who moved over 2,000 miles from one job to another. When the school board president of the new district got a call from an unidentified resident that the newly hired administrator was a "registered Communist," the board president asked for his dossier (which the man claimed to have). It never arrived. Fringe fighters are used to the smear campaign attack. It's one of the dirtiest games in town.

**THE POWER OF HUMOR**

The one weapon the school administrator has that is universal and understood by almost everyone is *humor*. And the one thing that the fanatics have is *no sense of humor*, especially about themselves. A person without a sense of humor has no perspective. They are unable to juxtapose their position or viewpoint with any other and to note discrepancies. The essence of humor occurs in this juxtaposition since many jokes end in surprises. The surprise is the unanticipated, the imperfection in human beings. But the fanatic is perfect, so nothing is humorous.

For example, the elementary school principal who had a problem with students. He used to play hide-and-go-seek with them but gave it up when nobody came and looked for him.

Or the teacher who said to the class, "Billie, where are the Azores?" When Billie responded, "I don't know, I didn't take them," the teacher dragged him off to the principal. When the principal heard the story from the enraged teacher, he said, "Look, I know Billie's family. If he said he didn't take them, he didn't take them." When the teacher confronted the superintendent in the hallway on the way to a meeting, he said to the teacher, "Look, I understand your problem. Just put your request in to the business manager and we'll get you another pair."

Or the one about the superintendent and the minister who decided to go fishing in the Rockies. As they were sitting alongside the creek, they heard a grizzly bear coming up the creek. The superintendent reached into his duffle bag and began to put on his tennis shoes. The minister said, "You fool, no one can outrun a grizzly bear." "I know that," snapped the nervous superintendent. "All I want to do is outrun you."

Defuse the fanatics with humor, particularly in public meetings and elsewhere, and you have got them at bay. They can't take a joke, literally. If they only had a sense of humor they *would be* perfect!

## CAVEATS, CODICILS, AND CONUNDRUMS ABOUT THE LUNATIC FRINGE

- The prudes today want more than *Catcher in the Rye;* they want the whole curriculum.
- If you have trouble with Phyllis Schlafly, you have the wrong attitude.
- Good teaching cannot survive the censors working to sterilize the schools.
- The fear of psychiatrists may be the most telling weakness in the agenda of the fanatic.
- Expose wackos and you expose their agenda. They are their own worst enemy. So take a wacko to a public meeting!
- Absolute certainty for absolute faith is a cheap promise—nobody can tell when it's been broken.
- The soil of science is doubt.
- The public schools' value to a free society is that they belong to no one faith—just like America.
- It is easy for the "joy" of one group's religious celebration to be the chains of persecution of another. Too easy.
- Fanatics can't take a joke because they believe they are perfect. The truth is if they had a sense of humor, they would be!

## CHAPTER 21

# Arch Rivals and Competitors

In the political arena, arch rivals and competitors are a basic part of life. Professional politicians have accepted this a long time ago. One minute they're blasting one another in the media, and the next, they smile and shake hands at a White House breakfast or a benefit ball. It's part of the game, part of the job.

And the field of education is no different. It can't be, because like political hierarchies, educational hierarchies are also pyramids. There are fewer assistant principals than there are classroom teachers; there are fewer principals than assistant principals; fewer assistant superintendents than principals; and there's only one superintendent in each district. Therefore, the closer to the apex of the pyramid, the fewer positions and the fewer openings—with more candidates competing for them. The competition and rivalry often get fierce, and when jockeying for positions internally within a district, the rivalry can get vicious and dirty.

### ET TU BRUTUS? KNOWING WHO WANTS YOUR JOB

Perhaps the most common rival is the person who wants your job. Depending on your title, that person could be your assistant, another administrator lower in the hierarchy, or even a classroom teacher. Knowing who in the organization had also applied for your position when you did will give you a list of your colleagues who wanted your job at some time and who may still want it. While this alone doesn't make such persons your arch rivals or competitors, it does suggest that they are potential competitors. Hitching that kind of aspirant to your star could make that person your most avid supporter. A good track record in having groomed your previous second-in-command or protégés to assume your previous positions or to assume other administrative positions is definitely an ace up your sleeve, and you ought to let your potential arch rivals know that it is there. Having others who want your job help you to vacate it through promotion is much smarter (and more pleasant) than having to fight them on a daily basis because they think that the only way to get your job is over your dead body.

But another kind of arch rival and competitor who is not as easy to deal with is the arch rival who has designs on a position not yet vacated and believes that you would be in the way because you would be competition. Therefore, getting rid of you now or somehow discrediting you in your present position would either eliminate you entirely, or at least head you off at the pass by weakening your chances later. Those folks look at the administrative hierarchy as a kind of educational "food chain," where those at the top feed on those at the bottom. They look at "advancement" as biological survival. Kill or be killed.

And, of course, there may be others who want your job, not because they want it for themselves, but for the same reasons why Salome wanted the head of John the Baptist on a silver platter. Something about you—perhaps your charisma, your success, your sheer joy on the job itself—magnifies their own unhappiness. A superintendent or a board of education president who must have limelight for energy as solar cells need the sun will not bask in the glories of a successful high school principal—even if they were the ones who had hired the person in the first place. Such a superstar may, in fact, be regarded by them as an eclipse, the superstar's very talent itself serving as the person's undoing. Most of the time such superstars must share the limelight with the solar cells within the district so that they feel charged, enhanced—if the superstar is to survive.

Knowing when to lay low and become "scenery" is especially difficult for superstars, but it is a survival skill that they must learn. Knowing when NOT to apply for a job, whether within the district or out of district, in order to offset the fear others may have of your talents or ambitions is often just as important for your survival than knowing when to "go for it." Another example of when to play "scenery" is to allow two powerful competitors to liquidate one another in a power struggle or to pass an "opportunity" when you have it on good info the position is "wired" for someone else. This keeps you from needlessly being publicly rejected.

## PLOTS, PLOTTERS, AND PSYCHOPATHS

In a way, it's easy to deal with those who either want your job themselves or want to eliminate you now in order to give themselves a clearer shot at a job not yet vacant and see you as a threat to their promotion or to their survival or both. At least their motivation has some logic. But when a person wants you professionally (and sometimes literally) dead for none of the reasons above, and, in fact, for no LOGICAL reasons at all, that's when you've really got problems because when you can't explain behavior through *logic*, you've got to look at the (psycho)logic.

Logically, the superintendent and board president who have hired someone who turns out to be a "Wunderkind" should feel good about themselves for making the right choice. But such a logical assumption is based upon several equally logical assumptions:

- Those in charge of school systems are committed only to enhancing the systems in their charge.
- Those in charge of school systems feel good about themselves in the first place.

But all systems, school or otherwise, are run by people—of all backgrounds, abilities, emotional needs, self-images, and most importantly, of varying degrees of mental health.

Anyone who has spent some time relating to other people while working at "people jobs," such as salespersons, waiters and waitresses, travel agents, etc., knows from experience that the mental health state of the union in our country overall is not good. And mental institutions, clinics, therapists, social workers, and the like deal with only the tip of the iceberg.

Tortured souls, angry and mean-spirited humanoids, sadists, bitter, jealous, empty, vindictive, small and truly ugly people are also among those who occupy bank presidencies, hospital directorships, college and university presidencies and deanships, high government posts, and are classroom teachers, principals, superintendents, and occupy seats on boards of education and on PTA's across this land. Some of these people are religious or political zealots, dishwashers, recluses, or average "quiet" family men and women. But for some reason, probably relating to their profound psychopathology, their malice and malevolence seem to be activated most by the purest of spirit, the most talented, the most charismatic, the brightest, and the most attractive. Those such as Jesus of Nazareth, Abraham Lincoln, Martin Luther King, Jr., John Kennedy, and Robert Kennedy are just a few of the most obvious examples of figures throughout history who have provoked the malevolent.

We're not suggesting that administrators require all those who surround them to submit to psychological tests. That's hardly possible, even if such tests could flush out the crazies. Nor are we suggesting that administrators react to each person in their professional lives as potential psychopaths. Each of the victims of assassins mentioned above had a fatalistic attitude about life—and death. Perhaps doing otherwise would lead to paranoia.

But we want school administrators to make a difference. That's what this book is about. That's what our lives have been about. And those who have the most potential for making a difference—the brightest and the best among us—are at highest risk. And yet it is they who must survive if schools in this country are to have a fighting chance of even coming close to reaching their potential.

### CASE STUDY: STANLEY FRIEND'S FIRST FAILURE

Stanley Friend is a high school principal in one of the largest city school systems in the country. He had worked his way up the administrative hierarchy of the sprawling system starting out as a classroom teacher twenty-eight years ago. Living up to his name, Stan was indeed a friend to everyone. He didn't have a mean bone in his body. A threat to no one, Stan was everyone's favorite—custodians, teachers, students, administrators—everyone.

Because Stan Friend had never met a person he didn't like, the Personnel Director had decided to re-assign Hank Larkin to Stan's school as assistant principal, replacing another assistant principal who had retired. This was to be Larkin's fourth re-assignment as assistant principal in the past seven years.

Stan knew all about Hank's track record and, in spite of the warnings that he had received about Hank from administrators in the District who had worked with him, Stan felt sorry for him. Hank had also been one of the old-timers who had started in the District with Stan. But Hank always seemed to be in the wrong place at the wrong time. His first assignment ended abruptly after the principal became ill and retired prematurely. The next person seemed to hate him at first sight and, after two years of fighting, Hank was re-assigned.

Hank's next assignment was to an inner-city high school. There, he established a reputation for treating minority groups harshly. It seemed as if he just couldn't win. At no time did he ever apply for one of the principalships which would become available periodically in the big-city system.

Stan knew about all this and about the rumors from the district grapevine that Larkin had few friends in the administrative hierarchy with good reason. But being the kind of person he was, Stan believed that Hank's major problem was not ever having the opportunity of working with a principal who would give him the benefit of the doubt. So when the transfer became official, Stan was actually glad to be the one who would show the system that everyone (including Hank) reacted favorably to being treated fairly and decently.

And Hank didn't disappoint Stan either. Sensing that he had at last found a kindred spirit, Hank responded by taking the school by storm. His presence set a new standard for excellence in the handling of student discipline. It seemed as though all Hank wanted was to serve Stan, whom he called "Sir."

Once again Stan's belief in the basic decency of human nature had been justified. But like magic, things began to change after six months. While making the rounds of the building, Stan had noticed that Hank seemed to be a "regular" at the ping-pong table in the faculty room. This was typical of Hank's gregarious nature. He was truly a people-person, but just the same, Stan felt that he had to talk to Hank and warn him that an occasional ping-pong game was fine, but he didn't want Hank to be one of the "regulars" in the faculty room whom Stan had to remind from time to time about being late to class.

Although Hank listened to his boss politely, nevertheless, every time Stan passed by the lunch time ping-pong crowd in the faculty room, Hank would be right there. Finally, Stan decided that he had to play tough. He referred to the importance of a balance between professional leadership and familiarity on Hank's year-end evaluation in June. Surprised that Hank signed it without seeing him about it, Stan was sure that Hank had gotten the message.

But things degenerated rapidly the following year from the outset. Stan had delegated scheduling to Hank, and there were many scheduling errors in student and teacher programs on the very first day of school, errors which weren't corrected for many months. Hank, throughout these many months, had never missed a ping-pong game. Moreover, Stan had instructed Hank to break up the clique at period 4 lunch by scheduling them for different lunch periods. He believed that the period 4 regulars at the ping-pong table began to take ping-pong more seriously than their teaching, which had become evident from their tardy arrival to their period 5 classes.

Yet, the period 4 clique remained intact—all had the same lunch periods. Hank explained that it was simply a "coincidence." Another coincidence was the fact that the coaches, who were members of what Stan now began to perceive as Hank's clique, also were scheduled to have free (unassigned) last period classes, even though the District's policy was that coaches were relieved of their after school extra help classes (which all teachers were expected to do), but were not to be intentionally scheduled to have a free period at the end of the day in order to get ready for their coaching duties.

Hank explained their schedules as being the "luck of the draw."

Stan began to feel uneasy. He found it more and more difficult to speak to Hank whose attitude seemed to be that he was accountable to no one. One administrator after the other in the large system would tell Stan that Hank was no friend of his, that he was bad-mouthing Stan in subtle ways and even openly all over the city.

Stan simply couldn't understand what was happening. No one had treated Hank better than he had. Yet, instead of showing some appreciation for what Stan was trying to do, Hank would not ever give Stan one ounce of effort beyond what was required of him.

To make matters worse, Hank also became belligerent. When Stan talked to him once again about the ping-pong and the full hour he was taking for lunch (rather than the period, which was forty-five minutes), Hank invoked the name of their union on technical grounds.

Moreover, Hank would leave the building almost on a daily basis to run errands (i.e., to the post office, to the bank, etc.). He would do this in addition to the full hour he took for lunch. Also, Hank would call in late on the mornings he would be absent from school, giving no reason for his absence.

But Stan began to understand what he was dealing with when he walked into Hank's office one morning after one of his absences when he hadn't called in at all. Stan had made inquiries within the district and had found out that Hank (who himself had forgotten about it till the last minute) was in attendance at an area administrators' conference, one of a dozen Stan had given him permission to attend to represent the district, but one which Stan had forgotten about.

As soon as Stan walked into Hank's office, Hank screamed at the top of his voice. He told Stan that he had no right to check up on him and then, with the door wide open, yelled obscenities at him, stormed out of the building into the parking lot, got into his car, and sped away.

Within a week, the same scene was repeated, only this time Hank was yelling at a seventh grader in his office, again at the top of his lungs. The scene got so ugly and Hank's temper seemed so out of control that another assistant principal opened the door, took the boy by his arm, and led him out and into his own office for his own safety. Later, Hank told Stan that he had "staged" the whole scene in order to "scare" the boy.

It was clear to Stan that Hank would not take direction from anyone. He was completely uncontrollable. He would call meetings with the department chairpersons about scheduling without telling Stan.

Once, when Stan was a few minutes late for his own faculty meeting, Hank began it and managed to get the meeting off on a sour note on discipline, skipping the other agenda items even before Stan got there. Moreover, parental complaints about Larkin's treating them rudely and abruptly and treating their children harshly increased in frequency.

Hank had refused to volunteer to supervise any evening functions, saying that he had to work on side jobs after school. Until late May, Stan and the other two assistant principals and the dean of students had supervised all of the evening functions themselves. Stan finally had to resort to ordering Hank to be at a minimum of two evening activities, which he reluctantly did.

Stan sought help from the director of the Troubled Employee Program in the district. It was clear from Hank's behavior that he had problems that were affecting his job performance and the school. But all the director could do was to advise Stan that somehow he had to get Hank to refer himself to the program for help.

The perfect opportunity came (or so Stan thought) when Hank had made two appointments with parents to resolve serious matters of discipline which had concerned their children, only to be absent from school on that day without ever having given any thought to cancelling or rescheduling them. Because fathers had taken the day off from work, Stan held the conferences himself in Hank's absence, conferences which lasted over an hour and a half each, since Stan had to gather facts from scratch.

Stan tried to talk to Hank about a pattern of his forgetting about appointments—the one when Stan couldn't find him and the most recent two. Hank's reply was that it was Stan who couldn't remember appointments, that Hank had expected Stan to take over the conferences for him in his absence as part of a principal's job. He also told Stan that the problem was that he was being hampered by Stan's style.

Driving home that day and thinking about how miserable Hank had made life for him since being assigned to his school, Stan tried to get some mellow music on his car radio to help him forget Hank and the unpleasant parts of the day. But the words to a song on one of the rock music stations made Stan take notice before he could even switch the station:

> A psychopath never
> takes a bath
> because he's afraid he'll
> wash away the hate . . .

Stan strained to understand more of the words which were being drowned out by the music:

> all you ever feel
> is bitter and twisted . . .
>
> all your life you've lived a lie

Stan knew exactly what he had to do. It took a great deal to get Stan to admit it, but he finally came to the conclusion that ALL human beings DO NOT react favorably to fairness, decency, and honesty. Hank had deep psychological problems including a well-spring of anger bordering on rage, the origin of which probably Hank himself did not understand. But Hank's pathology was the kind that was dangerous because it was cunning. Yes, Hank was crazy like a fox. Somehow, he was able to fool most of the faculty into thinking that he was the greatest thing since sliced bread. After all, he really "kicked ass" when they sent their discipline problems to him. And he took care of "his people" by giving them their preferences of classes, rooms, etc., and he was one of the boys, drinking with them on Fridays, bowling with them on Tuesdays, playing poker with them on Thursdays, and playing ping-pong with them every day. As a matter of fact, according to Hank, Stan's problem was that he was jealous of the intimate relationship that Hank had managed to develop with the staff in such a short time, a relationship, according to Hank, that Stan envied but was incapable of ever achieving because he wasn't a warm and compassionate person.

Only a handful of administrators in the district who had worked closely with Hank knew of his madness and of his viciousness.

Stan's path of action was clear. He had to excise the cancer before it was too late—before the malignancy would threaten his own survival. Stan knew that he couldn't help Hank. Perhaps no one could. He wouldn't respond favorably to anything. He was impervious to logic. He was beyond logic. You don't try to reason with cancer, you cut it out. And that's what Stan finally did.

The system didn't allow Stan to tell Hank to collect two weeks severance pay after cleaning out his desk and his office by noon and not to let the door hit his coat on the way out. In the real world, that would have been Hank's fate many years ago. In the real, non-tenured world, Hank would have been forced to get his act together in the first place because he wouldn't have been able to hold on to his craziness and to his job at the same time; he would have been forced to give up one or the other. The destructive side of tenure doesn't just affect teachers, it affects administrators, too.

Stan reluctantly agreed to allow Hank to be transferred once again, knowing that within six months to a year he would be up to his pathological tricks in order to prove to himself, once again, how superior he really was to his new victim. Stan really wanted to go after Hank's job, feeling certain that he was able to document enough to furnish the district with an excellent case, but the district's attorney felt that more documentation was needed. As it was, Stan furnished the district with the most comprehensive and well-documented year-end evaluation of Hank that Hank had ever received from anyone else before. At least that was a start. Hopefully, Hank's next principal would have the perserverance and the courage to further document Hank's pathology to a point where the district would feel that it had enough of a case against Hank to keep him away from children and out of schools for good.

## MOTIVATION FOR ADVANCEMENT

Hank had no motivation for advancement. He looked at the job in terms of dollars and cents for the hours and minutes spent in the office. The extra responsibilities, the aggravation of having "the buck stop here," having to make decisions where he couldn't always be the good guy, having to attend all those evening meetings and Saturday football games, and having to spend countless hours away from the Tuesday night bowling, Thursday night poker, Friday night drinking with the boys just wasn't worth the five thousand dollar pay differential. But being so clearly superior to the inept wimps he had to serve as assistant principal, Hank had decided to use his wasted talents to be a spoiler for the clods who held the titles which they weren't qualified for and didn't deserve.

Schools throughout the country are filled with Hanks, although hopefully, psychologically less damaged. Reasonably intelligent people cannot be expected to do the same jobs year after year without burning out, and teachers are no different, especially if they're good teachers, because teaching is emotionally draining.

Administrators who move from one level of administration to the next or from one district to the next know how stimulating such a career can be. But classroom teachers and administrators within a district who possess intelligence and talent need to be cultivated, supported, and encouraged to move on either within the district or to another district so that they don't stagnate and become embittered Hank Larkins, losing their souls and their sanity in the process.

School districts which maintain a balanced and healthy cross-current of upward flow encourage teachers within the district to develop and demonstrate their administrative abilities through

leadership positions, differentiated staffing, administrative intern-
ships, and administrative assistantships, and districts seriously consider them for administrative positions when they become available.
But healthy school districts know, too, the adverse effects of inbreeding (hiring only from within the ranks). A healthy crosscurrent
of outsiders with fresh ideas and "homegrown" talent in an upward
movement resulting from some administrative turnover is highly
desirable. However, most districts are not large enough to provide
the opportunities for advancement to those who already have the
motivation. Administrators within the buildings and within the
district must be their mentors and help them move on. And the by-
product of being a successful mentor, of course, is being able to
strengthen your power base so you've got nothing to lose by helping
someone else to become more powerful.

But when should YOU move on? That depends on the circumstances. Generally we get "antsie" when we get bored, when we
feel ourselves clicking into "automatic pilot," when we begin to feel
too comfortable, and often for us that's been anywhere from one to
three years in a new job. But how you feel about a job and how much
you are continuing to grow in a job should be more important than
how much time you do on a job.

And motivation for success must be assessed in light of other
things such as family dynamics and the needs of individual family
members. New jobs also impact upon those around you—especially if
it means relocating your present home. It is becoming more common—especially for those in the higher levels of administration—to
live apart from their families for parts of the week, being together
mostly on weekends and on holidays. While far from optimum, often
these compromises are better than uprooting entire families at the
expense of a spouse's career or the children's school career and
social lives.

Administrators are risk-takers. The deliberate choice of leaving
the safety and structure of the classroom for the uncertain and more
challenging world of administration is the first step on the road less
traveled. Administrators are a breed apart from classroom teachers.
Most of them embrace Alinsky's belief that "life is an adventure of
passion, risk, danger, laughter, beauty, love a burning curiosity to go
with the action to see what it is all about. . . ." And many of them
also agree with Dubois that "the important thing is this: to be able at
any moment to sacrifice what we are for what we could become."

Perhaps that's why so few of us hang around long enough to get
that gold watch for so many years of faithful service. Our watch is
internal.

## ASSISTANTS

It's hard to discuss assistants without thinking about all the men and women who have served as our assistants over the years. Between us, we've seen the gamut. Some were much older than we, others were younger; some were tall, some short; some slender, others obese; some intellectual types, others jocks; some men, others women; some black, others white; some very bright, others quite dull; some very talented, others completely inept. But the bottom line on assistants is that no matter what their age, sex, intelligence, body-types, or level of education, they all fall into one of two categories: assistants who can hurt you and assistants who can help you. There are no other kinds of assistants that we've come across.

### Assistants Who Can Hurt You

Without question, Hank Larkin is an outstanding example of an assistant who can hurt you. He can hurt you because he wants to hurt you, because that is the only way for him to feel self-worth. But most school districts have school board attorneys, boards of education members, and central office/building administrative teams which as a rule don't put up with the likes of the Hank Larkins of the world.

Many assistants who can hurt you really don't do it intentionally. Some high school administrative teams, because of their constant infighting and bickering, appear more like the keystone cops or the Marx Brothers than administrative "teams" to the faculties who watch their antics with amusement and disdain. The first order of business to establish is that a team is composed of team players who may let their hair down in the locker room, but once on the field, they play as one. Anyone who can't hack that is off the team—*no exceptions.*

Another assistant who can hurt you is the assistant like Bill the Bad described in Chapter 9—the assistant who is busy playing politics and building a little empire of his own through patronage and favoritism. Having two or more assistants of this type can actually lead to having a faculty or a district split into separate camps composed of the followers of these mini-kings and -queens.

Perhaps the most lethal assistant is the one who wanted your job before you got it, and wants it even more so now. Such an assistant, of course, will not go out of the way to make you look good; some will do just about anything to make you look bad. By working in a way similar to a drag in a fishing reel, they will make you exert a great deal of energy to gain very little "line." Very often they will be the source of the pipeline from your office to wherever it can do you the most harm. These assistants can be especially useful when you want to get "confidential" information to your adversaries on the "QT" through the pipeline which you're not supposed to know about.

Yet another kind of assistant who can hurt you is the happy "paper-pusher." Such a person has a bad case of the "papyrus syndrome," the Egyptian curse. The advanced stages of the malady manifests itself in the forms, correspondence, memoranda, etc., piled HIGH. It's people who give them fits. They just don't seem to know how to get along with them. Of course, if you have the luxury of having more than one assistant, the obvious solution is to lock the paper-pusher into a closet with piles of paper and away from people, while your other more gregarious assistants handle the people. One thing is for certain. No people-hater is going to do you nearly as much harm as a Hank Larkin because a people-hater will force you into the role of the good guy. Hank Larkins, on the other hand, save the roles of good guy for themselves, leaving you either as the bad guy or at least on the wanted posters.

There are probably countless ways that assistants can hurt you that we haven't mentioned here. What is important about what was mentioned is that not once did we give an example of an assistant hurting you because the assistant was smarter than you, more articulate, a better note-taker, a deeper thinker, or a better looker. And there's a reason for this. We have never been hurt, nor do we know of any competent administrator who has ever been hurt by an assistant who was superior to the administrator in any way. In fact, we believe that it is those assistants who are superior to us in some ways who enhance us the most. And the more superior they are, the more they enhance us.

We don't have to worry about one threatening the other. We "bounce off" one another, we complement one another—kind of like a good fit. It is those who are inept whom we *fear*. We fear them because they are dangerous to our survival. They weave elaborate webs of deception to cover their ineptitude. They are committed to killing off the best and the brightest in the organization because they are threatened by them. They know that they are in places where they don't belong and they know that as long as there is talent out there, they'll never be able to stay there through merit, they'll be able to hang on only through subtle or overt assassination. The only assistant you must *fear* is the incompetent.

Assistants are very much like secretaries in that they have the potential of doing you a great deal of harm or a great deal of good. After the secretary, perhaps it is the assistant who can make or break an administrator more directly than anyone else in the organization. And like secretaries, relationships with assistants must also be cultivated. But that is where the similarity ends. Secretaries aren't certified for your job (qualified, maybe, but not certified). And secretaries don't do things that give them power over teaching schedules, room assignments, duty assignments, etc.

Before delegating responsibility to an assistant, check to see what power you're giving that assistant and how the person will use that power. Hank Larkin used his responsibility of scheduler of the building to feed his political machine and as a lever to make people do what he wanted.

It's tough to be someone's assistant. Experts on stress tell us that the less control one has over a job, the more stress is experienced. That makes your assistant a better candidate for stress than you. And unless you're a complete jerk, you're not going to give your assistant the best aspects of your job, keeping only the worst for yourself. And who is the one who is expected to adjust to whose administrative style?

After your secretary, the person who can help you or hurt you the most is your assistant. There is no such thing as a neutral assistant; an assistant will either hurt you or will help you. The ones who can hurt you must either be eliminated such as in the case of Hank Larkin or they must be rendered powerless by being locked away in some closet. Some may even be trainable.

But those assistants who can help you will enhance you on the job and become your alter ego. Remember, the competent administrator does not want a clone. Complementarity is rooted in diversity, not similarity. The support and loyalty they provide are usually beyond price, but training them to be able to assume your job or one that is comparable to it seems like a good place to start.

## CAVEATS, CODICILS, AND CONUNDRUMS ABOUT ARCH RIVALS AND COMPETITORS

- All human organizations are filled with real and potential rivals and competitors.

- Some administrative "Wunderkinds" bring out the worst in rivals and competitors.
- Knowing when to become "scenery" is just as important as knowing when to "go for it."
- There's a difference between the logical and the psychological when seeking clues to ambition.
- The best gold watch is internal.
- Assistants come in only two types, harmful or helpful.
- The competent administrator isn't interested in a clone; he or she wants complementarity rooted in diversity.
- The only assistant you must *fear* is the incompetent. Those assistants who are superior to us in some ways *enhance* us the most.

## SECTION VI

# Surviving

## CHAPTER 22

# Knowing Who Is the Boss

**YOU DON'T WORK FOR EVERYONE: HOW TO TELL WHO IS THE BOSS**

It's amazing how many people in education don't know who their bosses are. Of course, there is some basis for the confusion. Educational hierarchies tend to have many chiefs and very few Indians. Secondary school teachers, especially, can be confused as to which of the chiefs is THE chief: department chairpersons, directors, coordinators, assistant principals, principals, assistant superintendents, etc. While each of these administrators might observe a classroom teacher's lesson and even write a formal classroom observation report, only one of them is THE chief of record—the person who writes the teacher's formal year-end evaluation (regardless of who has "input") and who recommends whether the teacher should get tenure or not. That's the person who is the leading actor or actress. The rest of them are bit players as far as the career of that classroom teacher is concerned.

Administrators, too, can lose sight of who really is the boss. Central office staffs also have their casts of characters: administrative assistants, executive administrative assistants, assistant superintendents, assistants to the superintendent, associate superintendents, business managers, directors of elementary and secondary education, and so forth. Working with a few or many of these chiefs during the year, one can forget who one's boss really is.

Here again, the answers to two questions should lead to the discovery of THE chief:

(1) Who SIGNS your year-end evaluation?
(2) Who recommends you for continued probation and eventually for tenure?

If there are two different answers to the above questions, then ignore question #1. The bottom line is that you really work for the man or woman who has your professional fate in his or her hands. That person is your boss. That is the person whom you must please. The rest are bit players who may or may not have influence with your boss. But if the boss wants you out, you're out no matter who else does or doesn't like it. The "who-elses" don't matter, only your boss matters.

**CASE STUDY: TODD LAKER KNOCKS 'EM DEAD BUT IS KNOCKED OUT**

Todd Laker was a restless assistant principal of a high school in Vermont. Not yet thirty-five years old, he was itching to get his own school to manage even before he became an A.P. Although the ink had not yet dried on his Ph.D. and his chair was not yet fully broken in (he had been an assistant principal less than two years), Todd was sending his resume all over the country.

It didn't take long before he got his first "strike"—an invitation to visit a high school in an affluent town approximately 800 miles down the coast. He packed a light bag and started out for an adventure— which is exactly what was awaiting him.

Todd appeared at Comstock High School thirty minutes early, refreshed after a good night's sleep at a nearby motel. He made the most of the time chatting with Miss Copasetic, the superintendent's secretary.

Dr. Sly Fox, the superintendent, saw Todd for a total of ten minutes. He told him that the school had had three principals within the past four years and that none of them had worked out for a variety of reasons. This time Fox had decided to have five different committees, each representing an important group within the school community, conduct the interviews of the candidates and rate them independently. If each of the committees happened to rate the same candidate first, then that candidate would be offered the job. But since that was unlikely to happen, Fox had hoped that the five committees could reach a consensus on one of the highly rated candidates. "Hell," Fox concluded, "they didn't like my last two choices, let's see what they can come up with on their own."

With that introduction, Todd met his first committee—the teachers' union. No sooner did Todd enter the room, when one teacher shouted, "Why do you want to become the next principal of Comstock High School?"

"I'm not at all sure that I do," was Todd's cool reply. "That's why I'm here—to find out."

Within the next hour the saga unfolded. Comstock was a high school filled with potential which was untapped because of internal bickering and the rotating principalship. Political factions within the community had spent their energies fighting one another.

By the time he moved to the next group, the "Community," he was ready for what was to follow. The "Community" group immediately had wanted to know what the union group had told Todd about the "situation." But before Todd could even begin to talk, they began to discredit the group's honesty, told Todd not to trust them, blamed them for the high principal turnover, and then launched into their version of the "situation."

When Todd innocently asked the question, "What happened to the last principal?" World War III was unleashed, and the group nearly came to blows. Half of them subscribed to one version and the other half had another version. Todd knew that the first order of business for the next principal would be to bring the warring factions within that school community together.

His third interview was a luncheon meeting with key central office staff and the other candidates for the position at a local restaurant. The other candidates took turns trying to outwit one another, while the central office staff took turns telling everyone how wonderful Comstock High School was and what a great opportunity its principalship would be ("a plum" they called it).

Todd then went on to meet the building level administrators within the district, including the assistant principals. There again, various versions emerged attempting to explain what had gone wrong in the past.

But the best committee, the dessert, was saved for the last. Todd finally got the chance to meet the student committee. They were bright and eager, dying for someone to make Comstock High School the kind of school they all knew it could be.

After that exhausting day, Todd was ready to begin his long drive back to Vermont. He hadn't seen Dr. Fox since his brief ten-minute meeting with him that morning and was sorry that he didn't get the chance to say good-bye. As he came closer to his red Porsche, he noticed Phil Rizzio, one of the other principals in the district standing there, obviously waiting for him.

"This yours, kid?" he asked. After Todd answered affirmatively, Phil continued, "Look, kid. You've got it all—looks, brains, charisma. Hell, you were better than the whole bunch of boring pompous blowhards we had to listen to all day. But let me tell you something. If they're smart enough to offer you the job and you decide to take it, do so with one thing in mind. Lay low, keep your mouth shut, and "yes" that turkey to death like everyone else does—

for about five years. The old bastard won't last longer than that.
Then when he's gone, you'll really have something. If you don't do
that, he'll ruin you."

Todd tried to think about Rizzio's advice on the way back home.
Obviously, he was no fan of Dr. Fox, but then again, Fox didn't have
that many fans on any of the five committees.

Within a week, Todd received a letter from Dr. Fox saying that
representatives from each of the five committees would visit his
school on a certain day during the following week. Sure enough, on
the designated day the delegation, which had flown to the nearest
airport and had rented a van, appeared. They roamed the building
talking to everyone in sight. Todd's staff joked with him that they
weren't looking for a principal, they were looking for a pope!

But during the process, several committee members had "leaked"
the news to Todd that he had been, in fact, the first choice of each
of the five committees and that the visit was just a prelude to the
inevitable.

No sooner had the committee left when Todd's support staff
walked into his office, closed the door, and sat on the available
chairs and on the floor. The three guidance counselors, the social
worker, and school psychologist looked like a solemn and somber
group. Evelyn Lowenthal, a guidance counselor spoke first.

"Look, Todd," she said, "they had their chance to look us over
and now it's our turn. We know you want your own school and we
know you were born for it, but don't take this one. You're going to
get the offer, and we're begging you as your friends not to take it.
There's a kind of pathology in Comstock. We can't agree, based on
just meeting that committee, on where it is, but we do agree that it's
there and it's deep. They've gone through enough principals to fill a
wax museum. Don't be the next victim. Stay here. Be patient and
wait for the right school, and take our advice—*that's* not it!"

But Todd Laker had visions of administrative grandeur and glory.
The quaint town of Comstock, the friendly people, the magnificent
kids, the huge school building with facilities Todd had only read
about. All this made him salivate.

Besides, he believed that the very fact that there were so many
principals in such a short time mitigated against such a thing happening again. And his being the first choice of each of the committees
would give him a ready-made constituency.

Within a week, Todd got the call that he had expected from
Dr. Fox. He told Todd that each of the committees had chosen him as
their first choice. He then offered him a three-year contract at a
starting salary which was twenty thousand dollars above what he

was making at his present position. Todd swallowed hard, took a deep breath, and told Fox that he needed a few days to think about the offer. He didn't want to appear too eager.

The rest is history. Todd took the job and took Comstock by storm. Not yet thirty-five years old and still single, Todd had the luxury of being able to work over fifteen hours a day, seven days a week. He went to everything—American Legion breakfasts for the football team on Saturdays, dances, athletic events, etc. He was grand marshal of the town's Columbus Day Parade, a member of the local service club, and probably among the best-known figures in Comstock.

School spirit soared. Todd formed an advisory board consisting of representatives from each of the political factions which had been feuding for years. Everything started to fall into place at the high school and in the town. Some members of the local political caucus even approached Todd with the suggestion that he run for political office in the county legislature.

Todd, working through his major constituency groups, had turned Comstock High School around in less than two years. Morale was up. Student achievement was up. And Comstock High School was once again in the running—for everything—athletic and scholastic.

But you wouldn't know that from reading Todd's first and second year evaluations. They were replete with backhanded compliments and damning faint praise. Dr. Fox would state one thing on one page only to take it away on the next. It was moving the pea right in front of his eyes on paper until he didn't know where the bottom line was. Todd had at first written these tactics off as being part of Fox's general manipulative ways. Eventually, he had written Fox off himself. He just got tired of having his ideas fall on deaf ears, of having his memos unanswered, of having to listen to his cynicism. After a while, Todd just did what he knew had to be done. He heard from Fox only when Fox decided to slap his wrists for one petty thing or another.

Perhaps Todd was on an ego trip. Perhaps he was suffering from hubris. Whatever the reason, he felt invincible. And the professional headhunters who had been hired to choose a successor to the retiring Fox didn't help matters either. The two well-known consultants had been in the district for about three weeks speaking to different groups representing various factions in the school community as part of their effort to compile a composite profile of the district so that it could be matched with the ideal candidate who could be compatible with that profile. The headhunters asked to speak with Todd. "Dr. Laker," one of them said, "we've been asking these same questions as part of these searches for eighteen years between us. In all these years, neither of us, after having asked what was good about the district, ever has gotten a unanimous response in the form of a person's name. Frankly, the question doesn't even call for it. So, when we asked the same question to a group representing the community and heard "Todd Laker, our high school principal" we were quite surprised. We just wanted you to know that whatever you're doing, you must be doing something right—keep it up!''

Todd Laker felt vindicated. Fox could put him down all he wanted in the months he had remaining as a lame duck. Laker's attitude had been, and remained, that each of the groups represented by the five committees that had selected him unanimously comprised one-fifth of the school district and their evaluation of him was superb! And since the whole was equal to the sum of its parts, those committees *were* the district and therefore Fox could go to the devil. Fox hadn't even been on any of those committees in the first place. In fact, he had given the job to the committees because he couldn't do it himself.

Todd Laker carried that attitude with him right into Fox's office on the afternoon Fox fired him. It was exactly two weeks to the day after the headhunters had told Todd how the community had felt about him. Fox's secretary called that morning and said that the superintendent wanted to see him in his office at 3:00 P.M. She said nothing more. Laker was convinced that the old buzzard had finally broken down and decided to give him a half-hearted compliment because of what the headhunters had told him. It would probably be a backhanded compliment said in a joking way as usual.

But Todd Laker was wrong. Dead wrong. Fox had simply wanted to inform him that he was not going to nominate Todd for tenure in six months and that he wanted Todd to have enough time to look for another job. Laker actually laughed, thinking that Fox was outdoing himself in the joking department, but the joke was on Todd. He went on to say that although Laker was a good principal, he was not an outstanding principal, and that he wanted his final legacy to the high school to be an outstanding principal. Since Fox would be retiring two weeks after Todd's tenure date, that didn't give Fox much time. Finally, he told Todd that it was his style that Fox had objected to and not his competence. As Laker was groping in disbelief, Fox told him that he had been sending out signals all along which Todd had chosen to ignore because he was a "sheltered babe in the woods."

In June, when Laker didn't get tenure, most of the community were outraged. The kids were heartsick. The staff was stunned. And when the school year was over, Todd Laker, the Golden Boy of Comstock High School cleared out his office, packed his bags, and looked for work.

## Todd Laker: Findings of a Job Autopsy

Perhaps the very selection process which led to Todd Laker's getting the job in the first place also led to his demise. It gave Laker the illusion that he had *five bosses*—each represented by one of the selection committees, and that the superintendent would be pleased as long as the five groups were happy. He was wrong! And Fox was absolutely correct in his assessment that Todd had been a "sheltered babe in the woods." HE DIDN'T EVEN KNOW THE PROCESS BY WHICH HE WOULD BE EITHER GRANTED TENURE OR DENIED TENURE! Only after he had gotten home from Fox's office on that fateful day did he actually pick up a book on school law and read the intricacies of the tenure statute.

ONLY AFTER FOX HAD FIRED HIM DID TODD FIRST LEARN THAT HIS FATE HAD BEEN IN FOX'S HANDS ALL ALONG. Until then, Laker never had to concern himself with such technicalities since in his whole career there had never been a question of his getting tenure.

Todd Laker had only one boss, and while he was knocking himself out trying to be the principal of Comstock High School, he was also "blowing it" with THE boss.

From the very first day on the job, be certain that you know

- who *signs* your evaluation, and
- who recommends you to the superintendent for tenure (if the superintendent isn't your immediate superior).

And no matter what else you do and who else you please, be sure that you are also taking care of business with THE boss as well.

Todd Laker should have listened to Phil Rizzio three years previously when he told him in the parking lot that if he took the job to "lay low for five years" and to keep his mouth shut. As it turned out, Todd would have had to lay low for only three years, after which time, he would have had the opportunity of working with Fox's successor.

### ALL THE PRESIDENT'S MEN: ARE THEY MEN?

Once you're sure who your boss is, the next thing to do is to take a good hard look at those people with whom your boss has surrounded him/herself. Who has your boss appointed to top leadership positions? Who are the members of your boss's inner circle or kitchen cabinet? How much like your boss are they? How do the members of your boss's team differ from him/her in age, sex, religious preference, race, educational philosophy, and intelligence? If your boss is a jock, are the members of the team also jocks? Does your boss recognize his/her limitations and purposely hire others whose strengths are the boss's weaknesses?

And most importantly, how *secure* is your boss? In general, the more secure a person, the more that person tends to want to be surrounded by the brightest and the best. On the other hand, those people who aren't very secure in their jobs are another story. Once again, Lee Iacocca provides us with some street smarts on the subject in his autobiography:

> When you have a guy who isn't very sure of himself on the job, the very last thing he wants is a guy backing him up who *is* sure of himself. He figures: "If the next guy is too good, he'll show me up—and eventually replace me." As a result, one incompetent manager brings along another. And all of them hide behind the overall weakness in the system.[1]

In other words, water and mediocrity seek their own levels. Perhaps that's why the greatest fear and abject hatred of the "good old boys" in an inbred system is reserved for the change agent, that superintendent or principal who opens the windows to let in some fresh ideas, fresh talent, new benchmarks for excellence—coming from people of sexes and ethnic, racial, and educational backgrounds which are different from what the good old boys have come to expect.

The important thing is that taking stock of all the president's people will serve as a vital clue to help you figure out more about your boss as a person and as a leader. And it will help you figure out where you belong in the organization—IF you belong there at all.

Not taking stock of all the president's men was one of Todd Laker's many mistakes. If he had, he would have realized that Dr. Fox's two major appointments were people who were alike in two ways which were obviously very important to him:

- They were both career seconds-in-command elevated from the ranks for reasons which were not obvious.
- They both had a "Rosemary Woods loyalty" to the boss.

### DOES YOUR BOSS WANT YOUR COMPETENCE OR YOUR STROKES?

Of course, once you find out the calibre of people with whom your boss has chosen to surround him/herself, you should have a much better understanding of exactly what it is that your boss really wants of you—your competency or your strokes. If Dr. Fox had wanted the best assistants for instruction and business that the district could afford to hire, he would have "gone for it" by advertising the positions in the *New York Times*, calling the best colleges and universities in the country for nominations, contacting professional organizations such as AASA, or even hiring professional consultants to help with the search. That's what he would have done if he were looking for sheer competence—very much like what he was forced to do to get Todd Laker because his handpicked principals weren't acceptable to everyone else in the past. But Fox didn't do any of these things because that is not what he wanted in his two closest assistants. He wanted people who were smart enough to learn those aspects of the jobs which they didn't already know before they got them. He wanted people who could handle the jobs, who could do the jobs. But first and foremost, he wanted people whom he knew and trusted, people who would be loyal to him first, last, and always.

And there's nothing wrong with that except for the fact that Fox used the two not as a base upon which to build an administrative team, but to stand on, like a pedestal. They, in turn, were committed to exclude everyone else or at least keep everyone else at bay—much like Ehrlichman and Haldeman were used by Nixon.

And into the middle of all this marches Todd Laker, fresh from the hills of Vermont, with his lofty ideas about putting Comstock High School on the map. But Dr. Fox wasn't interested in putting Comstock High School on the map. Fox was basically interested in remaining comfortable—which meant running things his way and not rocking the boat, and the other two "assistants" were interested only in giving the "old man" what he wanted.

All this, Laker missed by not being more aware. But Laker wasn't a very good listener either. Phil Rizzio had also provided him with a crucial bit of advice based upon bitter personal experience at the very beginning. He told him in very graphic language that the boss didn't want Laker's competence (or anyone else's). He wanted their strokes. Laker didn't have to knock himself out in the first place!

By not finding out who was his boss, his ONLY boss, by not taking stock of his boss's "people," and by not taking the time to ever find out what his boss really valued, Todd Laker spent most of his energy working hard. Perhaps if he had taken the time necessary to read this book, he would have worked smart instead—and saved his job in the process.

## WHO IS YOUR BOSS'S BOSS AND WHO CARES?

Everybody has a boss. Anyone who scurries up the administrative ladder in the hope of some day getting to the top in order to be the boss of bosses is a fool. That boss is God—and nobody with any sense would want *His* job!

But if so many people in education don't really know the identity of their bosses, they certainly wouldn't know who their boss's bosses were. Why is it so important to know the identity of your boss's boss? For one thing, like knowing who your boss's "people" are, knowing who is your boss's boss will give you a better understanding of your boss (i.e., where your boss may be getting some ideas, pressures, whom your boss may be trying to please, etc.).

Todd Laker knew the identity of Dr. Fox's boss—it was Rita Mundy, President of the Board of Education. Everybody in Comstock knew Rita Mundy, and she made it her business to know them. As a matter of fact, knowing everyone in Comstock was her business, since she was the director of the Welcome Wagon and the president of the Chamber of Commerce.

Rita was a real character. She was the Town Character. A more gregarious and affable person you couldn't meet. She loved people in general and kids in particular. She was the High School's athletic teams' biggest supporter. At soccer games, no matter what the call, one could hear her scream, "red ball," signifying that the call should be in favor of Comstock.

Rita was also a member of many service organizations. She was the Vice President of The Comstock Club, and the Treasurer of the Library Fund Board. She would use the influence of her leadership positions in these organizations to rally these organizations around the schools and to support town functions such as the annual crab cookout.

Yes, Rita Mundy was a character and a saint. And she was also an egomaniac. She was not an act or even the main event. She was the whole show. She needed to be loved by everyone. She was a celebrity in Comstock and she acted like one—and loved every minute of it. She was entitled. She worked hard for it.

It never occurred to Todd Laker that perhaps that was the reason why George Fox was so subdued and low-keyed—especially in Mundy's presence which had included Board of Education meetings. The monthly board meetings at Comstock were in every way "the Rita Mundy Show" starring Rita Mundy, with co-hosts Rita Mundy and Rita Mundy. Fox seldom had much to say except when he was praising her.

It never occurred to Todd Laker that Rita had aspirations beyond her titles of Queen of the Kids, President of the Board of Education, President of the Chamber of Commerce, Vice President of the Comstock Club, Treasurer of the Library Fund Board, etc. She also wanted to be mayor of Comstock, and in fact, she ran for that office, challenging the highly respected incumbent who had soundly defeated her.

When he had been approached to run for public office, Todd Laker was flattered, but he was not aware. He was not aware that his own popularity was being watched carefully by wise old loquacious Rita Mundy. And when the community sang his praises, Todd Laker felt good. He never felt cautious. And he never dreamed that the love that he had received from the students of his high school would make anyone else feel jilted. But then, he never realized that his love affair was actually a lovers' triangle.

Caution was a feeling or an emotion that was alien to Todd except when he was behind the wheel of an automobile. Because no living person on Earth had need to be cautious of Todd, it never occurred to him that he might have reason to be cautious of others—especially since he knew that he meant no one any harm. He indeed was an innocent, a babe in the woods.

Any sports fan can tell you that games (whatever the sport) are won or lost depending on the players' grasp of the fundamentals of the game—no matter how highly paid they are, and no matter how impressive their "stats."

So, too, your survival in a career as uncertain as school administration will depend on your grasping the fundamentals—no matter how good you are (and sometimes BECAUSE of it) and no matter how hard you try.

Always know from the very beginning who your boss is. And just as importantly, get to know what your boss is all about—who his/her "people" are, what your boss wants from them, what your boss wants from you. Know, too, who your boss's boss is and what that person wants. That doesn't mean that you have to compromise yourself and forget your values to keep a job. It does mean that you will always have a choice, and that YOU will make that decision.

Becoming more aware, more street wise and less of an innocent should be part of your training for school administration—including in-service training for veterans. Remember, not even the forest was safe for Snow White. She fell for the old apple trick. And you won't meet many dwarfs in school administration. Most of them have been knocked off except for the ones at the top, and they can be downright deadly.

**CAVEATS, CODICILS, AND CONUNDRUMS ABOUT**
**KNOWING WHO IS THE BOSS**

- Only the chief of record is YOUR chief.
- Your boss has got your whole world in his/her hands.

- The "who-else's" don't matter. Only your boss matters.
- The minute you feel invincible is the moment you are most vulnerable.
- If they can't get you on competence, they'll get you on style.
- Do you know the legal process by which you can either get tenure or get fired? If not, you don't know your job.
- Your boss's security is the key to your own.
- The good old boys hate change agents—a lot.
- Listen to your instincts—it's your survival gene talking.
- If you're working hard, you may not be working smart.
- Caution: your love affair may be a triangle.
- Water and mediocrity seek their own levels.
- Taking stock of "all the President's men" is the key to understanding what the boss is all about.
- Only God is the ultimate boss; everyone else has one.
- Not even the forest was safe for Snow White; she fell for the old apple trick.
- You won't meet many dwarfs in school administration; most of them have been knocked off, but the ones at the top can be deadly.
- Being street wise won't turn you into a streetwalker; it'll just give you a *choice*.

## CHAPTER 23

# Staying in Power and Staying Power

- In politics it is said, "It's the will of the people."
- In schools it is said, "That's politics."
- In business they say, "Nothing personal, that's business."
- In sports, "*The Turk* has struck again."

All of the above refer to a person in power being removed from power or being fired. *The Turk* is a pseudonym in professional football camps for being cut from the squad. "August is the longest month and one trilogy never changes. The sun broils you, your muscles ache and *The Turk* stalks you."[1] It happens to rookies and famous veterans. A note comes from the coach via the trainer with a message to see him and the fatal giveaway line "and bring your play book." If a player does not know when to retire gracefully, *The Turk* gets them all eventually. There are no exceptions.

So it is in school administration. As in sports, *The Turk* is never welcome. Sometimes there is a struggle. While football players can hide under the bed,[2] Superintendents have no place to hide. *The Turk* has claimed the biggest names in the education business. We think of a few:

- Robert Allioto, Superintendent, San Francisco City Schools
- Ruth Love, Superintendent, Chicago City Schools
- Wilber Lewis, Tucson Public Schools
- Robert Wheeler, Kansas City Public Schools
- Charles Bernardo, Montgomery County Public Schools, Maryland
- Mark Shedd, Superintendent, Philadelphia City Schools
- William Leary, Superintendent, Boston Public Schools
- Edith Gaines, Superintendent, Hartford Public Schools
- Ray Arveson, Superintendent, Minneapolis City Schools
- Barbara Sizemore, Superintendent, D.C. Public Schools

- Joe Carroll, Superintendent, Palm Beach County Public Schools, Florida
- Larry Cuban, Superintendent, Arlington County Schools, Virginia
- Linton Deck, Superintendent, Fairfax County Schools, Virginia

Many of the chief school officers visited by *The Turk* have gone on to other equally prestigious positions. For example, Mark Shedd became Commissioner of Education in Connecticut; Bill Leary, Superintendent of the Broward County Schools, Florida; Ray Arveson, Superintendent of the East Baton Rouge Public Schools, Louisiana. Many others are still superintendents in smaller districts. Others have become successful bankers, real estate agents, college professors, or consultants.

Our review of numerous clippings, personal knowledge of the circumstances, and the context of watching *The Turk* strike down the high and mighty have left us with these impressions and watchwords:

(1) It Takes a Combination of Errors to Get The Turk After You

Rarely does one decision, no matter how bad, do an administrator in. In the scenarios we've watched, it usually is a combination of decisions, misjudgments, or goofs that is fatal.

(2) Intellectual Issues Are Not Usually Fatal

An administrator may err on an intellectual issue or lots of them. Intellectual issues will never get one fired unless they become emotional ones. For example, an intellectual issue is the proper criteria for determining the reading difficulty of adopted textbooks. An emotional issue is "dirty books" in the schools.

We put some of these issues down to show the reader what we mean.

| INTELLECTUAL ISSUE | EMOTIONAL ISSUE |
| --- | --- |
| • the construction of a philosophy of education | • Does it include admission of God?<br>• Does it mean daily prayer? |
| • construction of a policy regarding student access to counseling services | • Will students have access to knowledge of abortion clinics if they are pregnant? |
| • development of a transportation policy | • Why can't my child be picked up at my front door? |

*(continued)*

| INTELLECTUAL ISSUE | EMOTIONAL ISSUE |
|---|---|
| • development of a grading policy for students | • Does a student have to maintain a "C" average in all subjects to play football or be in the marching band? |

A perfect example is school integration. Few are opposed to racial integration of the schools, at least not publicly anyway. However, many are opposed to "forced busing." When one is against busing, one is against integration, since in many school systems busing is the key to integration.

### (3) Emotional Issues Are the Harbinger of The Turk

It is the emotional issues, laden with values about specific actions, that are the galvanizing issues that unseat superintendents and other administrators.

The most emotional issues for parents are school busing, closing schools, or changing school boundaries. These issues are explosive. For teachers, the emotional issues are salaries, fringe benefits, class size, work load, administrative support (mostly lack of interference in teacher autonomy issues), and pupil discipline.[3]

For students, it is institutional reasonableness, sound expectation, and a caring faculty. Any administrator is in serious trouble who steps on the emotions of two critical groups normally acquiescent in most school systems, i.e., parents and teachers.

There will always be special parental interest groups or the union types for teachers. But the bulk of both groups are usually never active *unless* they are stirred up by actions or potential actions of the administrator on basic gut level emotional issues.

### (4) Special Interest Groups Are Not Powerful Unless They Trigger the Emotional Reaction of Parents and Teachers, the "Swing" Groups

The bulk of parents and teachers are *swing constituencies;* they can come down on any side depending on what's at stake for them, and they have to be "organized." Under normal circumstances, they are passive or apathetic about most school issues. With the issue confined to special interest groups and largely intellectual in nature, firefights are rarely fatal and sometimes fun. If these two groups become heavily involved, it is normally *against* the administration. They are, therefore, largely *reactionary.*

### (5) Pick Your Fights Carefully

Job survival means picking your fights carefully. The administrator who does this controls the way the issue is defined and hence reaction to it, the ground and territory (boundary) of the fight, and the timing of when the fight will occur. The administrator does this via agenda control and through long range planning. Boards don't plan. Administrators do.

So, define the issues in such a way as to free them from the emotional hot buttons that will set *The Turk* loose on you. Sometimes events are such it is not possible to control the events. Sometimes a naive board sets loose the emotional forces that result in a cataclysmic backlash. Such a backlash consumes the superintendent as a rule.

When the superintendent is fired, the modern day epic involves public disgrace of the vanquished on a page one petard. It is like the Gallic chieftain Vercingetorix captured by Caesar and paraded through the streets of Rome in chains. Superb educators have ended up victims of the crassest politics that can be played in the gutters of the nation's most glittering meccas of culture and pomp. Some of them have been our friends, and only those close to the battle know what really happened and what personal price was paid by those educators.

To assist the reader in knowing when one is in trouble, we have constructed a kind of index to understand the shifting political winds. Staying in power is like learning how to sail. One first has to know which way the wind is blowing. If the wind is blowing against you, one can skillfully tack into the wind and get where you want to go via a zigzag course. Too many administrators have never learned how to tack, let alone view power as going with the wind or skillfully against it. Power is not a force: it is gaining and keeping the momentum of office with and against all of the forces around it.

As long as the winds are blowing steadily and regularly the key to power is discovering their direction. However, if the winds are constantly shifting because the political forces that be are in a real state of flux, staying afloat and making headway are tenuous.

This is not to say that power is merely going with the flow. It is to say that knowing which way the winds are blowing is essential to maintaining any direction you select. It also means some directions are out of the question until the winds shift.

Our trouble-shooting guide is called the "Tar Baby Trouble Scale (TBTS)." It is named after that famous story by Uncle Remus with the Tar Baby that did in Brothers Fox and Bear. We've organized it in order of level of severity with a "1" being a "warning." A "2" means "this could be dangerous." A "3" means "danger." A "4" stands for "very dangerous." Finally, a "5" stands for "fatal in most cases."

### THE TAR BABY TROUBLE SCALE
### OR YOU KNOW YOU ARE IN TROUBLE WHEN . . .

1—WARNING SIGNS

- The teachers' union president calls for your censure in the union newsletter.
- Board members accept as a "fact" the wildest rumor in town about you or what your motives are for recommending a course of action.
- You receive anonymous "hate" mail on a variety of topics on which you have made public recommendations.
- Board members want the minutes of all your meetings with your administrators.
- The board consistently "surprises" you by introducing motions on items not on the agenda and looks annoyed when you are not prepared.
- Board members want to tour the schools and make un-announced "drop in" visits to faculty rooms and work areas.
- Your recommendations on a number of minor issues are debated at length and lost on split votes.
- A citizens' committee is formed to investigate problems in the schools.
- Board members state or imply they don't get all the facts or information from you or the administration on any issue.

2—COULD BE DANGEROUS

- The board wants to meet without you for an extended ex-ecutive session.
- The director of athletics is quoted in the local paper as saying "he's never seen you at a sports contest of any kind" and scores poor coaching morale as a problem.
- The school doctor is incompetent, but his wife is the board president who voted against your last contract renewal. The doctor certified some boys to play football without a real medical exam.

*(continued)*

- The mayor of the town wants you to hire an ex-principal who was fired as a racist and threatens to put him on the board if you don't do it.
- The American Legion has withdrawn its invitation for you to lead the Memorial Day parade after it discovered you were a pacifist and recently were spotted at an anti-nuke rally.
- The president of the board, the only one to vote against your contract, invites your secretary to lunch without checking with you first.
- Certain board members maintain a secret list of your "gaffes" at board meetings.
- The president of the principals' association "forgets" to invite you to the annual Christmas party.
- Certain board members, critical of your performance in the past, want to review your job description.
- The old superintendent begins to show up at board meetings.
- Retired board members begin to show up at board meetings to question your recommendations.
- Before straw votes in executive sessions, two board members always ask to leave to check their votes with the teachers' union president who awaits outside the door.
- Your "position" on some sensitive personnel issues appears in the teachers' union newsletter.
- The board refuses to evaluate you as stipulated in your contract.
- The PTA gives a "life membership" to a person who has publicly asked for your resignation.
- A board member releases your self-evaluation to the local press which publishes it entirely, including your self-confessed "areas needing improvement" in bold type.
- The town crank, a majority of one, suddenly is opposed to a unanimous administrative recommendation, and the board supports the crank on a split vote.
- The board wants more and more information before it decides on matters.
- The board has "spies" in your administration who tattle on you behind your back.
- Board members continually ask questions of you at public

*(continued)*

meetings until you can't answer them, then look triumphant with the "gotcha" look in their eyes.

- The board fails to discipline one of its own members who continually violates board ethics.
- The teachers' union president, working behind the scenes, promises you a different board president, but you end up with the old one on a split vote.
- Board members stray from issues at public meetings to attack you or your handling of a matter not related to the meeting at all.

3—DANGEROUS

- Board candidates run on a plank of getting rid of you.
- Your budget is cut by the board because some of them simply don't like you.
- Your personality becomes the issue, not the issue itself, and some board members vote against or for something depending upon which side you take.
- Your recommendations on anything are not accepted without having to do an in-depth report on the same subject for a later meeting.
- The board hires an outside consultant to evaluate the district and its operations.
- Certain board members keep sending announcements to you of positions open elsewhere signed "This looks good. Why not apply?"
- The teachers show up in force at a board meeting to protest your recommendation of an item on the agenda.
- Certain state department officials with regulatory authority begin calling, asking about possible financial irregularites in the district known only by your innermost cabinet of administrators.
- The president of the board asks for an administrator's personnel file who is loyal to you.
- The board socializes with other administrators, including the old superintendent, but you're not invited to the parties.
- When you're sick and stay home, the scuttlebutt is you're looking for a job.

*(continued)*

- The rumor on the larger professional grapevine is "you're in trouble."
- The board has to vote on whether or not to let you accept an invitation to give a speech at a state administrators' convention.
- The teachers' union gives you a public vote of "no confidence."
- Certain letters to the editor are published which contain information known only by you and the board.
- When you enter a school building, no one will talk to you; everyone looks the other way.
- Your phone messages suddenly drop off from people in the district. The only increase is from newspaper reporters.
- The board and the teachers' union want to meet without you present.
- The board has your telephone monitored.
- The board urges you to be tough on the teachers in negotiations even if they strike, but blames you after the strike for the strike.
- Board members agree to support your recommendation for closure on an issue behind closed doors and change their minds in public session to embarrass you.

4—VERY DANGEROUS

- The editor of the local paper calls for your resignation to restore harmony in the school system.
- The mayor of the town gives you a vote of no confidence on a critical issue.
- The board candidates running on a plank of getting rid of you are elected.
- The board fires your secretary for a conflict of interest without checking with you first.
- The placement director at your college calls to see if your file is up to date after talking with the board president.
- The board president asks you to call the board's attorney to discuss a possible negotiated buy out of the remaining time on your contract.
- The teachers present a petition signed by 97 percent of the staff asking for the board to get rid of you.
- The board forms a special sub-committee to review your

*(continued)*

expense vouchers, phone bills, and travel statements for the last few years.

- The board cuts your travel funds to conventions unilaterally.
- The principals no longer take your memos or meetings seriously.

5—FATAL IN MOST CASES

- Your contract expires in June and the board can't find the time to schedule a meeting with you to discuss a renewal in February.
- The board candidates running on a plank of getting rid of you are elected and constitute a majority.
- You return from a convention to find your office lock changed and all of your furniture removed.
- While at a convention you see your job advertised on a job board.

---

The press clippings tell us again and again the stories of superintendents hired and fired. It happens with such regularity that the news is enough to fill a column in the *Executive Educator* called "The Word: Who's Been Hired, Fired, Retired."

**REAL LESSONS FROM THE REAL WORLD**

*A Wingding in Wayzata*

Wayzata is part of the general suburbs of Minneapolis. Recently it settled with its superintendent of schools of barely two years, Shirli Vioni, by agreeing to pay her $35,000 and $10,000 more if she left by September 1, and an annuity of $1300.00 per month for life and severance pay of $80,250.[4]

According to a news analysis these cogent factors were pivotal in Vioni's problems in Wayzata:

- Four of the seven board members who appointed her left office within one year after she became superintendent.
- Vioni was forced to lead the cause for higher taxes which succeeded after the fourth election. Said one board member, "Positioning the new superintendent out there to lead the charge on the referendum was not in her best interest, it was a mistake. When leaders are out too far in front of the troops, they get shot in the back."[5]

- Another school board member said things started really
  unraveling when Vioni required teachers to do lesson plans
  and tightened accountability on the principals. "She
  appeared to have a short honeymoon with the school staff."[6]
- The community became polarized over the superintendent.
  Students were even wearing pro- and anti-Vioni buttons at
  the high school.

A letter to the editor spelled out in sobering detail the viciousness
of the infighting Shirli Vioni endured as superintendent:

> She has been continuously threatened through phone calls and
> anonymous letters. Her driving record has been investigated, her per-
> sonal finances reviewed, her long distance phone calls analyzed, her
> personal life scrutinized. Her professional reputation has been put at
> risk.[7]

Shirli Vioni called the Wayzata superintendency experience "a
poorly written soap opera."[8]

Vioni appeared to have alienated teachers early and brought the
bulk of the community out when she became *the issue* rather than
the sorry state of the district's finances. When these two constituencies were riled up, it was all but over.

*Conniptions in Kanawha County*

Superintendent Ed Lakey recently resigned to take a job with a
North Carolina medical supplies firm when he was voted by the
Kanawha County Education Association for the title of "the most
obnoxious superintendent." Teachers informally picketed Lakey
and did a lot of complaining about him. The veteran superintendent
threw the towel in.[9] Remember that the teachers are the "swing"
vote, and when they are galvanized, the results are never positive
for the superintendent.

*A Flap in Florida: They Wanted More Than Gatorade*

Barbara Newell was the first woman to head a multiple campus
state system of universities in the United States. As chancellor of the
Florida University system, her $97,790 salary made her the highest
paid woman on the state's payroll, some $22,000 higher than the
governor's.

After four years, Newell resigned because of "mixed signals"
from the system's board of regents. Described as an outstanding

planner in creating a master design for the Florida system, Ms. Newell had "a quiet style. She is not at all a back slapper."[10]

Florida State Senator Joe Carlucci noted, "She had the education. She had the background. She just wasn't a politician and I don't think the head of an institution should have to be a politician."[11] When it was announced that Florida would not do a nationwide search for Dr. Newell's successor, Carlucci commented, "They're going to go into the swamp and do a good ole boy search. And they're going to get exactly what they want."[12]

### HOW TO SURVIVE LOSING TO THE TURK: GETTING FIRED

There's a difference between losing one to *The Turk* and being a loser. Being fired is one of the most traumatic events in one's life. No matter who you are and no matter how it's done, some aspects are universal. You remember the date, day, time, and scenario. You remember the pain. Your pain and that of your family. And the pain is intensified by "friends" who evaporate into thin air, and you think about what your father or mother told you about the rough spots in life.

Said Harold Sperlich, former Ford executive fired before Iacocca, "It cost me a lot of money. It cost me a lot of friendships. It really disrupted my life and brought a lot of pain."[13]

When it's happened to us, the gnawing questions are hard to put down. But where was the board? Why didn't they resign? And we said to ourselves, "How can the board sleep at night?" And we note that Iacocca's board also was cowed. They hid behind the facade of "privileged information."[14]

But we note that the event forces one to grow—at an astounding rate. For perhaps the first time in one's life, you suddenly know what's important and what's not, who is real and who isn't, what matters and what doesn't. And you experience the love of your family in a way you haven't felt before. And you realize that you are one of the few persons on earth who knows absolutely who your friends are—and who aren't.

And finally, slowly, incrementally, but eventually you come to know someone you've never met before—yourself. You do things that astound you. Survival brings out things that you would not have thought possible. For the first time, self-reliance is more than just an expression. You experience it.

And when you've moved on, your values are different. You are different. You're no longer tolerant of incompetence, corruption, weakness. You don't care about being popular with or loved by the multitudes—only by those few who matter. And what you think of yourself matters most.

One becomes powerful by surviving a tragedy—and one does it mostly alone. You know you are all you need, all you ever needed. You have experienced defeat, humiliation, and the ultimate rejection. And like the fabled phoenix, you rose from the ashes. You can talk about it, write a book about it. You can help others through it. You can tell others how to avoid it.

A leader is a risk-taker, and good leaders have the courage of their convictions. They stand for something, and for some things, they have to take a stand. Remember, the role of the administrator isn't to tell the people or the board what they want to hear; it's telling them what they must hear. And if those who have paid the price for their convictions with their jobs at least once were to stand up and be counted, perhaps we would outnumber those who haven't. And if a leader has never paid that price at least once, how good can he or she be? What have they risked?

We like the statement by Teddy Roosevelt:

> The credit belongs to the man who is actually in the arena, whose face is marred with sweat and dust and blood, who strives valiantly, who errs, and comes short again and again, who knows the great enthusiasms, the great devotions, and spends himself in a worthy cause; who, if he wins, knows the triumph of high achievement, and who if fails, at least fails daring greatly so that his place shall never be with those cold and timid souls who know neither victory or defeat.

We want our school administrators like that. Many already are. Such leaders are inspirational and hardened. They are also street smart and have moxie.

We believe that Niccolo Machiavelli described men and women as they were, their foibles intact, so that we could learn how to be better. Ours is not a blind faith. Several social scientists have taken *The Prince* and Machiavelli's *The Discourses* and developed Likert scales that ultimately produced fifty items that discriminated between those people tabbed "High Machs" (high on Machiavellian characteristics) and "Low Machs" (low on Machiavellian characteristics).[15] Through a variety of tests the researchers found that:

- High Machs were better in bargaining contexts because they did not become emotionally involved and ego dependent on the issues. High Machs remained concentrated on winning and somewhat detached from the issues;[16]
- Machiavellianism is related to accuracy in perceiving others. High Machs were much more accurate in perceiving similar-

ities and differences between themselves and others than low Machs;[17]

- High Machs are preferred as partners, chosen and identified as leaders, judged as more persuasive, and appear to direct the tone and content of interaction—and usually the outcome.[18]

The person with a high Machiavellian tendency is one who has self-defined goals, can disregard any affective state that may exist, "attacks the problem with all the logical ability that he possesses. He reads the situation in terms of perceived possibilities and then proceeds to act on the basis of what action will lead to what result."[19]

It isn't that high Machs are more intelligent than low Machs. The researchers noted that it was within purely interpersonal situations which were unstructured and embedded in very complex situations where improvisation was required, that high Machs exhibited superiority.

To us, leadership is both involvement and detachment. One must be able to look at others and oneself as accurately as required to make decisions. Detachment is not from the cause, nor from the people as people, but their behavior and whether or not it will lead to the results we all want.

Sometimes a leader has to choose between a compromise that will lead to a result and one that won't. Sometimes the situation will prevent any compromise at all. In such circumstances don't be afraid to leave. Make *The Turk* pay his respects in the process.

### CAVEATS, CODICILS, AND CONUNDRUMS ABOUT STAYING IN POWER AND STAYING POWER

- *The Turk* gets them all. There are no exceptions.
- It takes a combination of errors to do one in; no one thing is usually fatal.
- Intellectual issues are never fatal.
- Emotional issues that involve teachers and parents are often fatal.
- Pick your fights carefully, choose your enemy, the issue, and the ground of the fight.
- Staying in power is like learning how to sail—you can make it, even if the wind is against you.
- The Tar Baby Trouble Scale should keep you out of trouble.
- Losing one to *The Turk* is different from being a loser!

## CHAPTER 24

# Idealism vs Ideology

## MACHIAVELLI AND DON QUIXOTE: THE ODD COUPLE

For one of us, the first encounter with Machiavelli's *The Prince* was approximately twenty-five years ago in an undergraduate course on world literature. The reading culminated in a paper titled, "Machiavelli's Ideal Prince: A Dictator." Its nineteen year old idealistic author described Machiavelli's ideal courtier as a ruthless, cunning, political animal devoid of conscience, scruples, heart, or soul. "Only in a totalitarian state," the young author concluded, "could such a leader survive."

The understanding instructor indicated that perhaps the student was a bit harsh with Machiavelli and ended her remarks by saying, "Why not tuck this paper away somewhere and re-read it and *The Prince* in about ten years? Perhaps you'll feel differently."

Although no longer nineteen, the author hasn't lost his idealism. And certainly, Machiavelli must have made quite an impression, since twenty-five years later, he had decided to re-read *The Prince* and the paper. The book was as he had remembered it, a survivor's manual for courtiers and would-be courtiers. But after re-reading *The Prince* and the paper written twenty-five years ago, it was easy to understand the purpose of the instructor's original advice to re-read the book and the paper years later because "perhaps you'll feel differently."

On the second time around, Machiavelli's prince did not seem to be a dictator who was ruthless and unscrupulous, but instead, a highly polished, sophisticated, street wise politician who had mastered the skills and who had acquired the knowledge without which courtiers would have perished in the shark-infested waters of court politics. In fact, it is this very sort of survivor's manual that school administrators and would-be school administrators need today for the same reason and that is why we wrote this book. It's amazing how much Machiavelli has matured in twenty-five years!

*293*

Of course, both the student of world literature and his co-author have also read *Don Quixote* by Cervantes and had easily identified with Quixote's idealism. And armed with our idealism, we pursued the glorious quest of the impossible dream, a quest that has taken us away from the safety and shelter of the classroom to the unsure political arena of school administration.

A bit older and a lot wiser than we were as college undergraduates, our quixotic idealism has been tempered with the wisdom of Machiavellian pragmatism. And it is this combination of idealism and ideology which we feel are the essential characteristics of effective school administration.

### IS IT CRASS TO CARE?

If school administration is political and if the political arena is shark-infested, then aren't conscience, scruples, compassion, and genuine caring definite handicaps? Isn't a person who manifests these traits vulnerable?

As long as school administration is a "people" business, the school administrator must be first and foremost a person, or, using the Yiddish expression, a "mensh" (an authentic human being). And the more compassionate, understanding, and caring—the more HUMAN the administrator, the more positively those who are affected by the administrator will react.

Besides, someone in the organization, any organization, has got to be idealistic. Someone has got to believe the organization can improve and will improve. And someone has got to tell the entire school community when the organization is improving. Someone's got to have a vision and share that vision with others whether it is a vision of a more perfect school or district or ". . . a grand and global alliance, north and south, east and west, that can assure a more fruitful life for all mankind . . ."[1]

Certainly those leaders who are remembered most and most fondly are those who had a strong sense of mission and who inspired others to internalize that mission themselves. Among these leaders are those who promised their constituents nothing but "blood, toil, tears, and sweat," who admonished them to "ask not what your country will do for you—ask what you can do for your country," who stood before millions of persons around the globe and declared, "I have a dream"—a dream they instantly realized was America's dream, still unfulfilled.

Is it crass to care? Education is a caring profession. How can its leaders do less?

## DREAMS VS PIPE DREAMS

Don Quixote's problems were not caused by his dreams; they were caused by his lack of practicality. No matter how certain we are that we're on the side of the angels, it's downright foolish to joust with windmills. Windmills are stronger. And besides, what does it accomplish anyway?

School administrators throughout this country have lost their jobs or are now in the process of losing them because they have confused pipe dreams with dreams and, like Don Quixote, they have jousted with windmills. And many school administrators will do the same in the future unless they acquire a proper education, proper training.

Dreamers must take into account that no matter how noble their purposes, schools are HUMAN organizations peopled with all kinds of human beings possessing the gamut of human frailties.

Dreamers must take into account that public schools do belong to the public. The students, no matter how much we may love them, are not our children. The funds which make up the budget aren't our money. The employees who comprise the organization don't work for us: they work for the same Board of Education we do—and even the Board can't fire a tenured employee without legal due process, which in many cases constitutes more *process* than seems *due*.

Dreamers must take into account that in real life the good guys don't always win and that bastards are not turned into saints by calling them "professional," "doctors," "deans," "professors," "presidents," "superintendents," "principals," "board of education members," etc.

And dreamers must take into account that no matter how divine or sublime their dreams may be, once shared, they become public domain. The dreams of Abraham Lincoln, Martin Luther King, Jr., John F. Kennedy, et al., were sublime. Their assassins were human.

The martyred leaders mentioned above were exceptional. Their dreams lived on beyond their lives—and they still live. Their wives and children would have much preferred their presence.

But if the rest of us lose sight of ourselves while being consumed by our missions, all will be lost—ourselves and our missions. This actual quote from a high school principal's yearbook says it all:

Dr. ------,
Much to my chagrin, you have proved something to me I have suspected for a long time. You can't really, deep down care about kids in this district and keep a job. Aside from being a great principal, you

are also a fantastic human being. You have showed time and again that you cared more about us than you did about yourself, or your job security. You are a member of a dying breed, you made my three years here a joy. You are a wonderful man. You made a great impression on the class of (date) and you will <u>never</u> be forgotten.

Thanks for caring,
Scott

The "fantastic" principal was not granted tenure, a casualty of a power struggle with the superintendent—a struggle that he didn't even know he was in till it was too late. And Scott was painfully correct when he said that the principal was "a member of a dying breed." Anyone who cares more about ideas, ideals, and dreams than about him/herself is by definition a member of a dying breed.

And that is why we have written this book. Caring, fantastic, open, idealistic, humane, authentic school administrators cannot become a dying breed. School administrators who are activists and reformers cannot become a dying breed. They are a rare breed, to be sure, perhaps even an endangered species, but they MUST not become a dying breed. Because if they die, if they don't make it, what breed is left?

## GUIDELINES FOR SUCCESS

We believe that we have outlined guidelines for success throughout this book—guidelines that you will not read anywhere else. But to underscore some of our major points and to assure ourselves that we have supplied our readers with practical "do's" as well as "don't's" we offer TEN COMMANDMENTS FOR GUIDELINES FOR SUCCESS:

1. BEGIN WITH A STRONG FOUNDATION: Know who you are. This is a serious and profound statement. Some people need years of analysis to find out who they are. Others have found themselves through the very process of life itself. Whatever it takes, be sure that you know yourself BEFORE you become involved in a profession where soon you'll be wondering who you are. Those around you will be eager to tell you. They'll want you to believe that you are the person who they want you to be because it serves their purposes. Know your hot buttons because others will find them. If you don't even know where they are, you won't know when others are pressing them!

   Part of your strong foundation should be a PRIVATE SUPPORT SYSTEM. A private support system composed of your family and your closest friends is essential for your own strokes, advice, perception—checks, counseling, etc. You won't get much of this on the job AND YOU SHOULDN'T. Your job will be to lead and give direction, not to make friends and cultivate a social life. Attempting to mix the two will compromise one or the other or both, and besides, you will never *really* know who your friends are while you occupy a position of power—EVER (unless you get into trouble).

The last cornerstone of your strong foundation should be *a plan*. You need to know where you want to go before you figure out how to get there. But perhaps even more important than knowing where you want to go is knowing WHY you want to get there in the first place. Without a very clear idea of who you are (a good self-image), knowing yourself in terms of strengths and weaknesses, having a strong private support system, and having a plan which is compatible with your spouse or anyone else who may be affected by it, you do not have a strong foundation upon which to build a career in school administration, or anything else for that matter.

2. DIVERSIFY: The largest and most powerful corporations in the world have learned this key to survival a long time ago. They don't put all their eggs into one basket—no matter how many eggs they have or how big the basket. Educators spend a lifetime telling kids that ability is transferrable, yet how many of them ever act as though they believe it?

As we bounced around and were bounced around over the years, we have had to do other things for a time to pay the bills between jobs. We have been consultants (and still are). We have formed our own company. One of us tried his hand at real estate and sold over two million dollars worth of residential real estate in the very first year. The figures become even more impressive when you keep in mind that there was no previous knowledge of "the field" other than knowing how to write a check for the monthly mortgage at the beginning.

We have done other things. We have EXPERIENCED that ability is transferrable. We're good at other things. We know how to make money. We come back to education because we CHOOSE to do this work; it is a labor of love, a calling.

Do you have any idea what a difference in attitude that knowledge has generated? Do you have any idea how confident you can be at *anything* with the knowledge that "I DON'T NEED THIS: I WANT IT"? Those who insure their security and survival by diversifying through investments, other avocations, etc., are the ones who need least worry about ever having to rely upon them. The knowledge that they're there will usually be sufficient.

3. TAP INTO THE MAINLINES: Actors and actresses looking for work in commercials, theatre, or film know what trade magazines and newspapers to read, what agents to approach, what contacts to pump, etc. Yet, many aspiring school administrators whom we have met just sit there and expect administrative jobs to fall into their laps. If you keep the pyramid in mind (Chapter 3), you'll constantly remind yourself that the higher you go in school administration, the fewer jobs there are and the more persons competing for the jobs. Therefore, you'll have to act like the hungry actors and actresses out of work. Use your present and past college and university professors as contacts—especially if they are influential. Be sure that your "credentials" are properly filed at your college or university placement office and have them send your papers anywhere you are applying for a vacancy.

As you reach the stage where you are looking for a superintendency or even for an assistant superintendency, you need to get to know some of the chief headhunters. Reading "Educational Career Opportunities" in the "News in Review" section of the Sunday *New York Times* for a couple of weeks in a row will tip you off as to who they are. Some of them offer "Career Workshops." Invest the money and take them, *and they will learn who you are.*

Join the trade organizations that matter. They will provide you with leads and keep you abreast of the latest in the field. Some of these organizations are: ASCD (Association for Supervision and Curriculum Development), American Association of School Administrators (AASA), National Association of Secondary School Principals (NASSP), National Association of Elementary School Principals (NAESP), and various other local and state-wide administrators' organizations.

4. DEVELOP A THICK SKIN: Perhaps because part of an administrator's job is to evaluate teachers, or perhaps for other reasons, teachers just love to evaluate us. And although much of this is behind our backs in teachers' rooms, much of it comes to us in the form of completely unsolicited advice, criticism, or even rage. The fact is that you're everyone's friend until you start telling the truth. When you tell people in writing that

they're not perfect, many can't take that kind of reality. And when you tell somebody that he or she can't do something they want to do, no matter what the reason, you'll begin to find out what your faults are, because they'll tell you. So you better know about them beforehand, rely upon your own private support system for positive strokes and let the blowhards blow!

5. INVEST IN YOURSELF—HEAVILY: Think of yourself as a company or better yet, a corporation. Corporations spend money to make money; it's not a one-way process. If you want to be more successful and more powerful (the same thing), you've got to invest in your own company.

Invest in the basics first. Be sure that you are physically fit. Physical release from pressure and stress is probably the most healthy kind of release for you. Exercise, playing tennis, golf, etc., are good ways to relieve stress.

Smoking is not a good way of relieving tension. As a matter of fact, it's an excellent way of building tension in others who are non-smokers, while assaulting your own body, which will already be under the attacks of stress and pressure of your job. Alcohol is another way some administrators "blow off steam." We've seen more than a few of them blow their careers in the process. No matter how sound your decisions, once you have the reputation for "hitting the sauce" at lunch or whenever, you will be second-guessed on those grounds alone.

Positions of leadership where stress and conflict are a way of life pose a daily threat to one's mental health. Therefore, anything you do that enhances your mental health will enhance your career. Jogging, walking, hobbies, outside interests, and avocations which keep your mind off your job when you're not doing it are good for your mental health. Others find yoga or Transcendental Meditation (TM) good for their sanity. For others, it's weekend trips or est or counseling. Whatever is good for your head—find it, buy it, do it. The most famous and the most public of our leaders, the President of the United States, doesn't stay in the White House fifty weeks out of the year, taking two weeks off in the summer. Compare our Ten Commandments with our present and recent past Presidents' lives and leadership styles and you'll see that these Guidelines have a broad application!

Invest in yourself by reading the *right* books, and by now we hope you know that we don't particularly think that the "right" books are books about education in general or educational administration in particular. We don't mean to suggest that you should ignore them. Keeping up with the profession via journals, attendance at conventions, etc., are givens. But other RIGHT books deal with communication/psychology (including "self-help" books), books that give you an insight into yourself and into other people or groups (group dynamics), books that give insight into management and leadership theories and practices in the corporate world—theories about motivation and morale among other things. Reading biographies and autobiographies about successful leaders might give you some insights into your own position. Those books and articles cited in the text and/or endnotes of this book are good examples of worthwhile readings.

Finally, invest in yourself by dressing for success. In no hierarchy does the leader look exactly like everybody else. Even in the insect world, you can pick out the queen bee from the rest easily. And even in organizations such as the armed forces, police departments, etc., where everyone wears a *UNIform*, the leaders' uniforms are *different*. The hats may differ or the number of stripes or even the color of the badge. Leaders LOOK THE PART. Women, especially, are becoming more mindful of this, and several excellent books have been written for them on this subject.

As educators, we all know that clothes have an effect on how people behave and on how others perceive them. Any teacher who has ever gone to a formal dance or prom can attest to this. Yet some of these same "professionals" dress like "officers" only on the day of their interviews for an officer's position and wonder why their candidacies haven't been taken seriously in their own districts!

6. PRAISE IN PUBLIC, CRITICIZE IN PRIVATE, AND GOSSIP NOT AT ALL: One thing no administrator ever need worry about is giving too much praise. There's no such thing. Presidents have won elections by telling people what they wanted to hear. History tells us that messengers have been put to death because they told people things they didn't want to hear. So don't worry about praising too much. Praise often and in public so that you can reap the extra "PR" as an add-on. But NEVER criticize in public. Public criticism makes you the bad guy or the fool or both. It's a no-win situation. If you're criticizing the whole group, it's as dumb as yelling at the whole class for the actions of one or some or even many. And if you criticize

one or a few in front of their peers, you make heroes or martyrs out of them and frighten the rest of the group into thinking they will be next. Saving your criticism for a private conversation may even result in the person on the receiving end resenting you less than if you had subjected the person to public ridicule.

Gossiping is another story. First of all, the ground rules of gossiping are different for administrators. While not everything that is said about a person by another person is considered gossip, when an administrator says something about another person, it is gossip. Our rule of thumb for adinistrators is: ASSUME EVERYBODY TALKS TO EVERYBODY ELSE. AND WHEN IN DOUBT, KEEP YOUR MOUTH SHUT!

One of the hardest things to get used to is that when you become the chairperson, director, principal, the assistant superintendent or the superintendent, etc., whatever you say suddenly has greater significance. If you do not as yet have such a position, you cannot know what we mean so you'll have to take this one on faith. For the rest of our readers, remember, too, the game of telephone. Not only will your remarks be magnified, they will also be distorted. So, with anything that even borders on gossip—keep your mouth shut!

7. BE OPEN TO LEARNING NEW TECHNOLOGIES: School administrators who aren't as yet comfortable with computers and who aren't, in fact, using them on their jobs are handicapped. Computers are rearranging clerical hierarchies. Those secretaries who know how to use computers and word processors are being paid more money, are getting higher titles, and are getting better jobs. It's obvious that this knowledge gives those who possess it more power than those who do not have it. School administrators who are at the mercy of others who have the skills of the new technologies relinquish to them some of their power as well.

But even if this were not true, new technology makes our jobs easier. We will have more control over more facets of our total responsibilities because they will be at our fingertips. All we need to do is learn how to use them to enhance ourselves. New management theories—especially from the business (real) world can often give us ways to increase the morale and motivation of those with whom we work. Many successful educational consultants are mostly teachers who are bright enough to know a good idea when they hear one and who know how to package and market it. Often, these ideas come from the world of "the bottom line."

8. YOU'RE ON THE AIR, SO ACT THE PART: Teachers know when they're "on." Secondary teachers usually do "five shows a day." When they're not in front of a class, they can let their hair down and relax—in the teachers' cafeteria, in the staff lounge, in their empty rooms. But administrators are always "on." Some administrators we know don't act as if they know this. They act as though they're never "on."

   The fact is that regular folks don't really like to see the officers doing regular things. Have your ever seen your teacher do the food shopping in a supermarket when you were a kid? Did you ever bump into a teacher at a movie or in a department store with their regular kids whom they were yelling at in a regular way? Did it change in college or even in graduate school?

   We're not suggesting that administrators have to put on shows or become affected. But we are saying that the one who's supposed to be in control has always got to act as if he/she is in control of everything—especially of him/herself. Officers don't lose their cool (in public). And officers don't drink with the enlisted men. When you socialize with a group as an administrator, you make that group the "in" group and that automatically makes the rest of the staff the "out" group. And while you're socializing, there are countless opportunities for remarks, or even body language, to be taken out of context to become your next problem. As a leader, you'll have plenty of problems without making yourself one of them.

   Finally, officers don't use foul language—at least an officer and a gentleman doesn't. It's amazing what words make people "freak out." It's not even the heavy duty stuff that seems to get some folks upset. Some folks feel violated if you say "hell" or "damn" in their presence. So if you are going to use anything in the vernacular, be sure it helps, not hinders, your message.

9. ALWAYS THINK BIG, BUT REMEMBER THAT IT'S THE LITTLE THINGS THAT'LL GET YOU INTO TROUBLE: In school administration—especially on the building level, situations become magnified. What administrator hasn't laughed in July at a problem that had kept him/her up for nights in March? The summer brings an opportunity to step back (and away) and gain per-

spective. But those of us who have a plan can weigh every incident against the yardstick: HOW IS THIS GOING TO AFFECT MY CAREER IN FIVE YEARS? With this yardstick in mind, incidents can be distinguished from crises. This will also help to keep you from jeopardizing the big picture over small potatoes. It's good for mental health because it helps you keep your balance.

Also, thinking big leads to acting big—or at least it puts a damper on acting small. And leaders ought to think big.

But, as one very successful superintendent who has been around says, "It's the little things that'll get you." By that, he means challenging the wrong person at a meeting, forgetting to greet one or more board members personally at a social function, being too busy to go out to lunch with a board member who shows up on the spur of the moment, the little hurts, the often unnoticed slights that then fester, only to create problems (some major) for the administrator later.

10. LUST NOT IN THY WORK PLACE!: No book on power and politics is worth a damn (excuse us) if it says nothing about sex. "Power," says Henry Kissinger, "is a wonderful aphrodisiac." *Playgirl* magazine agrees. In releasing its choices of the 10 sexiest men in the nation, *Playgirl* stated that the trend is toward "risk-taking, excellence, and power." Editor Tommi Lewis in a news release accompanying the list stated, "Whether cerebral, artistic, political, or athletic, power is a turn-on for today's woman."[2]

If you accept this statement to be true for many women (and we do), then it follows that powerful people, risk-takers, and those who excel (no matter what their general appearance, as *Playgirl's* list demonstrates) will be "a turn-on for today's woman." And women in positions of power will probably have the same effect on men (at least those who are sure of themselves).

We have seen many administrators lose their jobs, not because they were incompetent, but because they couldn't keep their thoughts above the waistline. We aren't trying to be funny here, nor are we trying to moralize. We stated early on that we have ". . . decided to deal with schools as we've experienced them. Not as we wish they would be or thought they were, *but as they are*." We personally believe that a person's sexual preferences and orientations or those of two consenting adults is their business. That's not what most school boards and school people believe. Even if the

Supreme Court says that they believe it (and they have said it) and even if school boards say they believe it because the law says that they must, you can take bets that their talk will be cheap at the local level.

In Commandment #1, we emphasized a strong foundation with a "private support system." It is altogether appropriate to mention that private support system again here. Sex should be part of that private support system with whomever, however, wherever, whenever—as long as it is PRIVATE.

Public officials do not have the same rights as others. Sex between two staff members in any organization is fodder for the gossip mill. But if one of the lovers is the boss, it's a scandal. Governments of nations have toppled in our lifetime because they could not withstand that kind of scandal. School administrators are far less powerful than those high officials and much more vulnerable.

### YOUR OWN GUIDELINES

In the final analysis, you can make up your own guidelines for success. Just observe very carefully the best administrators you have ever known and make a list of their characteristics. Or take a look at the worst you've ever come across and make a list of the opposite of their traits. But there's one major flaw here. The best administrators you've ever met may not be the most successful and the worst may not be the most unsuccessful. But, that's politics.

We were "born in the USA" as Bruce Springsteen proudly sings, and we have watched America's reputation for quality in just about every category that matters, from the quality of our automobiles and other manufactured goods as compared to foreign imports to the quality of our very lives and our standard of living itself, slip from the position of world leadership, where it was when we were born, to a position of mediocrity. And now we are even becoming worried about the level of literacy in the "land of the pilgrims' pride." We are, indeed, "a nation at risk," and a nation "in search of excellence." We have fought a World War to make the world safe for democracy, yet we have done nothing to make our schools safe for its propagation.

Our forefathers' legacy to us was a living will, the Constitution. Most of what was written over two hundred years ago has remained unchanged, a testimonial to their foresight. Some of it has been amended because the world has changed in the past two hundred years.

But perhaps giving away the power and the responsibility to educate to the states, which in turn have given it away to local communities, was a decision which must now be re-evaluated. Certainly, there is no such standard as an "educated American." The quality of education that Americans receive depends not only upon the states in which they reside, but upon the local communities within these respective states. And how can America be the land of equal opportunity, when the great equalizer, education, is itself *unequal*, and in many areas, substandard? The National Teachers' Examination should be considered as an implicit vote of no confidence by state education departments which are peopled with leaders who are literate enough to read the writing on the wall.

The richest and the most powerful country in the world didn't get that way by accident. Dozens of generations have dedicated themselves to make it so. And as Lincoln said at Gettysburg over a hundred years ago, "It is for us the living, rather, to be dedicated here to the unfinished work which they . . . have thus far so nobly advanced."

A much younger President, almost a hundred years later, said that he did not believe that any of us would exchange places with any other people or any other generation. We, too, are not ready to exchange places with any other people or generation. And we are not ready to leave a profession whose hands hold the very future of our precious legacy, a legacy which we want our own children to inherit.

But we are ready to change the way the game is played in our profession. And we are ready to profess that the future of our children and the very cornerstone of our democratic republic itself, our schools, are too important for such games. The future of our standard of living and of our very survival itself is too important to allow tenured incompetence to continue while careers of bright and dedicated men and women who are capable of leading their schools out of this morass are made or broken over fence post gossip or barroom handshakes.

Martin Luther King, Jr. was not the only great American who had a dream. His forefathers and ours had a dream for all of God's children. That if each of them were free to reach their full potential, they would lift America up by their own bootstraps, and so it would be able to help the rest of the world to do the same. It is this endeavor to which we must dedicate ourselves in the remaining years of this century, and we must begin *now* before it is too late.

And if we succeed, "The energy and the devotion which we bring to this endeavor will light our country and all who serve it—and the glow from that fire can truly light the world."[3]

We have already said that educational leadership, having a hand in the development of humanity is God's work, "and there will be times when you'll swear that you can feel His warm breath against the back of your neck." We sincerely hope that our labors, our passions, our experiences, and our advice will be of some help to a new generation of school administrators who are not only caring, open, idealistic, authentic human beings, but who are also activists and reformers willing to take whatever risks that are necessary to make our schools safe for democracy because our schools are its greatest hope.

We echo John F. Kennedy's pleas, "With a good conscience our only sure reward, with history the final judge of our deeds, let us go forth and lead the land we love, asking His blessing and His help, but knowing that here on earth God's work must truly be our own."[4]

And to this generation of educational leaders we pass the torch along with our prayers, our passions, and our undying support.

### CAVEATS, CODICILS, AND CONUNDRUMS ABOUT LEADERS AND LEADERSHIP

- As long as school administration is a "people" business, the school administrator must first and foremost be a *person.*
- Education is a caring profession; how can its leaders do less?
- Dreamers must take into account that public schools *do belong* to the public.
- If we lose sight of ourselves while being consumed by our missions, all will be lost—ourselves and our missions.
- School administrators who are activists and reformers cannot become a dying breed; they must not become a dying breed because if they die, if they don't make it, what breed is left?
- *The Ten Commandments for Guidelines for Success:*
    1. Begin with a strong foundation.
    2. Diversify.
    3. Tap into the mainlines.
    4. Develop a thick skin.
    5. Invest in yourself—heavily.
    6. Praise in public, criticize in private, and gossip not at all.
    7. Be open to learning new technologies.
    8. You're on the air, so act the part.
    9. Always think big, but remember that it's the little things that'll. get you into trouble.
    10. Lust not in thy work place.
- You will never *really* know who your friends are while you occupy a position of power—ever (until you get into trouble).

- Those who insure their security and survival by diversifying their resources are the ones who need least worry about ever having to rely upon them.
- You're everyone's friend until you start telling the truth.
- Your PRIVATE SUPPORT SYSTEM is an important part of the foundation of your career.
- To distinguish between an incident and a crisis, ask: HOW WILL THIS AFFECT MY CAREER FIVE YEARS FROM NOW?
- We have fought a World War to make the world safe for democracy, but we have done nothing to make our schools safe for its propagation.
- We sincerely hope that our labors, our passions, our experiences, and our advice will be of some help to a new generation of school administrators who are also activists and reformers willing to take whatever risks are necessary to make our schools safe for democracy because our schools are its greatest hope.

# Notes

## CHAPTER 1—POWER AND POLITICS

1. "Battle Tactics: Carl Icahn's Strategies in TWA Bid Represent a Model for Other Corporate Raiders," *Wall Street Journal*, p. 24 (June 20, 1985).
2. Richard Harrington, "Megastar Madonna Finds Fame in Fantasy," *Arkansas Democrat*, p. F.1 (June 13, 1985).
3. "Corporate Politics," *Inquiry* in *USA Today*, p. 9A (June 13, 1985).
4. Saul D. Alinsky, *Reveille for Radicals*, New York: Vintage Books, p. x (1946, 1969).
5. *Ibid.*
6. Morton M. Kondracke, "Second-Term Blues," *Newsweek*, p. 23 (June 10, 1985).
7. Attributed to Dean Smith, North Carolina basketball coach, from *Great Quotations*, Lombard, Illinois.
8. Lloyd Grove, "Crisis Negotiations," *The Washington Post*, p. D4 (June 20, 1985).
9. *Ibid.*
10. D. J. Tice, "Grace Under Pressure," *Ambassador*, p. 51 (July 1985).
11. Alinsky, *op. cit.*, p. xiii.
12. *Ibid.*, p. x.
13. James Reston, "Russian Proverbs Needed at Geneva," *New York Times*.
14. *Ibid.*
15. *U.S. News and World Report*, p. 65 (May 20, 1985).
16. *Ibid.*
17. *Ibid.*, p. 68.

## CHAPTER 2—ARE YOU READY TO PLAY THE GAME?

1. "How a Famous Canadian Wit Battles Against the Pretensions of Powertown," *Wall Street Journal*, p. 8 (July 29, 1985).

2. David Sullivan, "Canada's Top Envoy to Washington Cuts Unusually Wide Swath," *Wall Street Journal*, p. 1 (July 29, 1985).
3. "How Japanese Work Out as Bosses in U.S.," *U.S. News and World Report*, p. 75 (May 6, 1985).
4. Matt Moffet, "Media Consultant Sosa Tailors the Pitch of GOP Candidates to Gain Hispanics," *Wall Street Journal* (June 24, 1985).
5. *Ibid.*
6. *Ibid.*
7. "How Julio Woos a Woman," *USA Today*, p. 2D (July 18, 1985).

## CHAPTER 3—BUREAUCRACIES, BABUS, AND BAKSHEESH

1. Norman J. Ornstein, *Newsweek*, p. 9 (July 1, 1985).
2. UPI, "Missing Soviet Train Baffles Bureaucracy," *New York Times*, p. A3 (June 3, 1985).
3. "Missing the Train," *Time*, p. 50 (June 17, 1985).
4. Charles Mohr, "Secrecy and Democracy," *The New York Times*, p. C22 (June 13, 1985).
5. Jon Nordheimer, "One Death, Many Questions in Miami," *New York Times*, p. 12 (March 10, 1985).
6. Marilyn Adams, "IRS Accused of Shredding Mail," *USA Today*, p. 3A (May 17, 1985).
7. Michael Weisskopf, "Saga of Syria's Flak Jackets," *Washington Post*, p. A19 (June 20, 1985).
8. "Pursuing U.S. Is Like Spitting in the Wind," *U.S. News and World Report*, p. 47 (May 20, 1985).
9. Robert Kaylor, *U.S. News and World Report*, p. 44 (June 10, 1985).
10. Seth Mydans, "Gorbachev: Victor of Round 1 in Moscow," *International Herald Tribune*, p. 1 (July 5, 1985).
11. Van Cleve Morris, et al., *Principals in Action*, Columbus, Ohio: C. E. Merrill, pp. 149–156 (1984).
12. David Colton, "Bad Boy Stockman Quits," *USA Today*, p. 1 (July 10, 1985).
13. D. J. Tice, "Grace Under Pressure," *TWA Ambassador*, p. 50 (July 1985).
14. *Wall Street Journal*, p. 1 (July 17, 1985).
15. Stan Crock, "How to Take a Bite Out of Corporate Crime," *Business Week*, p. 122 (July 15, 1985).
16. Mark Mayfield, "Classic Coke Due Within a Month," *USA Today*, B-1 (July 12, 1985).
17. "Flying by Their Seats," editorial, *Wall Street Journal*, p. 14 (July 29, 1985).
18. Arnold E. Schneider, et al., *Organizational Communication*, New York: McGraw-Hill, p. 62 (1975).

19. "Crime in the Suites," *Time*, p. 57 (June 10, 1985).

20. Loretta Tofani, "Hutton Pleads Guilty to Defrauding Banks," *The Oregonian*, p. E10 (May 3, 1985).

21. Andy Pasztor, "Congress Widens Hutton Probe as Panel Learns Auditors Questioned Overdrafts," *Wall Street Journal*, p. 4 (July 22, 1985).

22. "Fresh Fish for Rickover," *Time*, p. 37 (June 17, 1985).

23. "Waste, Fraud and Abuse?" *Newsweek*, p. 22 (June 3, 1985).

24. Howard Kurtz, "9 of 10 Top Defense Firms Are Under Criminal Investigation," *The Washington Post*, p. A17 (June 20, 1985).

25. Francine Schwadel, "Three Indicted in Fraud Case Involving GE," *Wall Street Journal*, p. 16 (July 17, 1985).

26. Jeanne Dorin McDowell, "Job Loyalty: Not the Virtue It Seems," *New York Times* (March 3, 1985).

27. "Billy R. Reagan," *The Executive Educator*, pp. 13–16 (January 1983).

28. "Good News for Nerds," *The Pittsburgh Press*, p. A-2 (June 24, 1985).

## CHAPTER 4—THE COMMUNITY

1. J. R. Hoyle, F. W. English, and B. E. Steffy, *Skills for Successful School Leaders*, Arlington, Virginia: AASA, p. 65 (1985).

## CHAPTER 5—THE PTA

1. E. H. Jones and X. P. Mongenegro, "Climbing the Career Ladder: A Research Study of Women in School Administration: A Report to the National Institute of Education Minorities and Women's Programs, U.S. Education Department," Arlington, VA: Office of Minority Affairs, American Association of School Administrators (1982).

2. *Long Island Newsday*, reprinted with permission of the author (August 17, 1984).

## CHAPTER 6—THE STAFF

1. Sydney J. Harris, "The Most Infuriating Phrase, 'I Only Work Here,' " *The Morning Call*, Allentown, Pennsylvania, p. B-14 (July 21, 1985).

2. D. C. Lortie, "The Balance of Control and Autonomy in Elementary School Teaching," in A. Etzioni (ed.), *The Semi-Professions and Their Organizations*, New York: The Free Press (1969).

3. Harmon Ziegler, *The Political Life of American Teachers*, Englewood Cliffs: Prentice-Hall (1967).

4. "IBM Loses Innovator in Crash," *USA Today*, p. 2B (August 6, 1985).

5. "Bottom Up Management," *Inc.*, p. 40 (June 1985).

## CHAPTER 7—THE MEDIA

1. Siobhan Morrissey, "A Cartoonist Can't Worry About the Good of the Country," *The Washington Post,* p. B-3 (July 14, 1985).
2. Sara Solovitch, "What's Right to Teach? An Old Debate on New Subjects," *The Philadelphia Inquirer,* p. 1 (April 4, 1985).
3. Amy Dunn, "Teacher Suspended After Selling Candy," *The Miami Herald,* p. 1 (January 18, 1985).
4. David Margolic, "Students Allegiance Lies in Independence," *The Chicago Tribune,* p. 35 (December 7, 1984).
5. Lee Mueller, "Floyd School Chief Replies to Criticism," *Lexington Herald-Leader,* Section B, p. 1 (July 19, 1985).
6. Taken from Ink Mendelsohn, "How to Go Swimming in the 19th Century," Smithsonian News Service as reprinted in the *Globe,* Bethlehem, Pennsylvania, Section F, p. 1 (July 21, 1985).
7. *Sports Quotes,* Lombard, Illinois (1984).

## CHAPTER 8—STUDENTS

1. Sara Lawrence Lightfoot, *The Good High School,* New York: Basic Books, Inc., p. 342 (1983).
2. *Ibid.,* p. 350.
3. "Status in a Crowd of Professionals," *The Washington Post National Weekly Edition,* p. 38 (July 22, 1985).
4. D. L. Clark, L. S. Lotto, and M. M. McCarthy, "Factors Associated with Success in Urban Elementary Schools," *Phi Delta Kappan,* 61, pp. 467–470 (1980).
5. W. B. Brookover, *Effective Secondary Schools,* Philadelphia, PA: Research for Better Schools (1981).
6. Tinker V. Des Moines, See D. L. Kirk and M. G. Yudof, *Educational Policy and the Law: Cases and Materials,* Berkeley, California: McCutchan Publishing Corporation, p. 582 (1974).
7. Associated Press, "All Was Well in Texas Until the Report Cards Came Out" (March 19, 1985).
8. W. Baskin (ed.), *Classics in Education,* New York: Philosophical Library, pp. 639–640 (1966).
9. Lightfoot, *op. cit.,* p. 349.

## CHAPTER 9—CAREER PLANNING—THE LEGEND OF THE "CHAIRS"

1. Georgia Dullea, "On Corporate Ladder, Beauty Can Hurt," *New York Times,* p. C13 (June 3, 1985).

2. *Time*, p. 68 (June 17, 1985).

3. Extrapolated from an advertisement from TRW as it appeared in *Business Week*, p. 104 (June 24, 1985).

4. Ole Sand, *On Staying Awake: Talks with Teachers*, Washington, DC: NEA, p. 26 (1970).

## CHAPTER 10—RESUMES, HEADHUNTERS, AND INTERVIEWING

1. William Laas, *Monuments in Your History*, New York: Popular Library, p. 68 (1972).

2. Linda Chion-Kenny, "U.S. 'Dipscam' Nets Diploma Hawkers: Educators Named," *Education Week*, 4:36, p. 1 and 13, 18 (May 29, 1985).

3. Associated Press, "PUC Nominee Out, Had Mail-Order Degrees," *The Globe Times*, p. 1 (August 7, 1985).

4. Chion-Kenny, *op. cit.*

5. Jerome Cramer, "Meet the Power Brokers," *The Executive Educator*, 4:2, pp. 30–33 (February, 1982).

6. Richard L. Fleming, "Searching for the Right Search Firm," *PACE/Piedmont Airlines*, pp. 43–49 (November–December, 1984).

7. J. Donald Butler, *Four Philosophies*, New York: Harper and Row (1968).

8. Roger A. Kaufman, *Educational System Planning*, Englewood Cliffs, New Jersey: Prentice-Hall (1972).

## CHAPTER 11—ACADEMICS AND ABECEDARIANS

1. According to the *Guinness Book of World Records*, New York: Bantam Books, p. 434 (1982).

2. Donald J. Willower and Jack Culbertson (eds.), *The Professorship in Educational Administration*, Columbus, Ohio: University Council for Educational Administration, p. v (1964).

3. Roald Campbell, "The Professorship in Educational Administration: Preparation," in Willower and Culbertson (eds.), *Ibid*, p. 18.

4. Elliot W. Eisner, "Can Educational Research Inform Educational Practice," *Phi Delta Kappan*, 65:7, p. 450 (March 1984).

5. Philip H. Phenix, "Transcendence and the Curriculum," in Elliot W. Eisner and Elizabeth Vallance (eds.), *Conflicting Conceptions of Curriculum*, Berkeley, California: McCutchan Publishing Corporation, p. 122 (1974).

6. *Ibid.*, p. 2.

7. Arthur Blumberg, *The School Superintendent*, New York: Teachers College Press, p. xi (1985).

8. Judson T. Shaplin, "The Professorship in Educational Administration: Attracting Talented Personnel," in Donald Willower and Jack Culbertson (eds.), *op. cit.*

9. Elliott W. Eisner, *op. cit.*, p. 451.

10. *Ibid.*

11. Shaplin, *op. cit.*, pp. 2-3.

12. Eisner, *op. cit.*, p. 451.

13. Edward deBono, *PO: Beyond Yes and No*, Middlesex, England: Penguin Books, p. 40 (1972).

14. Joseph J. Schwab, "The Professorship in Educational Administration: Theory-Art-Practice," in Willower and Culbertson, *op. cit.*, p. 67.

## CHAPTER 12—THE JOB VS THE JOB DESCRIPTION

1. Leonard P. Ayers, *School Organization and Administration*, Cleveland, Ohio: The Survey Committee of the Cleveland Foundation, p. 82 (1916).

2. Ralph M. Barnes, *Motion and Time Study*, New York: John Wiley and Sons, Inc., pp. 7-12 (1937).

3. *Ibid.*, p. 12.

4. *Ibid.*, p. 14.

5. *Ibid.*, pp. 48-51.

6. *Ibid.*, p. 51.

7. Van Miller and Willard B. Spalding, *The Public Administration of American Schools*, New York: Yonkers-on-Hudson, World Book Company, pp. 317-320 (1952).

8. Lloyd E. McCleary and Stephen P. Hencley, *Secondary School Administration*, New York: Dodd, Mead and Company, pp. 176-178 (1965).

9. These three categories are the ones to perform job analysis. See Sidney A. Fine and Wretha W. Wiley, *An Introduction to Functional Job Analysis*, The W. E. Upjohn Institute for Employment Research, No. 4, 87 pp. (September 1971).

10. Time dimensions were taken from Van Cleve Morris, Robert L. Crowson, Cynthia Porter-Gehrie, and Emanuel Hurwitz, Jr., *Principals in Action*, Columbus: Charles E. Merrill Publishing Company, pp. 31-66 (1984).

11. *Ibid.*

12. *Ibid.*

13. Peter Drucker, *Management*, New York: Harper and Row, pp. 494-495 (1973).

14. William Adelbert Cook, *High School Administration*, Baltimore, Warwick and York, Inc., p. 109 (1926).

15. *Ibid.*, p. 110.

16. Daniel Burstein, "So New, So Now, So Sony," *United*, 30:8, p. 64 (August 1985).
17. *Ibid.*, p. 84.

## CHAPTER 13—PLOYS TO AVOID

1. See Cris Evatt and Bruce Feld, *The Givers and The Takers*, Macmillan Company, New York, for a detailed exploration of givers and takers in relationships (1983).
2. C. Evatt and B. Feld, *op. cit.*
3. C. Evatt and B. Feld, *op. cit.*

## CHAPTER 15—THE EMMETROPIA OF EVALUATION

1. For example, see George Drayton Strayer and N. L. Engelhardt, *The Classroom Teacher at Work in American Schools*, New York: American Book Company, pp. 387–395 (1920).
2. Susan S. Stodolsky, "Teacher Evaluation: The Limits of Looking," *Educational Researcher*, pp. 11–18 (November, 1984).
3. William C. Carey, *Documenting Teacher Dismissal*, Salem, Oregon: Options Press, p. 138 (1981).
4. *Ibid.*, p. 74.
5. *Ibid.*, pp. 76–77.
6. *Ibid.*, p. 78.
7. Jean Latz Griffin, "School Chief Stripped of Duties," *Chicago Tribune*, Section 4, p. 3 (August 22, 1985).
8. *Ibid.*

## CHAPTER 16—BUDGET SKULLDUGGERY

1. Barry M. Mundt, et al., *Managing Public Resources*, New York: Peat Marwick International, pp. 35–50 (1982).
2. "Forget the $400 Hammers: Here's Where the Big Money Is Lost," *Business Weekly*, pp. 48–50 (July 8, 1985).

## CHAPTER 17—TEXTBOOK TYRANNY, CURRICULUM CHICANERY, AND TESTING INSANITY

1. Patrick Reardon, "Dropout Epidemic Blamed on Policy," *Chicago Tribune*, pp. 1 and 20 (April 25, 1985).
2. We quote from a speech by Sizer to the AASA Convention in Tanya Barrientos, "U.S. Schools Are Failing, Need New Direction, Educator Says," *Dallas Times Herald*, p. 34A (March 9, 1985).

3. "Modular Plan Dies As Charges Fly," *Chicago Tribune* (April 16, 1970).
4. Shiela Mullane, "Northeast's Mod Plan Sought," *Evening Independent,* St. Petersburg, Florida (November 28, 1973).
5. "Rickards Parents' Group Hits Flexible Scheduling," *Tallahassee Democrat* (February 23, 1972).
6. We think of lawyer Shirley Hufstedler who was photographed in classrooms as the first U.S. Commissioner of the Department of Education and later William Bennett who was a guest teacher in some public schools.
7. Roger Farr and Michael A. Tulley, "Do Adoption Committees Perpetuate Mediocre Textbooks?" *Phi Delta Kappan*, 66:7, pp. 467–471 (March 1985).
8. Francis FitzGerald, *America Revised*, Boston: Little, Brown, and Company (1979).
9. As cited in David B. Tyack, *The One Best System*, Cambridge: Harvard University Press, p. 95 (1974).
10. *Ibid.*
11. Leonard Ayers, *School Organization and Administration*, Cleveland: Cleveland Foundation, pp. 100–102 (1916).
12. James Hertling, " 'Coherent Design' Missing in Curricula, Says Bennett in Call for Common Core," *Education Week*, p. 10 (March 20, 1985).
13. Fenwick W. English and Betty E. Steffy, "Differentiating Between Design and Delivery Problems in Achieving Quality Control in School Curriculum Management," *Educational Technology*, 23:2, pp. 29–32 (February 1983).
14. For a copy of the actual rating sheet see "Survey to Check for Quality Control Elements Present in Locally Developed Curriculum Guides," in John R. Hoyle, Fenwick W. English, and Betty E. Steffy, *Skills for Successful School Leaders*, Arlington: American Association of School Administrators, p. 91 (1985).
15. Bobbie Foust, "Marshall County Is a 10," *Tribune-Courier*, Benton, Kentucky, p. 1.
16. Daniel P. Resnick and Lauren B. Resnick, "Standards, Curriculum, and Performance: A Historical and Comparative Perspective," *Educational Researcher*, pp. 5–20 (April 1985).
17. Denise Worrell, "The Autobiography of Peter Pan," *Time*, 126:2, p. 62 (July 15, 1985).

**CHAPTER 19—UNIONS**

1. Facts pertaining to the AFT and some of the NEA were taken from William Edward Eaton, *The American Federation of Teachers, 1916–1961*, Carbondale: Southern Illinois University Press (1975).

2. *Ibid.*, p. 10.

3. Martha Woodall, "School Offer Would Raise Taxes 11 Pct," *The Philadelphia Inquirer*, 313:58, p. 1 (August 27, 1985).

4. Mary Ann Roser, "Senate OK's Education Package," *Lexington Herald-Leader*, 3:198, pp. 1 and 10 (July 19, 1985).

5. Muriel Cohen, "Role of Better Schools Center in Dispute," *Boston Globe*, p. 29 (December 19, 1984).

6. "Union Leader Claims Victory," *USA Today*, p. 2A (March 20, 1985).

7. Dan C. Lortie, *School–Teacher*, Chicago: University of Chicago Press (1975).

8. Kenneth H. Ostrander, *A Grievance Arbitration Guide for Educators*, Boston: Allyn and Bacon, Inc. (1981).

9. Harry F. Wolcott, *Teachers vs. Technocrats*, Oregon: Center for the Study of Educational Administration (1977).

## CHAPTER 20—THE LUNATIC FRINGE

1. Barbara Parker, "Stop the Censors," *New York Times*, p. 25 (August 29, 1985).

2. *Ibid.*

3. Amy Dunn, "Coalition Forms to Counter Battle by Health Text Foe," *The Miami Herald* (January 18, 1985).

4. Sara Solovitch, "What's Right to Teach? An Old Debate on New Subjects," *The Philadelphia Inquirer*, 312:94, pp. 1 and 10 (April 4, 1985).

5. Extrapolated from the *Phyllis Schlafly Report* (January 1985).

6. "10 Great Teachers," *USA Today*, p. 6A (September 3, 1985).

7. Sara Solovitch, *op. cit.*, p. 10.

8. The latest was Mclean vs Arkansas Board of Education in which "creationism" was declared unconstitutional.

9. From the *Los Angeles Times* (August 25, 1985).

10. See "Jerry Falwell's Crusade," *Time*, 126:9, pp. 48–61 (September 2, 1985).

11. David B. Tyack, *The One Best System*, Cambridge: Harvard University Press, p. 85 (1974).

12. Sara Solovitch, *op. cit.*

13. James Brooke, "A Suicide Spurs Town to Debate Nature of a Game," *New York Times*, p. B1 (August 22, 1985).

## CHAPTER 22—KNOWING WHO IS THE BOSS

1. Lee Iacocca, *An Autobiography*, New York: Bantam Books, p. 156 (1984).

CHAPTER 23—STAYING IN POWER AND STAYING POWER

1. Jerry Izenberg, "Nowhere to Hide from The Turk," *New York Post,* p. 71 (August 20, 1985).
2. According to Izenberg, some pro players actually tried to hide under the bed, *Ibid.*
3. Student discipline was a major strike issue in New Castle, PA. See Carol Colaizzi, "City School Discipline Code to Be Enforced," *New Castle News,* 299, p. 1 (August 30, 1985).
4. Jim Adams, "Vioni's Resignation Ends 'Soap Opera,' " *Minneapolis Star and Tribune,* p. 6A (May 11, 1985).
5. Mary Jane Smetanka, "Resignation of Vioni Caps Two Tense Years in District," *Minneapolis Star and Tribune,* p. 1 (May 11, 1985).
6. *Ibid.*
7. Letter to the editor of the *Minneapolis Star and Tribune, op. cit.,* signed by Alexandra Lucky of Plymouth.
8. Jim Adams, *op. cit.*
9. From "The Word," *Executive Educator,* 7:8, p. 3 (August, 1985).
10. Scott Heller, " 'Mixed Signals' from Her Board of Regents Caused Head of Florida's System to Resign After 4 Years," *The Chronicle of Higher Education,* pp. 1 and 19 (May 1, 1985).
11. *Ibid.*
12. *Ibid.*
13. Edward Miller, "Possible Successor to Chrysler's Iacocca a Tall, Thin, Quiet Contrast to His Boss," *Call-Chronicle,* p. D-2 (May 19, 1985).
14. Lee Iacocca, *An Autobiography,* New York: Bantam Books, p. 131 (1984).
15. Richard Christie and Florence L. Geis, *Studies in Machiavellianism,* New York: Academic Press (1970).
16. *Ibid.,* p. 208.
17. *Ibid.,* p. 234.
18. *Ibid.,* p. 313.
19. *Ibid.,* p. 358.

**CHAPTER 24—IDEALISM VS IDEOLOGY**

1. Inaugural address—John F. Kennedy (January 20, 1960).
2. "For Playgirl, Power Is Men's Sexiest Trait," *Long Island Newsday,* p. 9 (July 3, 1985).
3. John F. Kennedy, *op. cit.*
4. John F. Kennedy, *op. cit.*

# Index

Academics, 131
ADAMS, JOHN QUINCY, 86
ADLER, MORTIMER, 209–210
AFT, 231
Agenda control, 282
ALINSKY, SAUL, 8, 14–15
ALLEN, WOODY, 48
ALLIOTO, ROBERT, 279
Alphabet jungle, 137
Arbitrations, 235
Arch rivals, 251–252
ARVESON, RAY, 279
ASHWORTH, JOHN, 36
Assassins, 247
Assistants, 261
AYERS, LEONARD, 143, 212

Babus, 38
Bad news, 91
BAKER, JAMES, 20
Baksheesh, 37
BARNARD, HENRY, 24
BENNETT, WILLIAM, 316
BERNARDO, CHARLES, 279
Blunders, 44
Brahmins, 139
Bribery, 211
Boards, 46–47
Board groupies, 58
Body language, 226
Bogus degrees, 123
BOONE, RICHARD, 169
BOREN, JAMES, 38
Boss, 267
BOYER, RICHARD, 209
BREZINSKI, ZBIGNIEW, 20
Budget control, 201
Budget cuts, 207

Budget padding, 202
Budgeting types, 202
Bureaucracy, 35
BUTCHER, JAKE, 46
BYRNE, JANE, 31

CAESAR, 282
Camera, 90
CAMPBELL, ROALD, 131
Cannibals, 124
Career ladder, 18
CARLUCCI, JOE, 289
CARROLL, JOE, 280
Catholics, 246
Chain of command, 42
Chairs, 109
Chicago Teachers
  Federation, 231
CHRISTENSEN, D. LOUIS, 199
Chronocyclegraphy, 143
CHURCHILL, WINSTON, 8
CLEVELAND, GROVER, 117
CLEVELAND, MRS. GROVER, 63
Coalitions, 15–17, 24–25
Coca-Cola, 41
Community, 53
Competence, 186
Contractual constipation, 234
Contract negotiations, 206
Control, 146–147
Controlling costs, 205
COOK, WILLIAM, 147
Creative insubordination, 38
CUBAN, LARRY, 280
Curriculum alignment, 41
Curriculum, guides, 212
CUNNINGHAM, MARY, 1
Custodians, 226

Deadbeats, 127
Deadend, 127
DEBONO, EDWARD, 136
DECK, LINTON, 280
Democracy, 160
Detours, 127–128
DEWEY, JOHN, 100
Dipscam, 123
Dirty work, 185
DOHERTY, CAROL, 232
Don Quixote, 294
Doublespeak, 119
doubt, 245
Dreamers, 295
Dress, 300
DRUCKER, PETER, 146
DUELL, CHARLES H., 117
DUKAKIS, MICHAEL, 232

Easy generalizations, 86
E.F. Hutton, 45
Eggheads, 110
Educational mafia, 111
EISNER, ELLIOT, 132–133, 135
Emotional issues, 281
ESTRIDGE, PHILLIP, 78
Evaluation, 189
EVATT, CHRIS, 151

Faculty room, 82
Facts, 197
FALWELL, JERRY, 244
FBI, 123
FELD, BRUCE, 151
Flattery, 196
FORD, GERALD, 31
Frivolitigious, 236

Gadfly, 113
GAINES, EDITH, 279
GANDHI, RAJIV, 37
General Dynamics, 45–46
General Electric, 46
Getting fired, 289
GILBRETH, FRANK, 143
Givers, 151
GOGGIN, CATHERINE, 231
Good copy, 86
Good ole boys, 111
Good ole boy search, 289
GOODLAD, JOHN, 209–210

Good schools, 96
Good sports, 5
GORBACHEV, MIKHAIL, 37
Gossip, 64
Gotchas, 64
GOTLIEB, ALLAN, 30
GOTLIEB, SONDRA, 30
Grace Commission, 13–14
Grapevine, 42
Grievances, 235
Gripe sessions, 64
Growth, 189
Gut issues, 237

HALEY, MARGARET, 231
HARDEN, ALICE, 232
Headhunters, 124
Hiring, 172
Hispanics, 31
HOLLIDAY, FREDERICK, 171
Hubris, 164
HUFSTEDLER, SHIRLEY, 316
Humor, 248–249

IACOCCA, LEE, 7, 10, 274
ICHAN, CARL, 1
IGLESIAS, JULIO, 31
Indirect data, 191
Informal organization, 42
Infrastructure, 225
Instructional excellence, 192
IRS, 36, 40, 123

JACKSON, P. J., 242
Japanese, 30–31
Jive, 30
Job Description, 145
Job survival, 281
Jocks, 29–30
Jokers, 32
Judgments, 194
JUSTICE LEARNED HAND, 14

KANTER, ROSABETH, 48
KELVIN, LORD, 117
KENNEDY, JOHN F., 7, 105, 306
KENNEDY, ROBERT, 253
Kentucky Education Association, 232
Kickbacks, 45
King Arthur, 109
KING, MARTIN LUTHER, JR., 295, 305

KISSINGER, HENRY, 303
KNIGHT, BOBBY, 93
KOCH, EDWARD, 20

LADER, CURT, 70–71
LAKEY, ED, 288
Lawyers, 47
LEARY, WILLIAM, 279
Lebanon, 11
LEHMAN, JOHN, 45
LEWIS, DAVID, 46
LEWIS, TOMMI, 303
LEWIS, WILBER, 279
LIGHTFOOT, SARA LAWRENCE,
 96, 102
Likert scales, 290
LINCOLN, ABRAHAM, 53
Little Hitlers, 4
Little people, 73
LOVE, RUTH, 279
Loyalty, 47–48, 169
Lunatic fringe, 241

MACHIAVELLI, NICCOLO, 290, 293
Machiavellianism, 290–291
Macho males, 63
MADONNA, 1
Management by exception, 38
Management by memo, 9
MANN, HORACE, 24
Massachusetts Teachers
 Association, 232
MCAULIFFE, CHRISTA, 76
MCGREGOR, DOUGLAS, 178
MCKAY, JOHN, 23
Media, 85
Meta research, 135
Memo wars, 10, 158
MILLIKAN, ROBERT, 117
Mississippi Strike, 232
Moral Majority, 246
Morale, 82
MOORE, DIANE, 242
MORITA, AKIO, 148
Motivation, 259
Mugwumps, 209
MYERS, RICHARD, 242

National School Boards
 Association, 243
NEA, 231–232

NEWELL, BARBARA, 288–289
NIXON, RICHARD, 165

Old boy network, 110
OLIPHANT, PAT, 85
Organizational poker, 12

Paper power, 9
Parents, 281
Passing the buck, 143
Past Practice, 234
Patience, 11
Patronage, 238
Payoffs, 65–66
Pentagon, 36
People, 146
People puppeteers, 5
Placement service, 137
Post Office, 36
Pots, 103
Power, 8–9
Power base, 60
Power brokers, 225
Power conservatives, 5
Power-hungry-deprived, 4
Power plays, 11
Power structure, 54
Powertown, 30
Praise, 300
Pravda, 36
Prayer in the schools, 247
Principals, 60
Privileged information, 289
Professors, 138
Psychopaths, 253–254
PTA, 63

Quality circles, 160

RAVITCH, DIANE, 116
RAYBURN, SAM, 210
REAGAN, RONALD, 35
Regents Examination, 215
Religious fanatics, 244
Reporters, 88
Research, 132, 135
Resume, 119
RICKOVER, HYMAN, 45–46
Right people, 116–117
Risk-takers, 260
ROOSEVELT, TEDDY, 290

ROGERS, KENNY, 178
ROYALL, ANNE, 87

SALINGER, J. D., 241
SALMON, PAUL, 239
Salting evaluations, 199
SAND, OLE, 117
SAVAGEAU, DAVID, 209
SCHLAFLY, PHYLLIS, 242, 247
SCHWAB, JOSEPH, 138
Secretaries, 221
Secular humanism, 242, 246
Selling out, 187
SENECA, 101
Sex, 303–304
SHAPLIN, JUDSON, 133
SHEDD, MARK, 279
Shop stewards, 234
Sign language, 225
SINCLAIR, UPTON, 211
SIZEMORE, BARBARA, 279
SIZER, TED, 209–210
SONY, 148
Special interest groups, 281
SPERLICH, HAROLD, 289
SPIELBERG, STEVE, 216
SPRINGSTEEN, BRUCE, 304
Squatter's Rights, 115
STALIN, 7
STEFFENS, LINCOLN, 211
STEVENS, TED, 41
Strokes, 274
STOCKMAN, DAVID, 40
Stool pigeon, 81
Student power, 98
Superchargers, 79
Super-puff, 119
Superstars, 76–77
Swing constituencies, 281
Synergy, 75

Takers, 151
TAYLOR, ELIZABETH, 85

TAYLOR, FREDERICK, 143
Tax rate, 205
Teacher trades, 176–177
Teaching, 174
Teaching hospital, 95
Testing, 214
Textbooks, 211
THAYER, PAUL, 46
Theory of evolution, 245
Therbligs, 144
*The Turk*, 279
THURLOW, EDWARD, 40
TRAVIS, JOE, 232
Trouble scale, 282–287
TRUMP, J. LLOYD, 210
Turf battles, 159
TURNER, ADMIRAL, 36
Turkeys, 79–80
TUTELA, ALFRED, 171
TWAIN, MARK, 139

Unions, 231
Union busting, 238
Union leaders, 237
Union tactics, 233
University culture, 132

Vercingetorix, 282
VIONI, SHIRLEY, 287–288
VONNEGUT, KURT, JR.,
  27, 33

Wackos, 244
WARNER, JOHN, 85
WEBER, MAX, 35
WHEELER, ROBERT, 279
Wimp, 81
Winners grid, 28
WOLFE, THOMAS, 165
WOODS, ROSEMARY, 221
WRIGHT, RICHARD, 242

Zero sum game, 12

# Biographies

JOHN A. BLACK

John Black is a seasoned secondary school administrator, having served as Housemaster of Greenwich High School, Greenwich, Connecticut, and Principal of Northport High School, Long Island, New York, two secondary schools cited either by the U.S. Department of Education or other sources as being among the nation's best. Dr. Black is currently Principal of Robert Moses Junior High School in North Babylon, Long Island, New York.

Dr. Black is a native of New York City and received his B.A. and M.A. at the City College of New York. His Ph.D. was earned at New York University where his research dealt with whether instruction in general semantics would reduce ethnic prejudice in high school students. His dissertation received the Sixth Research Award of the New York Society for General Semantics, and the Promising Research Award of the National Council of Teachers of English. He has also published extensively in various journals dealing with general semantics and teaching.

FENWICK W. ENGLISH

Fenwick English is a nationally known author, speaker, and consultant. He has written over six books and 70 articles in a wide variety of national educational journals. He has been a superintendent of schools for five years in New York, an Associate Director of the American Association of School Administrators, and a partner in the international accounting and consulting firm of Peat, Marwick, Mitchell & Company. He is currently a Professor of Education at Lehigh University in Bethlehem, Pennsylvania.

Dr. English is a native of Los Angeles, California where he received his B.S . and M.S. from the University of Southern California and his Ph.D. from Arizona State University. In 1973 he received the Distinguished Professor Award from the National Academy of School Executives of AASA and in 1982 the Outstanding Consultant Award from the Association of Supervision and Curriculum Development. He has served as a consultant to some of the nation's largest school systems where he performed organizational studies and curriculum audits.

# To Our Readers

We welcome correspondence concerning this book. Our address is:

What They Don't Tell You
P.O. Box 83
Northport, New York 11768

—J.A.B., F.W.E.